Once Upon a Time A Boy Lived on Lake Minnetonka

D1521517

Harry Edwin Eiss

White Wolf Publications, Copyright © 2018

Friday
Night
Football

October, seven weeks after Dad's death — the bright orange, red and yellow leaves swirl to the ground. It's that time of year when the overly hot end of summer gets swept away by the fresh autumn air. For as long as I can remember, I've enjoyed the leaves' final burst of color, and I have good memories of the yearly traditions connected to raking and burning them, especially of sitting on the porch beneath the stars and talking with Dad while he patiently watches until the last whiffs of smoke die away.

It's never official or announced in any way. But, similar to how animals sense changes coming in the weather, the neighborhood intuitively knows the weekend it's time to rake. Then, on a Saturday afternoon one after another appears in their yards. The men take breaks to share a beer and talk. In the middle of it all, the women appear with trays of hamburgers, hot dogs, baked beans, potato salad and chips. The piles of leaves grow, the children and even some of the adults plunge in and roll about, laughing and joking about what idiots we all are, and after dark the burning leaves are perfect for s'mores.

Then things change. Once Dad gets sick, the autumn ritual loses its meaning. Perhaps there are reasons for people in town with carefully manicured lawns to clean away their leaves, but our yard next to a dirt road in the country hardly has a lawn and there is no real reason beyond the casually established social context.

Tonight, I don't notice the falling leaves as I walk through the cool air to the high school football game. I've made my way up Lane Five to Ward's Store and gotten about a fifth of a mile down Three Points Boulevard, just passed JoAnn's house, when a '57 Chevy passes me. I pay it no attention. Then I hear it squeal to a stop and turn to see why.

Someone exits the back door. I can't make out the face, but as he comes quickly across the road toward me, I realize it's Danny Ketchum. He's four years older, no doubt why he feels so emboldened.

"Hey, Kid! Where ya headed?"

"Football game."

"Yeah, you like football?"

"Yeah."

He reaches me.

"Well, Whadda-ya think of this foot in your balls!?" He tries to kick me as he finishes. My instincts take over. I reach out, grab his heel and lift. He falls hard on his back.

I look down, not knowing what to do next.

He's surprised and shaken. I can see it in his face, his startled eyes.

The wind gusts and a scattering of leaves whirls between us.

Then everything is still and silent.

I'm not one to run.

Five years later, I'm hitch-hiking on Highway Seven, just the other side of Mound, and he stops to give me a ride. He has no idea I'm the same person he once tried to bully, but I remember him.

His family lived on Lane Six, only a few houses down from Three Points Boulevard.

While Danny has an athletic build, his younger brother Milo is heavy-set. For a while, Milo plays in a band with Kim, and one night I happen to be at Kim's house when he decides to walk up to Milo's to jam. I remember them playing their versions of Ray Charles' hit *Georgia* and Tommy James' *Mona, Mona*.

I don't stay long. Feel out of place. There's a girl their age that latches onto me, at least for the night. We slip into the dark, walk down Lane Six, hugging and kissing as we go, eventually reaching the top of the hill above my bus stop. There we wander off the street into a yard where we continue our desires lying down. Nothing much, just some kissing, fumbling undoing of buttons and the fondling of breasts, the thrill of my mouth on bare nipples. I continue my kissing down beneath her breasts, across her stomach, below her belly-button, heading for the dark hair between her legs.

She pushes me off, as if she's suddenly awakened to what's happening. "What're you doing?"

It's fortunate. As we stand, Kim, Milo and others come walking up the road. Less than a minute more of exploration will have resulted in embarrassment. Maybe she pushed me off because she heard them coming. I'll never know for sure because it's the last I'll see of her.

That comes later.

Tonight, in the chilly autumn air, a startled Danny looks up at me and I down at him, neither of us knowing what to do next. Someone from his car yells at him to come back and leave. He gets up and scrambles toward the car. About half way across the road, he yells "I'll be back!" They squeal rubber leaving. It puts a scare into me and the entire walk to the football game I'm expecting them to return, but they never do.

Danny threatened me once before, in the middle of a bright summer day as I walked up Lane Five. That time as well he didn't follow up his threat, just stood and stared at me. I also made no move. For seconds that seemed like hours we stared at each other. Then he said, "Just you watch out!" and walked away.

They always walk away, even if they have a loaded weapon.

Dedicated
to
Harry Earl Eiss
and
Helen Henrietta Holmgren Eiss

To touch love
gently
as one would touch a flower
I reach out
trembling
to touch
the delicate beauty of you

I live in your warmth
Cry in your tears
And know joy in your laugh

I hear your song
a song sung
from the first unfolding of time
until the time
when time collapses
back upon itself

Apples

Frost clings to the lower third and the right edge of the living-room windows.

It's a crisp December morning. Other than the light gray smoke rising from a chimney on the next lane and a dog barking in the distance, the world is as still and silent as a Currier and Ives lithograph.

The top of a car appears above the small hill of our dirt road. Soon the entire automobile is visible. It slowly navigates the snowy road passed Porter's house, the mysterious, unoccupied house next to it, Strands and their aunt-and-uncle's houses. I watch it turn into our driveway. The engine goes silent and smoke from the muffler dissipates.

The peaceful engraving returns—a country scene meant for the cover of a Christmas card.

The car door scrapes open. Coach Haddorff emerges, slaps his winter coat, adjusts his ear muffs, opens the back door, leans in and emerges with a heavy box, one he needs to hold with both hands. He pushes the door shut with his left foot, carries the box around the front of the car and passes out of my sight behind the corner of the garage.

I turn away from the window and wait for Coach to make his way up the short sidewalk.

Within seconds, I hear the expected ka-lap . . . ka-lap . . . ka-lap on the storm door.

It's immediately followed by the wrenching sound of the front door being pulled open by Mom. I hear them exchanging greetings, Mom inviting Coach in, he refusing, explaining he has a number of deliveries to make.

"Eddie," Mom calls me to the front door. When I arrive, she moves out of the way and motions me through. "Coach brought us a box of apples."

I push passed her into the cold and reach between his arms to slip my own under the box.

Mom stays to exchange a few words with him while I carry the box into the kitchen and put it on the cupboard, next to the stove. Then she shuts the door and joins me.

"It's their yearly Christmas run."

"What do you mean?"

"Every Christmas they purchase a few dozen boxes of apples and bring them to those in need."

"Nice of them."

"Yes, they really are good people."

Table of Contents

Fishing the Milky Way

The sky fractures,
And fragments of other realities appear

Left of the Ticket Booth

The bough breaks
And down comes baby
Cradle and all

The Morning of My Life

When Miracles are still possible

The Mirror Shatters

The beginning of the fall into the Funhouse

An Examined Life

Any misrepresentation of people and events is unintentional, unavoidable, and impossible — all at the same time. As with everything, it depends on the context, and multiple perspectives cannot help but conflict.

I use the real names when I know them. For my name, I use Eddie, except in rare occasions, when there is a reason to use a different one.

This is the nickname I am given as a child, and my emotional attachment to it is the most real. As I go through school and enter the adult world, Eddie slides into Ed, and Harry becomes the name most people use. Remembering who uses which name becomes especially confusing during my school days, and there are times I no longer remember which name is used to refer to me, even by my friends, who sometimes used both.

Since I earn a Ph.D. in English and obtain a position as a university professor, I am generally referred to as Dr. Eiss by students and professionals in the field. I never have any emotional attachment to it, but find it a simple way of establishing my relationship with students and one it is assumed I should be called in academic circles.

I'm also given many nicknames. Some that immediately come to mind include Edgeway (a play on Ed), Head (a play on Harry and Ed), and Hedgeway (a play on both), Ice (a good but incorrect attempt by those knowing a bit about linguistics to guess the pronunciation of Eiss), also one sometimes purposely used to reference the connotations of ice — a pronunciation I've considered adopting (as my wife has done).

A couple of others that come to mind are Psychedelic Rabbit (a play on my football running abilities and my embracement of what becomes the Hippie Movement) and Spence (have no idea why). One week, I am called Pinkie, the result of my red-and-white football jersey turning pink when Mom washes it. There are others, the kind friends use to tease friends, and some that are downright mean, the kind enemies use to condemn me.

I agree with Socrates that an unexamined life is not worth living. A human life needs to be more than a mere physical passage. It needs to be a journey of self-discovery. If we cannot find the meaning and value of ourselves, then we are nothing but hollow men and women living in a spiritual and emotional wasteland.

Disconnected

You have to begin to lose your memory, if only in bits and pieces, to realize that memory is what makes our lives. Life without memory is no life at all, just as intelligence without the possibility of expression is not really intelligence. Our memory is our coherence, our reason, our feeling, even our action. Without it, we are nothing.

Luis Buñuel

You tell me: Can you live crushed under the weight of the present? Without a memory of the past and without the desire to look ahead to the future by building something, a future, a family? Can you go on like this?

Pope Francis

Memories are fragile, ever-changing and fleeting, yet they are the clay from which stories are shaped and molded into the life of a man.

How, after all, do we define a man? It seems it must have something to do with memory. What, then, if we lose our memory?

For a time, I lost all of my memories.

Tom says I landed on my head on the sidewalk.

That can't be completely correct. If it were, I'd be dead.

Is the alternative better or worse, alive with no memories, no past . . . no me.

I still don't remember the moment. I have a vivid memory to within seconds of it, then only a few scattered memories of the days and weeks that followed.

It's a cold morning — a light rain, more a mist; the sky a barely visible, pale blue; my footprints a trail in the dew covered grass. Not ideal weather for tree service. Wet bark is slippery. Best to wait for a sunny day. An electric line hangs near the tree, but I've not bothered making arrangements with the electric company to have it dropped. This is a simple takedown.

I just need to tie-in a takedown rope for Tom to control the fall. A quick climb. Nothing to it. I don't even bother with my saddle or hang rope.

As I reach the tree, I drop my spikes and they clatter onto the sidewalk. It's nothing to buckle them over my climbing boots. I wrap the end of the manila rope around my waist and tie it in a loose knot.

Tom has already found a suitable tree on the edge of the lawn to wrap his end of the rope once I have mine in place. He slaps his chest. "All set! Let's get at it! It's cold!"

I stick my right spike into the bark and began my climb.

That's where the memory stops.

My first guess is that the power line touches the wet tree, sending electricity through it. But I'm not sure if that's even possible. Maybe I touch the wet line.

Maybe I slip. Nothing more than that. Makes sense, except I would not have landed on my head on the sidewalk, would not have landed on my head at all. I know how to roll. If I were conscious, at worst I might break a leg or an arm.

Though he saw it all, Tom has nothing more to offer. According to him, I fall about twenty feet and land on my head on the sidewalk. This means I was unconscious when I fell. I circle back to electricity. Somehow, I must have gotten a shock big enough to knock me unconscious.

It's not likely I will ever remember this lost moment and resolve how it happened. And it isn't important.

I have three clear memories of my time in the hospital. I know they're real, though they have the sense of a dream.

The first is walking with a nurse down a dimly lit hallway to a bathroom and urinating in a man's off-white urinal that stretches to the floor. I'm not embarrassed that the nurse stands in the bathroom door and watches me, but the entire experience has a surreal quality.

The second also has an unreal feel. In the middle of the night, I wander out of my room, confuse another patient's room for my own, and launch into a profanity laced tirade at the unfortunate woman in it to get out of my bed. Later I'm told that profanity is normal with brain injuries.

The third is a doctor telling my mom and I that my heart is unusually located precisely in the middle of my chest.

Do these scattered memories mean anything? While I'm prone to analyzing, I suspect there is little more to them than that my brain is struggling to regain its normal functions and these thoughts happen to stick.

I don't remember leaving the hospital, and I'm not certain of the events over the next few weeks.

I think I go straight from the hospital to stay with Mom. Deirdre has a full time job and Mom is a nurse, so that makes sense. All of my memories from my stay have to do with me creating things. I make a wall hanging of one the "tall ships" from the age of exploration by pounding tiny nails into a board and stringing wire from one to another. I make another of an owl using yarn. I turn large section of a tree trunk cut about 4" thick into a table. Mom helps me make a huge, heavy quilt out of a variety of different squares of cloth.

As with my hospital memories, these are scattered, though in both cases, they are vivid.

I don't how long I stay with her. It's probably less than I've thought through the years, probably less than a month, perhaps less than two weeks.

Somewhere during this time, I remember Deirdre deciding to try and get me health insurance, I suppose because we don't have any and the emergency has alerted her to our need for it. The result is not what she hopes. Instead, I get blacklisted and am told I cannot get insurance from anyone because of my recent fall. Apparently, all of the insurance companies have access to this list, but it is not available to the general public.

After I've moved back to my own place with Deirdre, I am still not completely recovered, even remember going golfing at the University of Minnesota golf course with John while I have double vision. I recover from this. I've also lost my sense of smell, and I never regain that.

What's even more frightening than my scattered memories of the immediate time period is that I lose my memories of my entire life.

I am certain of this, because I remember regaining my memories.

Random scenes start appearing of a boy. In the first ones, the boy is about three. He has short, blonde hair. He's playing in the sand at a lake. He has a small, yellow, plastic shovel and a small, red, plastic pail with a white handle. He looks at the camera and laughs.

Other scenes follow — not in chronological order. I'm wandering through the scattered fragments of someone else's life. That's the main thing. I'm not regaining the memories in the sense they are mine. It's more as if I'm watching movie scenes of some other boy.

I don't know how long I remain in this transitory state. The years I spend studying psychology and neurology suggest it's probably a rapid transition, and it likely happens while I'm still in the hospital.

She steps carefully through the tall grass and a patch of pussy willow. She has used its bark many times to help him ease the aches in his shoulders, but has none with her tonight. The children have gone and the crickets have stopped their chirping. A light breeze lifts the strands of hair hanging over his forehead.

"Perhaps it's best to leave it be," she says as she reaches the fallen tree trunk and begins to rub his back just below the neck. She has done it many times and knows where the muscles tighten.

He doesn't look back. There is no need. He knows her touch, her smell, her aura, knows her so well he sensed her approach without hearing or seeing it. And his muscles anticipated her wise fingers before they began pushing out the tensions.

She feels the familiar warmth of his skin. "Once the mirror is smashed the fragments are too jagged and sharp. Even the most careful, caring fingers get cut and bleed trying to gather them."

He looks at his hands. Indeed, they are the hands of one who has bled many times, hands that hold stories, stories he needs to tell before they are lost.

She leans her head into his neck and kisses him lightly. "Come, you did what you could. . . . Come, the children have gone home. . . . Come, the lake will refresh you. . . ."

He turns to look at her over his shoulder and smiles. "You should have given up on me years ago, and yet here you are, still trying to draw me away."

"Come, no one will question you, no one will deny you your rest, your time of reflection and peace."

He places his hands on the rough tree bark to brace himself and leans his head into her breasts. "You well know I cannot let him go, so you might as well stop your soothing temptations."

"Aaaaough!" she growls softly. "You're impossible!"

"Thank you! We just have to be patient. Let him work through the fragments. Once he has time to collect them and see them all around him, we can help him piece them together."

"You make it seem so simple. But you know a broken mirror cannot ever be new again!"

"And you know there's another world on the other side of that broken mirror, so stop juggling words with me!"

"Even if that mirror is the entire sky!"

He laughs. "Look." He points into the night sky. Barely visible in the moonlight.

Author's Note

While this memoir is the story of a boy who grew up in Minnesota, it is also the story of a boy who got thrust into another reality, one that cannot be found on a map. If you choose to read it, be forewarned that it is not a traditional biography of a boy growing up on Lake Minnetonka or any other literal place, but the story of a boy who got lost on the dark side of the mirror and ended up in the Funhouse.

I have no illusions as to how fragile story is and know that I never will get completely out of the Funhouse. I'm no longer confident I could live outside of it. Its strange, dark truths are far more comforting to me now than the safe truths I see on those rare occasions when the mirrors briefly become windows.

Thank You

I appreciate and thank everyone who has offered advice in my attempt to map out meaning and value. I insist on mentioning a few by name. Noreen for her expertise and for being my wife. Dr. Norton Kinghorn, the chair of my Ph.D. department, my advisor, my friend, and a man I hold in the highest respect, for being the first professional to see and support my early drafts. And Lori Sawicki, an excellent writer herself, for being kind enough to give me endless feedback and support as I worked toward my final draft.

Because
the earth is round
or nearly so
Because the past is meaningless
except it be given a story
Because the wind must blow
and the cradle must fall
baby and all
Because love cannot be explained but does exist
and refuses to be ignored
Because all things must end
except eternity and its twin sister infinity
and these are where reality and illusion intersect
Because life is more than a carefully crafted joke
or a meaningless conundrum
of physics and mathematical constructs
Because there is a difference between being alone
and being lonely
Because I've been told that one day
I'll fish among the stars of the Milky Way
Because others have asked God to bless me

Fading

The puck slides to the corner right of the goal. I lean against the St. Louis Park player to take his weight onto me and then let up, causing him to lose his balance and slide into the boards on his hands and knees. As he does, I dig the edges of my skates into the ice. A wave of ice crystals sprays over his legs as I scrape to a stop. In one continuous motion I slide my stick over the loose puck, pull it out of the frantic grasp of his leather glove and turn for an open shot at the goalie, immediately realizing I can deke him to his right, draw back the puck and flip it into an open net.

It's easy. I lean to the right. The goalie instinctually shifts to match me. I pull the puck to my left.

My right skate hits wood. Nothing can be done. I fall headfirst into the huge leg pads of the goalie, the puck left to slide aimlessly toward the sideboards, the beautiful moment destroyed by the St. Louis Park player disparately thrusting his stick into my path.

I quickly gather myself, rise to my skates and turn on him.

He has also risen and readies himself for my expected response.

In an explosion of anger, I bring my stick down squarely on his helmet, breaking the stick in half!

Time stops.

The arena disappears. Everything is silent . . . and distant.
I skate slowly into the open center of the rink, trying to hang
on, to stay visible, but I know it's
happening, know I'm disappearing . . .
feel myself fading . . .

T

Fishing in the Milky Way

Papa, why are you rowing the boat so far from the shore

Don't worry, son
I'm just going fishing

But Papa, you're rowing past the horizon
Right up into the sky

I'm going to catch some fish along the Milky Way
It will be a great adventure

But Papa, don't leave me here
Take me with you

Not this time, son
But don't worry
One day you too
will fish among the stars

Fishing the Milky Way

The she sky fractures,
And fragments of other realities appear

T

The Death of a Child

Mom waves to catch my attention. She motions me to refill Simon's feeding tube. The formula has already been mixed and is sitting on the kitchen cupboard — one cup powdered milk,

T

two cups whole milk, one teaspoon salt, two jars strained baby meat (beef, liver, pork), one jar strained baby vegetables (green and yellow alternately), one cup skim milk, one half-cup strained orange juice, and water added to make five cups, totaling 1100 calories.

In addition to feeding Simon a carefully controlled diet, it is necessary to make sure he gets Dilantin (four cubic centimeters every morning and five cubic centimeters every evening), Phenobarbital (two teaspoons every morning and evening), and Nortec (Chloral Hydrate, one teaspoon three times a day.

Simon is terminal. He has Hurler's disease. In addition, he is paralyzed in the throat and must be fed cereal through a gavage every three hours to keep up his energy. Because of all his mucus, it's necessary to do Diehl suctions with a catheter throughout the day.

Mom is on the phone, talking with Dr. Johnson. Susie is dying. "Yes," Mom says. "Okay, just a minute." Mom cradles the phone between her cheek and shoulder, picks up a folded piece of notepaper from the desk with her left hand and uses both hands to unfold it. "Okay, here it is," she says. "At 5:30 last night, Susie received eight ounces of Similac. By 6:30 her rectal temperature was 107 degrees plus, Fahrenheit. Her skin was hot; her breathing fast and labored; her eyes fixed, and her muscular contractions relaxed. I gave her two-and-one-half grams of baby aspirin and began continual sponge baths. When I contacted you at 7:00, you ordered a five-gram suppository of aspirin every four hours. At that time, her rectal temperature was 106 degrees, Fahrenheit. Shortly after that she vomited her supper and had diarrhea. By 8:15 her rectal temperature had fallen to 100.2 degrees. She still had labored

T

breathing, and her fingernails were blue. By 9:00 her fingernails had gained some color and were pink. Her breathing was easier, and her rectal temperature was 97.2 degrees. She had some muscular contractions, and she had some diarrhea and saliva.

I went to bed. At 3:15 in the morning her rectal temperature was 98.4 degrees, Fahrenheit. She was resting peacefully. At 5:15 her rectal temperature was 89.1 degrees, and she continued to rest peacefully. She had a small amount of diarrhea. At 7:15 her rectal temperature was 97.8 degrees. There was no change in her condition. At

8:45, her breathing was shallow but peaceful. Her temperature remained at 97.8 degrees. There was still no pulse."

I pour the formula into Simon's tube. Susie is a hydrocephalic. When Mom took her on, Susie was six-years-old and not expected to reach seven. She is now nine. She will not reach ten. She likely will not be alive tomorrow. It's sad. Mom is too busy trying to keep Susie alive to cry now. But Mom will cry when it's over. I will cry, too, but not as much as Mom. Mom has been caring for Susie day in and day out, night in and night out, for three years – feeding her and washing her and trying to give her some joy, some reason for having been born. For Mom, the large head, the languid eyes, the atrophied limbs, the hole in the throat – all repulsive to outsiders – have become the identifying marks, part of the personality of a real human, someone who can laugh and cry, someone to be cherished.

When Mom nursed Dad, there was a difference. Dad had a sharp mind until the very end. And he lived a healthy life for over 37 years before getting cancer. Yet the unfairness remains. It is not fair that Susie should be born mentally and

T

physically deformed only to die at the age of nine. It is not fair that Dad was suddenly stricken with cancer and died a painful death before his full life was lived out.

The same can be said about the other welfare children in Mom's care. Mary is a micro-cephalic with severe mental and motor disabilities. When she arrived two years ago, it was necessary to give her a half a teaspoon of Versapen twice a day for a decubitus ulcer on the right side of her head. The ulcer cleared up and the Versapen was discontinued. The other medicines will continue until she dies — Phenobarbital (six cubic centimeters four times a day), Valium (one milligram three times a day), and Nortec (five cubic centimeters prn). Her meals consist of eight ounces of Similac four times a day and eight ounces of fruit juice every morning.

She was a pretty, thirteen-month-old baby when she arrived — curly, light brown hair, brown eyes, high cheekbones, small, pouty mouth. Her parents and grandparents were all very appreciative of Mom's willingness to care for her. They tried to do it themselves but found it too much of an emotional strain. Besides, Mary required the constant attention of someone with medical expertise, something her parents did not have. She was classified as terminal, and sadly but honestly could only hope to die quickly and painlessly.

Peter was four-years-two-months old when he arrived. We've only had him for three months now. He is not terminal, but he is blind and subject to grand mal seizures. He was dropped when he was only two weeks old and suffered a subdural hematoma. Tongue blades and Phenobarbital are to be used in case of a seizure. The Phenobarbital, along with potassium chloride and penicillin, is also to be used at Mom's discretion. Peter has black hair and large blue eyes. He is

T

severely disabled and spastic. He can't walk or talk, but he can sit up and roll on the floor. He eats pureed food and drinks liquid from a bottle.

Charity is only six-days-old and has no real physical problems. She has been voluntarily given up by her parents. We're not told why. Within a few days or perhaps weeks, Charity will be placed in a permanent home through the Children's Home Society in St. Paul. She was born bald and has a very round face. She cries a good deal, especially at night, and in many ways has the worst personality of them all. But Mom enjoys Charity. After all, Charity is a normal child, a breath of fresh air.

Of course, there are Jimmy and Johnny, the twins. Mom was given them in 1963, straight out of the hospital, when they were two weeks old. They were born prematurely; Jimmy weighed four-pounds-eleven-ounces, Johnny three-pounds-ten-ounces. Both have blond hair, blue eyes and dimples, and fit the category of cute babies; however, we are told in the terminology of the times, it is believed they will be mentally disabled or at least "slow learners," since both the parents are. On a regular basis, they must be brought to the Minneapolis Clinic of Psychiatry and Neurology to see a neurologist and have encephalograms. Their medicine consists of ten milligrams a day of Mellaril (thioridazine), a sedative used for schizophrenia. They are extremely hyper. It is becoming apparent that no one is going to adopt them. They're going to become a permanent part of the family.

Since Dad didn't have medical or life insurance and his fight with cancer resulted in thousands-upon-thousands of dollars in hospital bills, when he died, Mom faced bankruptcy, but she refused to declare it. She believed in paying her bills.

T

However, Mom had not had a job since she married Dad some thirteen years previous to his death. She did not want to go back into nursing. She said her training was outdated and it would be impossible for her to go back to college at her age. Instead, she tried working at a furniture-making factory. The job was both tiring and dangerous. It lasted only a few months. Then she took a job working on the assembly line at Tonka Toys. Once again, the job lasted only a few months. Mom was not cut-out for factory work. She next took a job as a waitress at the Ambassador Motel and Restaurant located on Highway 12 in St. Louis Park. She seemed to like waitressing better, but she hated the drive home at night.

Her fears were not unfounded. There was a real possibility of the car breaking down every time she drove it. Not only was it old and rusting away, but she had no idea how to maintain it, not even such simple things as changing the oil, replacing a battery or keeping the radiator filled, and though she had no fear of physical labor, she would not have known how to change a flat tire on the side of a road at night, even had she a working jack, lug-nut wrench and spare tire that wasn't flat itself. This was a real concern, as the tires were old and ready to go at any time.

But her greatest fear was that men would follow her home.

She was deathly afraid of being raped. More than once she arrived home from her late-night shift, turned off the lights and rushed John and me into a dark corner of the basement.

Sometimes a car would slowly pass the house, turn around at the end of the lane and leave. There was no way of making certain whether she was being followed or not, yet there is no other explanation. We lived at the end of a dirt road that no one would be driving immediately after her unless she was

T

being followed. And even if the men in those cars never stopped, it made sense to think they might stake out the house for a return visit. It never happened. She never was attacked, but her fear was real.

I felt it – that eerie, unsettled danger as we crouched beneath a blanket in a damp corner of the basement. Still and silent, we huddled together, watched the quiet road beneath the yellow streetlight and listened for the furtive car. If I looked away from the road at the shadows surrounding us in our dark basement, I could partially make out the broken chairs, the tattered cardboard boxes of clothes and the random stacks of old lumber. There was a large Victorian style lamp without a cord and a broken window fan and a sled without one of its runners. There was a brown teddy-bear-without-eyes-and-only-one-ear and there were untold other dark forms that could not be identified. Sometimes, if I shifted just right, the light would catch the glass eyes of an old, stuffed owl. I wondered if ghosts were present.

After about a year at the Ambassador, Mom quit and took a job at Woodhill Country Club. It was still waitressing, but the drive home was cut in half. The problems remained. A drive home at night, even half as long, was still a drive home at night. Besides, waitressing did not bring in enough money to pay the monthly bills, much less begin the huge task of paying the past debts.

Then came the idea of taking care of welfare children. Mom loved and was good with children. Plus, she had been a nurse. If she could get enough welfare children, she could start paying off the debts. Furthermore, she could stay at home – something she dearly wanted.

T

The idea seemed a godsend, at least at first, and Mom began taking in welfare children. In the beginning, she only had one, two or three at-a-time — all relatively normal children, easy to care for. They had been placed in a welfare home because the parents simply did not want them or because the parents had been deemed unfit to raise them. They were nearly all less than a year old. There was no psychological damage, at least nothing noticeable, and Mom enjoyed caring for babies. Unfortunately, the extra money brought in for such normal children was still barely enough to keep the most meager food on the table, not enough to pay the standard monthly bills, certainly not enough to tackle the larger debts.

The years since Dad's death had barely begun the very slow digging out from poverty (from the splitting of one pound of hamburger a month between the three of us as our only meat, the using of a cheap, white margarine that both looked and tasted like lard on homemade buns made of the cheapest ingredients, and the eating of oatmeal with water for our daily diets to having an occasional meal of chicken and even pork chops), but we were a long way from catching up on the bills and leading anything close to what might be considered a middle-class or even lower middle-class existence, anything close to the life style of our neighbors and friends.

Fortunately, the welfare department needed someone with Mom's expertise as much as we needed their money. By 1965, Mom had been given a license to care for five children in addition to the twins, and this had been done with the idea of giving her the critical young children — those who were physically deformed, had serious mental problems, needed special medications, and often were expected to die soon —

T

children such as Peter and Mary and Charity and Susan. Many had been born with their
hardships, some had suffered a serious accident, and some had been taken from their parents because those parents beat and molested them.

Eventually, Mom would get a severely retarded six-year-old girl, whose parents had visiting rights, and the right to take her to their own home over the weekends. It was obvious to Mom that these visits were resulting in sexual intercourse with the child, and Mom reported it. The Welfare Agency said that nothing could be done. That would be the standard reply for such incidents in a series of battles that eventually would lead Mom to quit, retaining only her care for Jimmy and Johnny, the unofficially adopted twins.

Mom hangs up the phone. Nothing to do but wait. Unfortunately, it's Saturday. At 1:00 Mom must take Jimmy to the doctor in Wayzata; at 2:30 Peter's parents are coming to visit, and at 4:00 Mom has to take Charity to the doctor in Hopkins for a measles shot.

Saturday is the main day for such errands, since either John or I will be home to babysit. Mom has tried to find other babysitters, but no one is willing to care for such children, even for a short period of time. I can still see the frightened faces of potential babysitters as they quickly excuse themselves upon being introduced to the children. However, it would be misleading to say John and I were enthusiastic babysitters. We weren't frightened, but, at least to us, we had "better" things to do on a Saturday, or any other day, than fill feeding tubes, change diapers, flush their disgusting contents down the toilet when necessary, and process them through the ever-running washer and drier.

T

I sit down on the ragged cushions of the living room couch and look out the windows through the trees to the lake below. The sunlight sparkles off the water.

Our house is about to witness yet another death. I watch the wind ripple through the tree leaves, imagine the gentle rustling sound, the feel of it on my skin.

"Eddie," Mom says as she enters the living room. "I'm going to cancel all appointments for today." She doesn't say why. It isn't necessary. We both know why.

At least we have our own phone line. It isn't that many years since we were on a party line, nine houses all connected to the same line, all able to listen to the others' conversations, all having to wait until the line is free to use it.

Mom sits down on an old armchair across from me and takes a sip from her coffee. She is a constant coffee drinker and has developed a taste for instant coffee, black. "It's a good thing football hasn't started yet. I'd have to miss your game," she says and smiles.

"That's life," I reply. I would have understood. Even at that age I know there are more important things in life than a football game.

I don't play much baseball. Baseball in our town is controlled by the good old boy system, and I don't have a father to be one of the good old boys (that situation will cost me in all sports, and in other areas of life, often without me realizing it until years later). However, I've already established myself as the star athlete in my grade, partially because of natural abilities and partially because I'm so competitive – all out all the time. It's my battle zone, a place with rules that make sense, nothing ambiguous – at least that's what I felt at the time.

T

"Want to play Chinese Checkers?" Mom asks. She's the best Chinese checkers player I ever knew. Chinese Checkers and Scrabble, those are her games. John and I are good at cards, but Mom always wins her two games. Unfortunately for her, we seldom play her games. We like cards. I was playing Canasta and Five-hundred (a game similar to Bridge) before Dad died, and after he died, John and I often played Five-hundred as partners against Mom and one of the neighbors, if one could be found to play with us.

For a while, Mom went with Harold Lundby, a nice man who lived across the street for a few years, and he would come over and be Mom's partner. John and I usually won. And there was a famous game, where we were so far behind we had to bid and make ten-no-trump two hands in a row to win, and we did.

Harold Lundby was a retired painter who had moved to Three Points after his wife died. Of the few men Mom dated after Dad died, he was the one John and I liked the most. I remember a nephew of his coming to stay with him one summer, and the two of us connecting, spending a good deal of time swimming off my dilapidated dock and make-shift raft. Harold Lundby truly fell in love with Mom. Even at my young age, I could see it. It was the closest she would come to remarrying. She even took him to meet the relatives on her side of the family. (We had almost no contact with Dad's relatives.) Unfortunately, Harold was older than Mom, and he had gray hair. Her parents and siblings teased her about going with such an old man, and she could not get passed their teasing. It was the kind of thing they did, if not intentionally, the result of being insensitive. Curious how extremely intelligent people can also be so inhumane. And

T

their opinions still influenced her, even though she had separated from them long ago and they had shown little interest in helping her through the hard times during and following Dad's death.

It's strange to think of Mom as being rebellious, a black-sheep, independent person, who stood up to her parents, put herself through college, becoming a nurse instead of the teacher her mother had been and wanted her to be, but, in truth, she was. Behind the innocent county girl, who went to church and had a simple faith in God, the somewhat shy woman who only wanted to be a wife and mother, was perhaps the most liberal, independent person I ever knew.

I still remember the Saturday a neighbor came rushing to our house genuinely intent on saving us because he had seen a Black couple pull up to our door and enter. He was sincere in trying to be a good man and protect his neighbor. Of course, that's how many such people think. If one is prejudiced, it all becomes obvious, and then one just adds in the sexism, and it is easy to see how a White Woman is in severe danger having a Black couple enter her house. It never occurred to Mom. She had taken on a Black welfare child, a good-looking baby, and the parents were there for their first of what would be weekly visits. Our town had no Blacks in it at the time. Mom, without even considering the hugeness of what she was doing, had broken a barrier.

It was all so natural for her. She did not struggle with the ethics or the complications of it. People were not to be judged by their race. People were people.

And it wasn't just in terms of race. She had that same approach to everything. Her simple faith in her religion did not include a condemnation of other religions. And because this

T

prejudice did not register for her, she had gone against her family by marrying outside her church. She and her family were Methodists, and Dad was Lutheran, not a strikingly different religion, but, nonetheless, for her family, marrying a Lutheran was a sin. She did it because she fell in love. It had nothing to do with either rejecting or embracing a narrow religious prejudice.

Later in life, still poor and in need of a job, she began working as a janitor at a private school. The other janitors were men, and they did not believe a woman should have such a job; it was man's work. They made sure to make life as difficult for her as possible. It was one of those scenarios often stereotyped and thus made more comfortable in news reports or fiction, of a victim, in this case a poor, good hearted, hard-working, older woman, finding herself in a position of being not just taken advantage of, but purposely hurt, isolated, forced to do far more than her share of the work, condemned for it, and pointedly made aware she was going to be not just physically but psychologically a victim as long as she worked there.

In her case, there is no need to soften the truth, no need to complicate the reality of it with complex philosophy or commentary. Rather than a detailed drawing of lines and colors, it is a silhouette. She works alone in the night, a dark shadow in the dull, yellow light of the classroom or the cold white light of the moon, while the men gather in other buildings and socialize over coffee and cigarettes.

Not only was she living in this world of blatant prejudice, but this was another job requiring her to drive at night, and now the drive was even longer than those of the past, involving more freeway driving, something she hated, holding the added danger of her weakened sight, especially at night, and a

T

return to a home she lived in alone. I cannot help but think of the fears she must have known.

At this time in life, I was living in another state, and only communicated with her by phone. But the sorrow came through. Wish I could have done something, but in the reality of life there was nothing for me to do but listen, listen to the stories of how she had to re-wax floors because the men "accidentally" scuffed them after she had finished, the stories of how her boss assigned her three buildings to clean, while two or three of the men had but one to do as a group, the stories of how she was purposely given the heavy furniture to move by herself, while the men moved it in twos, and then condemned her for failing. I was not able to give her much real, physical, economic or hands-on help. I was as poor as she, had a family I was trying to support and a career that required me to live far from her. I was also busy fighting my own nightmares.

Are these just excuses? I don't think so, but my demons of guilt sometimes, often, make me wonder. I can't shake my thoughts of her driving nearly blind in the night, trying to merge onto Highway 100 from the onramp, guessing more than knowing if cars are coming, arriving at work shaken from the drive only to face her cruel co-workers, or unlocking her front door after the trip home to enter a dark house, not knowing if a man has broken in and is waiting for her. On a good night, sitting in her dark house alone with but her ever-present dog and the television to keep the emptiness away.

While she was facing real on-the-job sexual prejudice, she had absolutely no interest in the Feminist Movement going on all around her. She saw nothing wrong with the traditional roles for women and men, and worked outside of the home, not

T

because she was against being a housewife (it's what she wanted to be), but because she had no choice.

I'm convinced that her living and believing in things from a naïve perspective intuitively held a profound understanding of life. Unfortunately, it also opened her up to those who don't understand this deeper ethos, and they often saw her as less than she was, taking advantage of her trust, which, in turn, would make her sad. She couldn't understand why people would purposely do bad things, and it wasn't until late in life that she accepted it. The longer I lived, the more I realized how all this worked and wished I could have found a way to resolve or at least lessen it for her, but I never did.

I continued to visit her every summer and fly her to wherever I was living for Christmas, until there came the year she got too weak to make the trip and told me she had to stop. It was the first year after the Twin Towers attack and airport security was extreme. She had had a stroke, one leaving her left arm nearly unusable and though she could still walk, she did it with a noticeable limp. I remember the two of us standing in a confused crowd of slow-moving lines until she finally had to tell me she could stand no longer. I still hear her saying it, "Sorry, Ed, but I have to sit down." Ahh! I felt terrible! I hadn't realized how hard it was for her! My guilt prompted me to action and I aggressively led her through the crowd to the front.

Airport Security was not friendly, but I was insistent. She had to have a wheelchair. Once they realized I was not going to let it go and allow them to fade us back into the crowd, they suddenly turned nice, smiling and offering condolences. Almost immediately, one appeared with a wheelchair and helped her into it. That was the extent of their sympathy. I was coldly

T

dismissed — blocked from following as they quickly turned her about and pushed her through the gate. It was a disjointed goodbye. I suppose we had already said goodbye several times over, whether we actually spoke the words, but that final abrupt separation felt incomplete.

I watched as they wheeled her away from me down the large, nearly empty hallway. She was so small and weak my eyes filled with tears that ran freely down my cheeks. Who cared if the mass of people surrounding me saw my sorrow.

Her Christmas visits were a much-anticipated event, not just because everyone enjoyed seeing her, but because she had always made Christmas special, not for either its religious or its commercial aspects (for a few years after Dad's death we continued our tradition of attending the Christmas Eve service, but once I got my Confirmation through Sunday School that also ended, and though Mom always spent way more than she could afford on Christmas, that still didn't amount to much). What made it special was that it meant so much to her. It was a childlike joy she connected to the holiday, a sense of it being a time of family — whether it be an evening sewing popcorn into long strings to hang on the tree or an afternoon making a floury mess of the kitchen and dining-room in a wonderland of homemade Christmas cookies, especially the sugar cookies.

Dad had figured out how to cut out the tops and bottoms of tin cans, keeping the rims, cutting the barrels about an inch down, and then bending them into various shapes, perfect for making his own cookie cutter designs, and though we accumulated a few commercial cutters through the years, we still liked to use his. We had a whole cardboard box of tin Christmas shapes — angels, stars, bells, camels, Christmas trees,

T

Santa Clauses, snowmen, candy canes, deer, wreathes. On JoAnn's wedding he made a number of different sized hearts, and those always also got included, whether or not they really belonged to the world of Christmas. After we got our cut shapes onto the trays, we spread colored frosting, shook on colored sprinkles and put them in the oven – hoping not to burn them (always had to burn a sheet or two, was part of the experience).

In addition to his larger jobs improving the house and yard, Dad did these smaller creative bits that tended to go unnoticed. I still remember the dozen two-to-three-inch replicas of fish he cut out of quarter-inch plywood on his jigsaw, carefully painted with delicate details, and glued to the walls above our bathtub. Certainly, they were a poor-man's decoration, but they were well done. He also made me my own Tonka Toy trucks when a shipping box of the toy's wheels fell from one of their trucks and bounced into the weeds along Highway 12.

Sure, his trucks weren't the real thing, but he could cut and paint wood well enough to satisfy my needs, and the hill of sand in our yard from digging out the basement was just the thing for my own toy truck fantasies, an ideal place for me to create my sand highways and entertain myself for hours.

He also made me a wonderful, small tool-table for my own wood building tasks. Guess I'm not to know he built it. On Christmas Eve there was a ringing of Santa's bells outside, and when we opened the door, the exciting tool-table was sitting there with a big red bow. He had put some time into it. There were slots for a hammer, a screwdriver, a saw, and a pliers, and there was a drawer; and of course, my present under the tree was a small set of tools to go with it.

T

Another Christmas he satisfied my desire to have the toy Alamo set that was being featured on all the commercials by building me my own out of scraps of pine and hardboard. When I think back, his version was actually much better than the store version. His was a carefully constructed set of buildings and walls (much like a castle's surrounding walls), with small, lookout walkways for my toy soldiers and even tiny hinges so I could open and shut the front gate. I didn't have the right toy soldiers for the Alamo, but I was okay with my collection of odds-and-ends cowboys and WWII figures. I could dispense with the obvious contradictions in my imagination, and I spent many an evening in the dim yellow light of our living-room making up my own versions of the story. Sometimes I would shoot rubber bands at the soldiers to simulate battles, but in truth that never really worked, and in the end the main thing was to construct the scene.

He also found a discarded basketball hoop, built a wood backboard, and found a way to attach it to the old building we used as a garage. Many years later, after he died and we tore down this building, I managed to attach that homemade backboard to a large tree that grew between the house and the road, and I spent many, many evenings shooting baskets in the dim yellow of the street light, pretending to have contests where I took on the roles of different players.

After decades of clinging to the house she and Dad had embraced as their own, Mom finally had to admit that she had grown too old, had to accept that it was no longer safe for her to stay alone in this old, make-shift house filled with endless dangers, and though it was a hard surrender, she made the decision and moved into Presbyterian Homes and Services, a highly rated senior citizens center in Spring Park.

T

I think it was the death of her latest cocker spaniel, named Skipper as usual. He had been her companion in the house and now it was empty. This aloneness was accented by the changing make-up of the neighborhood. Those that had been part of her and Dad's world were mostly gone, and those replacing them brought a different atmosphere. Three Points was no longer a place for poor people to live in rough-hewn buildings. The public land we had all shared along the lake was privatized, and a new wave of wealthy business men and women who worked in Minneapolis began building their million-dollar homes on Lake Minnetonka. The road connecting the peninsula to the mainland was raised in the stretch where it crossed through the swamp and had flooded over each spring, much of the swamp was landscaped, and Seahorse Apartments now stood where once I had hunted turtles through the bulrushes.

It was no longer possible to tie an old manila rope to the branch of a large cottonwood and use it to swing over and into the water. It was no longer possible to gather discarded wood and build a boy's fort in nearby woods. It was no longer possible to informally stake a claim to one's own dock simply by building it. Now it was necessary to get a license and conform the dock to the township's rules, which meant the old wooden posts that had been sturdy enough to be left up all winter for decades had to be replaced with metal ones that needed to be taken down each autumn, stored somewhere away from the shore over the winter, and put back up each spring. The length, style and color of these docks was carefully controlled, and such things as the diving board I had hammered into place at the end of ours were no longer allowed. The number and types of watercraft that could be kept at the dock were strictly regulated. A

T

yearly license was necessary, and inspectors began making random checks. The raft I had built and found to be such a perfect fit for our bay would no longer be allowed. There were rules, and they weren't about to allow homemade anything.

This new world of regulations extended well beyond the use of the lakes. It was no longer possible to dig out one's own basement and use the dirt to level out the yard, as Dad had done, or haul it in a wheelbarrow across the gravel street to create a walking path through a swampy woods, as Bill Howell had done – land someone must have owned, but no one knew who or thought it necessary to find out. For better or worse, the roads were no longer dirt. Wealthy people want asphalt roads, and now they had them.

Mom's friends were mostly gone. Her best friend Vera, her coffee confidant, had died. Dad's friends no longer gathered informally as the sun began to sink toward the horizon, often holding a beer, talking about their baseball or bowling leagues or how to come up with the money to fix their worn-down brake pads.

In the autumn, neighbors no longer leaned on their old rakes to commiserate at the end of a day of coaxing leaves into the ditch along the dirt road. It had been a ritual going back beyond memory, and it had developed certain rites – a huge pile of leaves for children and even adults to dive into, roll about and end up laughing for no real reason; a bag of marshmallows, a box of graham crackers, Hershey bars, the fun task of finding fallen branches or small saplings suited to filing into a point with a jack knife for roasting the marshmallows over the burning leaves and making s'mores, a challenge because there was a talent to getting the marshmallows just melting, not burnt (depending on one's

T

taste), and not having them fall off into the fire, not to mention the clearly undignified task of maneuvering the sloppy combination of melted marshmallow and chocolate barely held together between two fragile crackers into one's mouth without it dripping on clothes and the even greater dangers of burning lips and tongue. Indeed, the ceremony of standing or sitting late into the night to make sure the leaves burned without incident had turned a task into a memory. I still smell those burning leaves when I remember sitting on the porch with Dad beneath a clear sky of stars.

Of course, any community is going to have its arguments and constant complaining, yet there was a general acceptance of it being a community. Children considered the entire neighborhood common ground, playing games such as capture-the-flag on a field that stretched through blocks of people's yards without it occurring to anyone it might be necessary to ask permission.

Now that world, Mom's world with Dad that she had so desperately held onto, was gone. The new neighbors had little interest in the older woman living in the poor house they wished would get condemned and replaced. If she should bring over a plate of cookies, they put up with her or might even be rude. They didn't understand such customs, thought them the quaint, eccentric actions of a nuisance they didn't want to bother them.

John deserves a lot of credit. While we were both still living there, and Dad's death had resulted in a feeling of the three of us against the world, we had been constantly finding ways to solve whatever needed fixing in that old, outdated house. There was no one to turn to for help or even advice, and there was no money to purchase materials or tools. It never occurred to us

T

that we should either reach out for help or give up with these easy excuses. Instead we innocently assumed we could and would solve the problems with what we had. And we did. Not only that, but Mom took the cliché of a woman wanting to constantly move the furniture around rooms to a new level, and we literally knocked down and rebuilt walls! Why not? That's what she and Dad had been doing all along.

But I was growing out of this world, spending less and less time in it, and though John was not as prone to adventure out, both of us grew less and less willing to spend our free time helping keep up the house. During my years attending the University of Minnesota, I lived close enough to continue to help, and my visits became a matter of how many of the needed repairs I was willing to take on. It was similar for John, and from then on, we shared the mixed frustration of knowing Mom always had lists of projects that we had to either do or feel guilty about not doing. After I moved out of the state and my visits became less frequent, though the lists were still there for me when I did visit, her needs still involved weekly help, not help once or twice a year, and much of this would fall on John's shoulders.

John would also move too far away for such constant help, but not for long. After moving to International Falls for a few years, he moved back to the Minneapolis suburbs, close enough to help her out, soon moving to Long Lake, less than a half hour drive away. So, he became the one to have almost daily contact with her. By this time, he had married Bonnie and adopted her daughter Lisa, and the three of them would share the joys and tasks of helping Mom maintain her life.

But an older woman living in an older house alone grows more and more dangerous. And this house held even more dangers than most. Add to this her continual fearless tendency to pick up a saw or a shovel or an axe and take on whatever needed doing, and it's amazing she never had a serious accident. Eventually, her fears of driving on freeways at night turned into the reality of her not only not being able to drive at night but not being able to drive at all.

She had fought to keep the house. Refused to give it up. It had taken on a matter of principle. No one was going to force her out of the house she and Dad had shared during the best years of her life.

While both John and I could step back and see it all through a different lens, we were determined to leave the decision to her. We understood.

But now, finally, she knew.

And as wrong as she might have been to so stubbornly cling to that house, by the time she gave it up, it really did mean she was giving up on her life. Yes, the senior citizens center had all of the amenities, everything to make her life safer and more comfortable, yet there can be no doubt but that sitting in her special, comfortable bed watching a big screen television, rather than falling asleep on an old couch watching an older, often unwatchable television, meant her life was over, meant she was just waiting for the end.

Though my Christmas gatherings with her were done and she no longer lived in the house, my summer visits continued, and with each one I saw her growing noticeably older. Soon she began the shaking that comes with Parkinson's and she worried about it getting worse. She talked more and more about how she was afraid she would end-up tied to a hospital bed in some nightmarish existence and urged John and me again and again to make sure that didn't happen.

T

Of course, it didn't. We couldn't even conceive of such a horrible thing. But for some reason, this dark vision continued to haunt her.

Eventually her health deteriorated so much she could no longer get out of bed, and my visits became nothing more than an hour or two of sitting by her bedside, just being with her until she fell asleep. Her kidneys stopped working completely. She complained she couldn't swallow, but the doctors ignored this for months before realizing there really was something wrong. Even though John had gotten her set up with a large television to watch and I had taken her to purchase a special bed, things grew worse. More than once I would call, hear the phone get picked up, followed by a soft bang and no answer. I would speak into my phone, "Mom? Mom? Are you there? Mom?" No answer. It made no sense.

Months later it sadly crystalized. She had picked up the phone, been too weak to get it to her ear and dropped it. She couldn't reach it. There was nothing more to be done. How horrible. It breaks my heart.

During her years at the center, she collected angel figurines, and for her final birthday, I gave her one depicting an angel and two lambs. It didn't seem to mean much to her – she had reached the point where nothing mattered anymore. Guess it was selfish of me to want her to still care, to appreciate what I felt was a thoughtful gift. I tried to get her to tell me about her life, partially for her and partially for me. I wanted to flesh it out, to understand her more, and I knew time was running out. But it was hard to get her to have any interest. She was done with this world. It was time to go.

Then the doctors started giving her strong drugs, and she began hallucinating. She told me some of these. In one, her bed

T

stood on end and rushed her across the room to slam against the wall. She said she both experienced it and yet knew it was not real at the same time. Must have been a terrible psychological state.

Is it even possible to relate to being so sick one does not have the strength to use a television remote, has to take drugs that cause bizarre, frightening nightmares, cannot swallow or urinate, cannot do much of anything, and yet have a mind still sharp enough to know it — minute after minute, hour after hour, day after day, week after week, month after month?

But all of this is the future.

Today Mom is busy trying to ease another soul into Heaven, dealing with the death of a child she has spent years comforting, finding ways to make laugh, and falling in love with as she tried to give a lost soul a bit of joy in a world that still moved through the shadows of the death of her own husband.

Even as young children, John and I both want her to find another man, to fall in love again and marry. But she never will.

In the end, it isn't her family's teasing that stops her, or anything more than a very simple truth, so simple that people often don't believe it; and at the time, John and I are far too young to understand. Mom's not finding someone else and remarrying is the result of her deep love for Dad. She just cannot get herself to have sex with another man. Dad has been her true, true love, and with his death goes her desire for romance, or at least her ability to satisfy it. Rather, she will spend the rest of her life in mourning.

T

Another part of this truth is that she is badly shaken by his death and never is the woman she has been before it. Three times in the first few months after he dies, she is involved in car accidents. No one is hurt, but the closeness of tragedy surrounds her.

"Well! Are you going to answer me or are you just gonna sit there like a fence post and ignore me!" Mom says.

"Oh, no, no, I don't feel like Chinese Checkers," I say.

Mom takes another sip of her coffee. She has dark brown hair, very fine hair, and brown eyes. She used to keep her hair curled at the ends, but in recent years she has lost interest in doing much of anything with it. She has an oval face and a thin figure, but these, too, are not what they once were. The facial skin is no longer as soft as it was even a few years ago, the body not as spry.

"Well," Mom says, "since you're just going to be a stick-in-the-mud, I'm going to go back and check on Susie."

I look out the window and think about going down to the raft.

What am I to do?

It seems I should do something, but what?

Susie is going to die.

No one can prevent that.

She has already outlived the time she's been promised.

Everyone dies.

What was it Barney Strand said between his sips of beer, "There are only two certainties in life, death and taxes"?

But then what?

After death?

Heaven?

T

If Heaven is so wonderful, why don't people yearn to die, instead of crying and mourning when it happens?

It's a beautiful day, blue skies with huge cumulous clouds. I can see the waves rippling across the lake. I can imagine their sound as they lap against the shore.

It's my sanctuary. Sure, others trespass in and on it, but not many and none are as attached to it as me.

What to do?

I'm no help to Mom. Perhaps I can visit with her between her nursing duties, but I'm not up for it. Making small talk while waiting for Susie's death?

We have no air conditioning, and the hot day is also humid. I decide to walk down to the lake, not sure if I want to go swimming or maybe lie in the sun on the dock. When I get up from the couch, a loose wire in the armrest catches the back of my pants, resulting in a five-inch rip in the left leg. Oh great, I think, my one pair of pants without a tare.

"Eddie," Mom calls and the rip is quickly forgotten. Susie is dead.

In less than half-an-hour, two police cars arrive. I sit in the living room and gaze out at the lake. Susie looks no different dead than she looked an hour previous, when she was still alive. I remember the waxy look of Dad when I saw him in his coffin. His cheeks were overly red, as were his lips.

The police go into the dining room to make out their report. I pay them no attention.

Then, I hear one of them calling to me. "Hey, boy, you hear me! I said come in here!"

"What? Why?" I mumble, pulling myself to the present.

"Don't get smart, boy! Just get in here!" he orders.

T

This command strikes me wrong. "Sure, sure, sure," I say sarcastically.

But before I've stood up, the policeman is leaning over me. "You listen, boy, and you listen good! There's a dead body right through that there door! For all I know, you're responsible for its death! You know anything about death, boy! Of course not! You're too young to know anything about death! Well, you listen to me! Death is a serious business! Now you just get your ass in the dining-room and answer some questions, so we can fill out our report! You understand me, boy!"

This outburst is the spark that starts Mom crying. The other policeman walks over to her and says, "Listen, Mam, maybe it would be best if you asked your son here to leave until this is all over with. Joe, just let the boy go outside. We don't need anything from him."

The policeman leaning over me stands up. "Damn kids! Think you're so damn smart! Have no respect for anything! Well, go on, get the hell outta here!"

Mom mumbles through her crying, "Eddie, why don't you go swimming for a while. The coroner will be here shortly, and this will all be over with."

The policeman steps back just enough for me to rise. When I do, he shoves me toward the door.

I slam the door and turn toward the dirt road, muttering under my breath, "Don't trust the bastards; they'll probably plant a gun in the crib and accuse you of shooting, what did he call Susie, the IT!"

The coroner stops his car between the two police cars and calls out, "Is this the house that phoned about the death?"

"Yes," I reply. "The police are drilling my mom right now, seem to think IT was killed!"

T

The coroner frowns and rushes past me. For some reason it strikes me as wrong that he has left his car sitting in the middle of the street. No one could have driven through anyway, since both the police cars are also left in the middle.

I walk slowly down to our dock. I'm still wearing my ripped pants, but it won't be the first time I've swum in long pants. I take off my shirt and throw it up the road in the direction of the house. It lands in the road. I'm barefoot – standard in the summer. In fact, the souls of my feet have become so tough that I barely feel the stones on the gravel road.

It's late in the summer for swimming, but this year an Indian summer has settled on Lake Minnetonka.

Our road ends about twenty yards past our house. The end of the road is followed by a fifteen-foot wooded decline to the lake. We've built wood stairs down this drop to our dock.

A year previous the telephone company replaced the telephone pole outside our house and gave me the old pole. I sawed it in half with a dull board saw and nailed some of the old two-by-fours piled in our back yard crosswise to build a swimming raft. It's ten feet long and eight feet wide, and the top of it floats three inches above the water. I found an anchor on the bottom of the lake, took a piece of used clothes line, hammered a spike halfway into the end of one telephone pole, tied one end of the line to it, and bent the spike over to secure the line to the raft. Then, I tied the other end to the anchor. Finally, I took two old wooden oars from when Dad was alive and slid them into the water under the raft. The relatives took Dad's two outboard motors but had no use for the unmatched oars. They're fine for my purposes. All-in-all, the project turns out well. My raft is ideal for swimming. It always stays just above the water line, no matter how many people are on it.

T

It's a way for me to escape, to be securely separated from everyone. All I have to do is row or swim it about fifty yards from shore and drop anchor.

I finish my walk down to the raft, untie it, and swim it to the middle of the lake. The sky is a pale blue, and a hot white sun glistens on the lake surface. I drop anchor and lie down on the raft. Within minutes the sun dries my skin and hair. Even my pants will be dry in less than a half hour. Though a bright sun reflecting off Lake Minnetonka can burn the uninitiated in minutes, my skin has turned a rich, dark tan over the summer, and there is no chance of that happening to me.

I cover my eyes with my arms to block out the day and let the gently rocking raft lull me into a half sleep. A radio blares from the shore: "Be not too hard, for life is short, and nothing is given to man . . ." I recognize Joan Baez's voice. Children yell and laugh from the small beach at the end of Lane Three, just before the shoreline bends away to give the bay the shape of a dog's back leg.

The water laps against the raft, a soothing lullaby – lap, lap, lap-lap, lap, lap, lap-lap-lap . . .

I remember the night Reverend Voll comes to the house. Dad has become ever more emaciated, but we still believe the latest chemotherapy will work, will save him. It's late at night. I've been sent to bed long ago and am assumed to be asleep. But I hear the minister at the door and sneak out of bed to see what's up.

Mom and the minister go directly into my parents' bedroom. I quietly cross the small, darkened hallway and look in the partially open door. Dad is sleeping, breathing in a faint, rasping manner. Mom stands by his head. The minister stands

T

at the foot of the bed, his back to me, a Bible open in his hand. I listen as he prays:

"Dear God, we beseech you in your infinite mercy, please let this man . . . die quickly!"

My internal scream is deafening, the last shred of hope gone, the prayer not for life, but for death!

That memory, that moment in time, will never leave me.

After Dad's death, I try to figure out death. Many nights I lie awake, forcing myself to be as honest as I can. Death I decide is simply nothingness. That is the final truth all of our religions and other occult systems try to hide from us, because it is too harsh a truth for us to handle. We die and that's it. Nothingness. Within perhaps a generation we are completely forgotten, as if we never even lived.

Such is the deep insight of a ten-year-old.

I think about Susie, a child born with only a very short life to live, a life that could not have the full workings of a complete, healthy, human mind. In many ways, she was more like an animal, a dog, than a human. She would never talk or walk or comprehend even simple words. Yet, she certainly could feel sorrow, and joy, and even love. Now she is dead. Many will say she is better off, that she has gone to a better world. That will be Mom's thought.

I fall into an uneasy sleep.

I see Susie alone in a maze. Brick walls rise above her. She looks about, using her misshapen arms and elbows to turn herself as she did when alive. Her large brown eyes are filled with fear. She opens her mouth and a high-pitched noise comes out. It startles me.

I lift my hand. It has dropped into the water as I dreamed. I'm back on my raft. Somewhere in my hazy mist I realize a

T

speedboat has just passed me. The raft rocks on the waves. The radio from the shore broadcasts . . . "Police have used teargas, and several of the protestors have been arrested. It is an almost surreal scene, hard to grasp on American soil. Windows are broken, cars overturned, people walking about with blood on their shirts. A minister is standing off to the left with a gathering of some fifty people, delivering a sermon of some sort: 'Blessed be . . . Blessed be . . . Blessed be . . .,' he keeps applying the Biblical passage to the current situation."

I try to concentrate. Try to remember my Sunday school teachings. Blessed be the meek, for they shall inherit the earth. Blessed be the . . . how did it go? . . . I can't remember and lose my way.

I see a deformed young woman, a child. Her hands and feet are bound to a hard hospital bed. There are electric wires connected to her head.

People in white hospital gowns move about the bed. The child cries.

Then the bed is floating on water, like a raft. And the binds are gone. The child crawls over to the side of the bed and right into the water! I call out! "No!" But no sound comes out. I can't understand it and call out again. But my voice is mute.

I'm under water. I see Mom standing on the floor of the lake, in a room that extends beyond my vision. Beds of children with catheters attached to feed them stretch in all directions. Susie floats down straight into Mom's arms. They're both smiling.

I'm at a graveyard, the graveyard where Dad is buried. It is a clear day, hot, but with a nice breeze. Mom is there. John is there. Dave and JoAnn are there. Susie's parents are there. Some birds are chirping from the nearby woods, and occasional cars pass by on the country road that runs along the west side.

T

A minister reads last rites: "And He weeps for all the children of the world, weeps for the child who cannot eat, for she must be fed, weeps for the child who cannot walk, for she must find passage, weeps for the child who cannot talk, for she must have her voice, weeps for the child born unable to control her hands, for she must reach out to know the touch of another, weeps for the child born blind, for she must know the beauty of His world, weeps for the child without thoughts, for she must know herself, weeps for the child born only to die, for she has not had the chance to live. But most of all, today, He weeps for this child, Susie, and He blesses her and takes her in His arms and smiles on her."

I wake up, startled . . . hear the children at the beach laughing. I roll off the raft and into the cool water to wash away my tears.

T

Chemotherapy

Sometimes death enters quietly and softly shuts the door behind her. Then it can be hard to know she's in the room. But if one learns how to sense the shades of silence . . .

Mom, John and I rush through the dim night lights and cold rain of the parking lot, heading for the doors beneath the blue neon lights that spell out Visitor's Entrance. Mom has opened an umbrella and keeps trying to get us all under it, but it's hopeless.

The previous day and much of the night, she sat alone in the waiting room while the doctors did their best to fight the latest surge of cancer. Shortly before the sun rose, one of them found her and told her things went well and a nurse would be by to lead her to Dad's room, where she could sit by his bed while he slept. He didn't wake until late morning. Since he was still too drugged to talk and the various nurses and other hospital personal kept coming in to do one thing or another, Mom and Dad agreed she should leave and return with us that night.

So she drove home in the early afternoon, took a short nap, picked us up from the neighbors and headed us through the rain to the hospital. John sleeps in the back seat most of the way. I sit in the front seat.

Once we get onto the highway, Mom tries to explain the situation. "The doctors have prescribed a new program of chemotherapy involving cytotoxic agents."

"What's cytotoxic?"

"Cells that kill the cancer cells. It will be necessary for Dad to go to the hospital every so often to be given these chemicals that will fight the cancer, but these same chemicals will make him weak and sick, even cause him to lose his hair."

I try to imagine Dad bald and it makes me laugh.

"What's so funny?" Mom asks.

"Bet he won't be happy about being bald! But, if that's what it takes to get well, he's gonna have to put up with my teasing!"

"I wouldn't tease him tonight," she says.

I wish she hadn't said it. I know this is serious.

I glance at her face. She stares intently at the road through the slapping window wipers. Her barely visible, worn profile matches the serious tone of her words. She looks tired. She looks frail. She looks old.

I lean against the door and look out the side window. It's night and it's raining, so there isn't much to see, just an occasional blurred light. Soon, we reach the downtown traffic, and after a few stop lights, Mom turns into the hospital parking lot.

Our quick rush through the rain and into the entrance leaves us wet. Mom folds up the umbrella. "Brush off the rain. Like this." She quickly runs her hands over her light coat and we attempt to imitate her.

"This way." She points to three elevator doors in a hallway on the other side of a large reception room. The ceiling lights give the room a quiet, yellow feel, and the soft, ambient sounds create a comfortable quiet that complete silence would not.

Two older women sit behind an information desk. Both hold large coffee mugs and take turns sipping from them while the other talks just above a whisper. As we pass, one is saying

T

something about a Senator Kennedy. It has something to do with the possibility of a Catholic getting elected President. I don't understand the difference between Catholics and Protestants, but I know Mom's family was really upset when she married a Lutheran, even though Methodists and Lutheran are both Protestants. I wonder if God knows what I'm thinking. Would he be upset if a Catholic were elected President?

Before we reach the elevators, I hear a dull ding and see the doors of the middle one slide open. Three nurses emerge and walk towards us. One is complaining about a patient who uses a lot of profanity. "Seems there should be some rule that people can't use such language in a hospital," she says as they pass us. Hmm . . . I wonder. Makes sense. There's something about a hospital that's similar to a church. Both have a hushed atmosphere. I act different in a church than I do other places and I wouldn't swear in either a church or a hospital. If I did, I would have the sense that I had done something God would disapprove. I wonder if even thinking profanity is a bad thing. If God knows my thoughts, then there's no hiding anything. Maybe, if I keep my thoughts inside, it's okay. But why would that be okay? I know there's something Jesus said about lusting in the heart being a sin. Wouldn't other kinds of thinking be the same thing?

Is that how Jesus said it? In the heart? Is that where lust takes place? People always connect the heart to love in a positive way. I know lust and love both involve sex, at least this kind of love, but I'm not sure how to untangle these.

By the time we reach the elevator, the doors have shut, so Mom pushes a button and we wait for them to open.

T

We're all born in sin. Right? Isn't that what the whole Garden of Eden story is saying? But! But, Jesus is the way out! Right? His death is the key! It's so confusing . . . Since Jesus is the son of God and God let Jesus die, we can be saved if we believe in Jesus. So . . . when we die, if we believe in Jesus, we will go to Heaven. . . . Why? . . . And it doesn't even matter if we are bad people in life? . . . That makes no sense.

Most say it does matter. That we get into heaven if we are good people and that we go to hell if we are bad people. That makes sense.

Believing in Jesus is hard to grasp. What does that mean? I cannot question it. It's a matter of faith, not logic.

The elevator dings, the doors slide open and we enter. Mom pushes the third floor button and the elevator lurches up. No one else is using the elevator, so when it jerks to a stop, we are at our floor. The doors slide open and we exit into another quiet, dimly lit hall. Mom directs John and me to sit in the waiting room to the left while she talks with a clerk at the reception desk.

John and I walk into the waiting room and sit in two chairs next to a small table covered with tattered magazines – Better Homes and Gardens, Life, The New Yorker. An older couple sits across the room, and a woman about Mom's age sits against the wall to our left. All of them have their eyes shut. The man's head is bowed as if he's in prayer, though I realize that's not likely. He's probably either asleep or wishing he was.

Everything is quiet.

But there are different types of quiet. Sometimes quiet is soothing . . . refreshing . . . comforting. Sometimes quiet is ominous . . . frightening. How can I explain the quiet of a hospital?

T

A hospital is the place where what science knows blurs into what it doesn't know. Much the feel of a church, yes, the two meet in the same spiritual landscape – a brain fed by blood and oxygen merges with a mind, a spirit, a soul, a world beyond mass and matter. Can a brain exist without a mind? Can a mind exist without a brain?

What is the mind? Is it the same thing as the soul? The spirit? If I lose or replace other organs, I still exist, am still me. If I lose my brain, that me inside is gone? Isn't it?

Does that mean my soul or spirit is also gone? If so, doesn't that mean "I" am gone?

The air conditioner kicks on and I'm reminded of the air conditioner coming on in church.

The minister tells us all to bow our heads in prayer. I hear but cannot decipher the whispered prayers of the others. It's as if their invisible mutterings have an energy, a texture that influences the air. How to explain it? This is not the same air I breathe in the grocery store.

The air conditioner comes on.

Think it through . . . think it through.

How to merge? I feel it, but it is a disappearing liquid air and flows away from me.

It is real! I know it is real!

How do I explain it? make others understand?

How do I explain that which is beyond explanation?

I don't know why, but instead of math and logic, I intuitively know I need to find a poetic bridge. This realization cannot be explained.

Am I copping-out with this claim? Do I believe it's true because I want to believe?

T

By the time the minister ends the group prayer and tells us to open our hymnals, I've tangled myself in the following: "The air tiptoes quietly through the soft white light and the people speak in whispers as if we are all part of a never-ending prayer."

I am but eight. Is that a legitimate excuse for such a clumsy attempt to express the quality of the air in a church? Don't know. Perhaps more important is the web of questions concerning why I find it so important. Why does it matter? Why do I separate myself from the activity instead of simply participating?

I'm not much older as I sit in the hospital, sensing and trying to understand the quality of the silence it holds. I remember watching a man on television say something about the ghost in the machine, say it is that aspect of humans that means they're more than merely animals, say that the ghost is the spirit or soul within each of us, the god in us that science cannot explain. He says that those who truly believe have passed through the doors of perception.

Is that what I've done, passed through the doors of perception? Am I sensing an invisible reality within the silence? Is that what makes some kinds of silence different? Why people automatically respect certain kinds of silence? Because they can sense that other reality?

Yes, I decide, there is something about the atmosphere in the hospital — the sense that I'm in a place where there are invisible powers and I must be respectful of their presence.

In Dad's room, the atmosphere is not as ethereal. The lighting has harsh contrasts and the battle for life is more real. The unkempt man in the bed is not Dad, not the Dad I know. A long tube is taped to the back of his right hand and leads up

T

to a half-full plastic bag hanging from a stand. His face is drawn and in need of a shave. His hair is mostly covered with a cloth held on by two straps tied behind his head. He breaths slowly, a raspy, rhythmic breathing. Tears fill my eyes.

Then he sees me. His dull, flat, empty eyes struggle to find a sparkle.

Mom leans over him and kisses his cheek. They whisper something to one another. Then Mom stands back and pushes John and me towards the bed.

"Hi Johnny! Hi Eddie! It's good to see you. Here, come over by the bed. Let me have a good look at you. Still have your tans. You guys get the darkest tans I ever saw. Eddie, come here. I hear you won your first football game. And Mom says you scored two touchdowns!" His voice is nothing more than a forced whisper.

I smile, try to see his face as the one I know. "What do you expect from a superstar?" I respond.

Dad laughs, a scratchy laugh, but that's okay. "Just like his old man!" he says. A familiar phrase, a connection with the past, with the Dad I know or knew. Then he starts coughing and Mom quickly moves between us.

"Okay, boys, you can sit in those chairs by the window. Go on." Her back is to us. We wait, anxious. Then Dad stops coughing. Mom turns, "Go on now! Here, let me take this one." She pulls a third chair from the wall over by the bed. "Now, you two," she points again to the chairs by the window, "sit in those!" We comply.

She sets her chair next to Dad, and they start talking in whispers. I try to "sit patiently and not make a lot of noise." At first, I strain to hear what Mom is saying to Dad about the possibilities of radium treatments. Is it the same as what she

T

told me on the way in? Seems similar, but she is using more words I don't know and her soft whispers fade in and out. I can't follow her and reluctantly give up the attempt.

A burst of rain snare-drums against the window. I like the rain. When I'm inside, rain often makes me feel cozy and secure. If it's not too hard, I like to walk or even swim in it, though I've been warned not to do either during a lightning storm.

I remember the time Dad and I are fishing near the swamp, around the bend of Jenning's Bay, by the beaver lodges, and a sudden lightning storm breaks over us.

As usual, we've been catching crappies by the dozen. Suppose that's why we don't notice the ominous clouds from the west. But we see the flash of lightning and hear the clap of thunder. Dad immediately brings in our lines and jerks the starter rope on the trolling motor. It kicks in – plat . . . plat . . . plat . . . plat-plat-plat-plat.

Within seconds, the rain hits. It's a cloudburst. Even at the slow speed of a trolling motor, our dock is but twenty minutes away, but the rain is so heavy it threatens to fill the boat before we get there.

"Eddie! Use the bucket! Bail as fast as you can!"

I pick up the metal pail and scoop it into the water gathering at the bottom of the boat. I go too deep, and it hits a wood brace.

The boat slows and the motor begins to sputter. His blue work shirt clinging to his chest and back and his feet covered with water, Dad wills the boat forward.

Lightening hits across the bay! Its sharp white light cuts through the dull, dark, beating rain, accompanied by a crack of thunder!

T

The brilliant flash leaves the thick rain even more blurred and blinding. I can't see the dock, can barely see the dark shadow of the shore.

The motor sputters . . . . Dad opens the clutch . . . it roars then hesitates. He lowers the intake . . . back and forth . . . back and forth . . . sputtering . . . catching . . . sputtering . . . catching . . . .

I concentrate on bailing water – scoop, splash, scoop, splash, scoop, splash . . . .

Thump! The boat hits a dock post!

The sudden stop causes me to fall on my side!

Dad cuts off the motor and grabs the post!

I turn, press my chest against the side of the boat, bend my arms and push myself to a kneeling position.

Dad pulls the boat against the dock and holds it there by sliding his left arm around the post.

I grab the boat seat, now covered by water and pull myself to a standing position.

Dad shoves his right hand into the water beneath the front seat, latches onto the manila rope, pulls it out of the water and loops it over the dock post.

Lightning slices through the rain! Thunder cracks!

"Come on! Forget the gear!"

He grabs the dock post and wills himself up onto the dock. "Come on! Come on!"

He bends his knees and reaches down toward me.

I splash to the front of the boat. "Here! Take my hand!" Our forearms lock. He yanks me out of the boat, straight into his chest. I instinctually cling to his shoulders as he immediately rises and turns toward the shore.

Lightning fractures the sky! Thunder cracks the air!

T

He carries me rapidly down the dock to the shore, sets me at the base of the stairs and pushes me up the wooden steps. Then he grabs me from behind by my arm pits and drags me up the dirt road toward the house.

Lightning strikes!

It hits the oak tree next to the top of the steps, less than ten yards from us! Crack!

I instinctually turn to look, see the tree split, half of it crashing over the steps we've just come up!

I'm stunned!

It registers as if in slow motion.

One of the few memories that remain.

There's the time in the car. I'm in the back seat. As usual Dad drives and Mom sits next to him.

Que Sera, Sera (Whatever Will Be, Will Be) comes on, and Dad turns up the radio. "Like this song."

"Yes," Mom says. "Like everything about Doris Day."

"You can sing like her when you want," Dad says.

"That's what you keep saying," Mom says.

"I actually like your singing better. Has more of an angelic quality," Dad says.

"Well ... I'm *not* Doris Day," Mom replies.

They listen to it. Dad starts whistling along.

When the song ends, Dad turns down the radio. "Eddie, do you know how to whistle?"

"No."

"Just curl your tongue," he says. "Push it against the top of your mouth, and blow." He whistles again. Seems simple. I curl my tongue, push it to the top of my mouth and blow. A spurt of breath and spit comes out, but no whistle. "Hey," he says, "watch it! You just washed my neck! Curl the tongue and blow through the curl. Don't worry about pushing it against the roof of your mouth." I try again, and I hear it, the whistle. Weak as it is, I have just whistled. "I got it!"

Dad laughs. "Well, it's a start. You're gonna need some practice."

"Diet," the nurse says.

She walks John and me down the hall to a waiting room. "Put your father on the right diet, and he'll get better."

I look up at her. She has a thin face, more serious than friendly, but she seems pleasant. "No meat, eggs or fish. Only honey or maple sugar. No white flour, spices or pickles. Feed him celery knobs, leek, tomatoes and salads."

When we reach the room, she stops and looks down, "Potassium free, sodium free – that's the key. Let the body heal itself."

The rain surges against the window. I look over at John. He's slumped against the arm of his chair, sleeping. My thoughts drift back two years to a hot summer night when I sit on a mound of clay beneath the yellow light of a hanging work-lamp and watch Dad and Al Carlin swinging picks, their backs glistening with sweat.

Al and his family live on Lane Two. I'm not sure how he and Dad became friends, but I remember a few gatherings of the families.

Tonight is one of many I get to help what seems an endless task of digging out the basement by pick, shovel and pail. I'm not much real help, but I take it seriously. While the adults might see it as work, I see it as fun.

As usual, Dad and Al talk, share stories, tell jokes and laugh while they work and drink beer. Dad even lets me drink

T

some of his beer. I'm not sure I like the taste, but I like being treated as an adult.

I will always remember the clay, the pockets of sand, the rough, round timber posts, the two-by-six crossbeams and the light from lanterns flickering against the tunnel-like beginnings of our basement.

Dad stops swinging his pick and leans on it. "Sure as hell is humid," he says and draws his bare arm across his forehead to wipe off the sweat trickling into his eyes.

"Hot as a whore in heat," Al responds and leans his shovel against a dirt wall.

Dad gives Al a wink and motions toward me.

"Oh! Sorry!" Al says. He walks over to the battered, metal icebox, lifts the lid and digs a can of beer from the chunks of ice.

"Toss me one!"

Al swings it behind his back.

"Show off!"

Dad catches it and snaps the top. His sweat continues dripping in his eyes, so he sets the can on a small ridge in the clay wall, picks up his tan shirt and wipes his face. "Damn humidity." He tosses his shirt aside, retrieves his beer and finds a place to sit.

"I'll never forget our hunting trip last fall." Al says and takes a swing from his can.

Yes! I know how it works. They take a break, open a beer, one of them brings up something, seemingly out of nowhere, and they start talking. It's the best part of these evenings.

"That was a fun trip," Dad says. "Remember when Bob shot that mallard and it landed in a beaver's pond."

They both laugh.

T

"Goddamn, that was funny! I can still see Bob doing his tightrope act out on that beaver's dam trying to fetch his bird!"

"Yeah," Dad cuts in through his laughter. "And then the beaver slapped the water with its tail, startling him."

"Startling, my ass, it scared the living hell out of him!" Al exclaims.

"Whatever it did to him, he sure as hell made a splash when he hit the water!"

"A classic back flop!" Al adds. They both laugh.

"But that was nothing compared to the exit he made when that beaver came after him!" Dad says.

I only partially understand these stories, but it doesn't matter. The laughter is all that really matters. I laugh, too. I can't help myself.

"What a hunter!" Al says. "Remember when he came on those three grouse alongside the road out by Leach Lake?"

"Yeah," Dad says. "Blasted 'em with his twenty-two from about five feet."

"Blam! Blam! Blam!" Al says, imitating shooting a rifle.

"Puff! Puff! Puff!" Dad adds. "Nothing left but feathers!"

They both laugh. I laugh so hard it hurts my stomach.

Dad downs the last of his beer, crushes the can in his hand and tosses it toward the pail. It misses and lands in the dirt.

Al follows suit. "Well, I guess we'd better get some work done," he says. Soon the steady thunk of the pick and scrape of the shovel fill the night.

I watch for a while, then decide to continue the road I'm making for my toy trucks in the pile of sand near me.

The basement has taken the form of a tunnel leading from the stairs under the top of the "T" to the pump room, a closet

T

like room extending beyond the house toward the lake. While I sit on a mound of dirt, listening to the talk and watching the slow progress of the digging, I can smell the clay, taste the sand and dust and see it layered in the dim yellow light. Sometimes Al helps. More often, it's just Dad and me.

Night after night after night, I watch Dad's strong, muscular back drip with sweat and dirt as he finishes digging out the basement that summer, wedging tall, rough wooden posts on cement blocks to hold up the house as the clay and sand pockets are slowly hauled out.

Bucket by bucket up the stairway or out the holes that will eventually become windows – the dirt is hauled, emptied into the waiting wheelbarrow and then dumped in the southwest corner of the yard, slowly leveling off the land. As Dad progresses, he wedges rough posts along the edges and crosses the ceiling with 2 x 6 planks to hold up the house. Days pass, weeks pass, months pass. Once enough of the dirt is out, cement is mixed with sand and water – wheelbarrow load by wheelbarrow load – and cement blocks are laid, row upon row. Frames for basement windows are built and the windows installed. Sections of the dirt floor are leveled and a sand bed put down. Cement is poured, section-by-section, and carefully smoothed level. Two bedrooms are created by putting up frames and chalkboard. A furnace is put in.

Eventually vinyl floor tiles will cover the cement floor, but that will be a task for Mom and John and I. Dad will no longer be able to help. We never will finish covering all of the clay basement walls with bricks or the entire dirt floor with cement. The pump room will remain a dirt room without a door, more like a cave than a room, though the top of it will have a wood roof.

T

"Eddie! Eddie, wake up!" Somewhere in the rain I hear Mom's voice. "Eddie, it's time to go. Come on. Wake up. Johnny! Come on, Johnny! Stand up. That's right. Listen, boys. Dad'll be home by Friday. Okay?"

"Okay," I respond.

"Okay, Johnny?" Mom asks.

"Yeah,"

"Maybe," Dad says, "we can go to Dave's football game. How does that sound? Sounds fun, huh!"

When Mom tells us Dad will be home by Friday, I think she really believes he will, but he won't.

Though Coach Gove will let Dave bring home films of the football games for Dad to watch, Dad will only see one more game in person, and that looking through a chain fence from the front seat of our car. I still remember trying to make out the small forms moving up and down the lighted field over 100 yards away. I have no idea what's happening, and no one else does either, though Mom cheers every time the announcer says Dave's name, and since Dave is the quarterback, we hear it every offensive play.

T

A Dream of Death

"We never dream we die," Janet says.

"Really?" Carol responds.

"Saw it on TV. A psychiatrist explained that we cannot dream it because we can only dream about the possibilities of the world we experience while we're awake."

"So . . .," Carol pauses. "So, dreams are about what happened during the day?"

"Yes. When we fall asleep, our conscious mind is no longer thinking, so our unconscious mind thinks. That's what a dream is. It's the unconscious mind sorting out and working through what happened the previous day."

"Makes sense. Obviously, we cannot dream about dying, because we'd be dead."

They aren't paying any attention to me. I just happen to be walking down Lane Five with them.

It's the first time I've heard it. There's no reason to doubt what an expert says on television.

Dave confirms it. That evening he's shooting baskets with me, and I mention what I heard. "Makes sense," he says as he turns to grab the ball before it reaches the road. He tosses the ball to me, "Your shot."

I file it away.

When Dad gets sick and I start thinking more about death and that reality beyond the conscious world, I wonder how dreams fit. The ones I remember don't make any sense. But usually I can relate them to something from the previous day.

One day when Lynn and I are lying on the raft, I tell her what I've heard.

"Dreams are wishes, you know, the Disney song. A dream is a wish the heart makes."

"That makes sense . . . But what about nightmares?"

She doesn't respond.

A motorboat passes and its wake rolls through the ripples causing the raft to rock in a languid rhythm.

I open my eyes and bring my upper body to a sitting position.

Lynn notices and also assumes a sitting position. "That's when the conscious and unconscious are fighting. The conscious is upset about something and the unconscious is trying to find a solution, but the conscious won't let it."

"What?"

Lynn slides into the water.

A large cloud blocks the sun.

I also slide into the water.

One day I read that the Aborigines of Australia think of the spiritual world as the dream world, what they call the dreamtime. I don't understand, but it's clear they connect dreams with the spiritual world. If so, then, when we dream we're entering the world beyond life. We live in that world, even though we're dead in this world.

But . . . no . . . because they believe that, when a child is born, during pregnancy, the dream spirit enters the child. So the child does not live before that spirit enters it. And by extension, there must be a form of nonexistence.

But . . . if it is in the mother's womb, then the mother's dream spirit might also be its dream spirit until it gets its own. In a sense, the child in the mother and the mother are the same being until whenever it is that the new dream spirit enters the child.

T

I ask Tim, and he isn't sure if we can dream we die. He's more interested in telling me a dream he keeps having about his mother having two fallopian tubes, which he interprets as symbolizing her having sex with his real father and his stepfather. It seems too obvious, artificial, and I wonder if he made it up as a clever metaphor, rather than actually dreaming it.

At one time or another, I ask Jim, Frank, Mike, Brian and others, and they're in general agreement that it makes sense we do not ever dream we die. None of them remembers ever having such a dream.

It's accepted. A curious thing, perhaps, but with some validity. After all, it comes from a psychiatrist, and they're the ones who know.

We cannot dream we die.

Humans never dream they die.

There's logic to it.

Then I wake from a dream.

And at that twilight moment I remember it. Not all of it. But enough.

It's dark, the first break of dawn. An army advances across a rural landscape, similar to what surrounds my own town, specifically Highway 101, just outside of Mound, though I don't remember a specific detail to confirm it. There are houses with smaller yards mixed with small farms. Shadowy soldiers with rifles rapidly approach, climbing over fences, and scrambling through trees, patches of undergrowth and tall grass along the roads. Others parachute randomly from the barely visible sky. I can hear the hum of airplanes.

We're not soldiers. We're civilians, people caught in the front lines of an advancing army. Explosions and the rapid

T

tat-tat-tat-tat-tat of machine guns mixes with a deathly silence. They kill us in bursts as we try to scramble away. I see dozens of shadowy civilians collapsing as bullets take their lives.

I trip over a branch and fall backwards.

A soldier sees me.

There is no escape.

He swings around his machine gun and fires.

There's burst of red, yellow and orange.

The dream fragments.

I struggled to retain it.

I force myself back into it.

I'm above the scene.

I'm in the sky.

Looking down.

There!

In the weeds!

I see my dead body!

Then I lose it.

That world is gone.

But I can still remember.

I've brought some of it back with me.

I know I died.

I've found an answer.

Found it is possible to die in a dream.

What does it mean?

Mrs. Blood laughs. "A silly superstition. People dream of death all the time."

"Yes," Mr. Bones adds. "It's a standard dream symbol of transformation. We die to one state of being or consciousness in

T

order to be reborn to another. A child dies to its psychological state of dependence in order to be reborn into an adult's state of self-responsibility."

T

Fishing

It's impossible for me to know that this will be the last time, the one I will remember all of my life.

I wedge my back into the prow of the wooden boat, set my heels against a worn rib of the frame along each side for leverage and bring my knees halfway to my chest against the chilly morning air. It probably seems careless or even stupid to those not familiar with my world. All I have on is a white tee-shirt and the threadbare, cut-off jeans I often use for swimming. But I'm young, the cold doesn't bother me much, I know it will get hot quickly once the sun rises, and even at my young age I've already developed an aversion for having to keep track of anything more than absolutely necessary. I would have hated to have been a woman constantly burdened with a purse.

A Caspian tern circles slowly above the main part of the lake that lies to the west. Its slow circling floats on the quiet hours of the morning, hours that rock gently on the blue, green and white ripples of the lake. While this is my first time on this lake, I've spent many a summer afternoon sitting or lying in the hot sun on the end of our own wooden dock, watching the terns, seagulls, mallards and Canadian geese gliding serenely over West Arm.

Dad flips another practiced cast, this one splashing lightly into the moment near a clump of rusted-yellow swamp grass. Without a wasted movement, he begins slowly reeling in his line. It's familiar and comfortable. He's fished all of his life and has been taking me along since before I could walk. I don't need to watch or listen for the sudden hit. It's become so much a part of me that I can sense it.

Instead, I let my thoughts wander and take in the waking world around me. For a while I watch the tern riding easily on its current, seeming to share my relaxed moment. But then I find I'm wrong. Suddenly, it folds its wings, plunges almost straight down into the lake, grasps an unwary fish in its sharp claws, rips it out of the water, and climbs back into the sky. Within seconds it disappears into the gray horizon. It's a jarring energy that seems out of place in the peaceful moment. But rather than shattering my serenity, it affirms it. I've witnessed nature's violence many times, participated in it. It's expected. All it means is that the morning is that the morning is as it should be.

I watch Dad slowly reel in his line. He has not noticed the dramatic catch of the tern, is content with his own thoughts and familiar fishing routine.

The sun breaks above the tamarack and blue spruce along the top of the steep cliffs surrounding three sides of the inlet. To the east, three buckskins, dead trees with but a skeleton of branches, rise boldly above the living trees — more majestic in death than the others are in life. Don't know how this name came to be associated with such trees; but whatever the etymology, a buckskin is more than just a dead tree. It's a tree that has gained a stark dignity in its stubborn refusal to succumb to the changing seasons of life.

The sunlight begins to reflect off the water just below the canoe-birch, and soon I can see the rippling reflection of white trees dancing on the surface. I like the water, like the lakes that are so much a part of my life. They're always in motion,

T

and since I've grown up so close to one, spent so much time in it and on it and by it, I know its rhythms and moods, know the currents, not just the expressive surface currents, but the more powerful, more mysterious movements beneath. At different depths currents flow at different speeds, in different directions, and Lake Minnetonka is crystal clear, so I can look down into it and watch the different currents as they cross beneath me. I can even open my eyes underwater and see the different worlds each level holds, the fish, turtles, snakes, water-rats, frogs and seaweed. It's a part of me just as I'm a part of it.

But my life is about to change.

As the morning light turns the dark shadowy forms into their daylight personas, I see the red crowns and bluish gray bodies of two sand-cranes standing perfectly still in a thicket of tall swamp grass in the quiet water along the edge of a string of large limestone rocks. One of these rocks, the size and roughly the shape of a coffin, lies above this bank in a bed of dark green moss, purple coneflowers and shiitake mushrooms, as if an impressionist painter with the skills of Claude Monet has decided to create this scene with his small, deft strokes; but no, it's not the handicraft of a man, not a human creation. It's nature's own artistry, a perfect scene capturing the pristine spirit of the northern woods of Minnesota — perhaps, if one believes, the living beauty of God.

A light breeze flirts with the drooping peddles of the coneflowers, causing them to flutter coquettishly — and the smooth, dark-green surface of the lake begins to dance, a delicate, rapid interplay of light and shadow.

I watch the ripples rush toward the boat and dissipate.

All is as it should be.

Surely, this is as close as one can come to experiencing God.

T

But wait.

Something moved in the ripples, disturbed their uniform brushstroke across the water's canvas.

I focus, study the lively surface — see nothing out of the ordinary.

There it is, yes, now I see it — the yellow-and-black-striped head of a turtle less than fifteen feet from our boat, its shell and legs barely visible beneath the surface — nothing of importance, nothing frightening, a comfortable companion, a watery playmate.

Yes — all is as it should be in my world.

Small birds began to flit about the bushes and lower branches of the trees — chickadees, titmice, cardinals, blue jays, sparrows. A couple of robins hop about the grass, searching for worms.

I look into the clear water. The bottom of the inlet is covered with large, squarish rocks interspersed with small clumps of thin, sinuous weeds. For a moment I think I see a large dark form moving through the underwater shadows. I flinch, not much but enough.

"What's wrong!?" Dad says. He sets down his rod-an-reel and leans toward me.

"Oh! Nothing!" I answer, realizing that the startling form is only a sunken tree trunk. A cool breeze cuts through my shirt and I instinctively shiver.

Dad, more practical than I, has brought his wool, lumberjack shirt, the kind with the black-and-red-checks. "Here, this will warm you up."

"No, no thanks." It's wool, and wool always makes my skin itch.

He smiles and shakes his head. "It's *your funeral*."

T

I smile back, shrug and look away. I can already feel the sun's rays. Soon I'll be sweating and might even splash into the lake for a swim.

The soft droning of an outboard motor breaks through the sounds of nature. I scan the still gray edges of the lake for the source, but see nothing. The lake is filled with small islands, some with spruce, pine, tamarack and birch, and consists of a number of bays connected by channels and small inlets similar to ours, so it's not surprising I cannot see the boat. Still, I'm pleased when the sound fades away and all I hear is the lapping of the water against the boat. I like the sense of being on the lake alone with Dad.

I return to my lazy observations and follow a bed of yellow coneflowers meandering like a fragile stream of warm flowers through the colder, green, wood-grass. The white blossoms of a dozen Juneberry trees gently fall into it like soft, summer snow.

Everything is so quiet and peaceful that sounds normally drowned out by the noise of civilization come across the water in clear, sharp detail. I hear the muffled-drum-like-whirr of a grouse staking out his territory, and the jarring caw, caw, caw of a crow.

I watch the still, dark shadows along the edge of the inlet and think about Dad's cancer. Years from now, after Dave and JoAnn move out, I will begin sleeping in the basement, and many nights I will wake with the feeling that something, sometimes I sense it's Dad's spirit, is moving about the dark shadows. Now, sitting in a small boat fishing with him, I feel his presence without looking, as if there's something in the air, an energy, a life force, a reality that's greater than rational, empirical explanations, neither a coldly scientific reality nor

T

an illogical unscientific reality, rather a reality that partakes of the mathematics, both real and broken, of a Beethoven symphony.

The early wake-up was easy. I slept little in the rented cabin and was eager for the day to begin. But now the excitement is wearing off. The sounds of nature become a familiar lullaby while the boat gently rocks on the water, and soon I fall asleep.

I see a huge fish slowly swimming along the bottom. Other fish are scattering away. It turns and sees me. I swim quickly to the surface.

The water stretches in all directions.

Something comes across the surface towards me. I strain to see what it is. Soon, it gets close enough to make out that it's a raft with someone on it. No. Wait. Not a person. It's Pinocchio! And there's Jiminy Cricket!

Close behind it is the big fish, much bigger than it was a moment ago. It's going to swallow the entire raft, including Pinocchio and Jiminy!

Wait! That's right! Geppetto is inside the whale! Pinocchio has come to save him!

The whale opens its huge mouth. The raft flows past the whale's large teeth and over its tongue, disappearing into the whale's belly!

I'm also in the belly. But I'm not a part of the happenings. It's as if I'm watching it unfold on a movie screen.

I see Geppetto, but no! What? It's not Geppetto. It's Jonah from the Bible. What? I don't know how I know, but I know it's Jonah.

T

Pinocchio says he must save his father and become a real boy.

Jonah asks what it means to be a real boy.

Jiminy Cricket says it means Pinocchio has to stop telling lies and misbehaving.

Jonah says Pinocchio is too late. Geppetto is dead.

This is wrong. Geppetto doesn't die. Pinocchio saves him.

They continue to talk, but there's too much noise. I cannot hear the rest of their exchange.

What is that story about Jonah and the whale? I read it in some children's book in Sunday school. Jonah gets swallowed by a big fish. The book doesn't say it's a whale. It's just a big fish. And he survives . . . after being in the fish's belly for three days, he comes out alive, just like Pinocchio and his father Geppetto.

No, that's not right. Pinocchio dies. Pinocchio saves Geppetto, but dies in the process.

Then, because Pinocchio sacrifices himself to save his father, the Blue Fairy brings him to life as a real boy.

"Eddie, Eddie, wake up," Dad says softly, leaning across the middle of the boat and gently shaking my shoulder.

"What?" I mumble.

"Enjoying the outing?" he asks. There's a wry smile on his face.

"Oh! What? Yes!" I say and smile back my embarrassment.

"Well, then, come on, time to get at it." He sets his rod-and-reel against the inside of the boat.

Still half asleep, I turn away to look over the prow of the boat. I know the fishing is better in the early morning, but we have the whole day. There's no rush.

T

Nevertheless, Dad isn't as willing to let what's left of the morning slip away. He steps across the middle of the boat and picks up my rod-and-reel. "You're never going to catch anything with your lure in the boat. Here," he says, "see if you can land this thing over by that dead log."

I take hold of the rod-and-reel rigged with a lure and ready for use.

"You see it?" he asks, directing me to follow his broad finger. "Right along the edge of the shore. Bound to be something settled in there."

I cast and miss the spot by a good ten yards.

"Nice cast, Superstar," he says and laughs. "It's a wonder you don't catch your limit every time with that kind of accuracy."

I smile, embarrassed. "Well," I say, "it's a tough life for us superstars, always having to purposely make mistakes just so people don't get jealous."

Dad laughs. "You seem to have your Clark Kent disguise down pat. I'm not so sure about the Superman part."

"Well, Dad," I reply, "I notice you haven't caught a single fish – not exactly what one would expect of a superstar."

"You're right," he says. "I guess it's time both of us take off our Clark Kent suits and show what we're really made of."

This trip is special. The excuse for it is my ninth birthday, but I know there's more to it. We don't normally rent cabins up north. We have our own lake filled with fish, and cabins cost money we don't have. I'm not sure what's going on, but I sense it's connected to Dad's cancer. There's a shadow just beneath the surface, an urgency under the fun Mom and Dad are having.

T

Though nothing is biting, there's plenty to occupy my attention. After a few more casts, I replace my lure with a hook, slip it through a chub, set my weight so the bait will be about a foot from the bottom, and cast near a promising patch of cattails. While I wait for a bite, I look into the clear water. A school of small, silver fish swims left of the boat, their scales flashing briefly in the sun and then becoming dark forms as they swam north of me. When they reach the edge of my vision a larger fish appears, scattering them, likely making a meal of some.

Mom and Dad love living in the country. They want a traditional marriage. While Mom has a nursing degree, when she meets Dad, she quits nursing to be a wife and mother. He works his job downtown Minneapolis, and she takes care of his two children from his previous marriage and has his dinner waiting when he gets home. On weekends, he works on the house and yard, and she makes the meals, nothing special, mostly the fish he's caught or the standard hamburgers, hotdogs, potato chips, baked beans — corn-on-the-cob dipped in butter at the end of summer. The house is but a small cabin from his first marriage, no indoor plumbing, no basement, but they have plans. He's going to fix it up, dig out the basement, eventually get it in good enough shape to sell and buy another he can also fix up and sell. I guess the idea is that each one will be slightly better than the previous one, this process eventually leading to more money, but I also knew that whether or not they can make money isn't the main reason. Just doing it is what attracts them. He likes to build, and she likes to be a part of it.

I turn my attention to a daddy-longlegs crawling slowly across the prow of the boat, his long skinny legs awkwardly centered by a small gray body. I wonder how such a helpless

T

creature survives at all. It seems that all the daddy-longlegs should have died out years ago. One day, I kill one on his sidewalk, and Keith Frahm tells me that it will rain if anyone kills a daddy longlegs – within an hour we have a sun-shower. That is strong evidence for his claim, but I still only half believe it.

Not enough to stop me from squashing the senseless spider crawling across the boat and flicking it into the water. I have a momentary doubt. I've just tempted fate. One thing I don't want today is a storm.

Its almost weightless body makes tiny ripples on the surface. As I watch them, I notice the skater bugs zigzagging across the water. "Talk about a pointless life." Maybe it's good to tempt fate.

Years later, while listening to the rock-opera Jesus Christ Superstar, I remember the verbal jousting matches Dad and I share and how we laugh when we can catch each other in the middle of a verbal knockout. Admittedly, I'm usually the one who loses, though I do win a few. Whenever I win I feel clever. Looking back, however, I've come to believe that even the times I win are not the result of my being clever, after all, but rather, are silent gifts from Dad. Too bad he dies before I grow clever enough to return them.

Dad continues casting for about an hour after I stop, but then he also slips a chub on his line. For a time we both sit in silence. I suppose he might also be watching the pointless zigzags of the skater bugs, I'll soon find he has other things on his mind. I gaze absentmindedly at his thick, black hair with what I later realize is considered by his generation to be a very attractive wave down the right side and across the forehead. I, on the other hand, have inherited Mom's fine, straight hair, and though she has dark brown hair, I've inherited a blonde color from her side of the family. Later in life, when I spend less time in the sun, my hair also turns brown, but it will never be the rich black color of Dad's hair.

Three large turkeys appear from the fine, thread-like leaves of fescue growing among the pine that edge a small opening above a grouping of gray rocks. One spreads his tail feathers, puffs out his chest and begins strutting.

"Eddie," Dad says softly and points to three mallards flying over the south edge of the lake.

"Too bad we're not duck hunting," I say. Dad has taken me duck and pheasant hunting, though he doesn't let me carry a gun. Sometimes, however, he's let me shoot at a piece of paper tacked to a tree.

I remember the last time we went hunting with Dave.

I can still hear the two rifle shots pierce the wet stillness of the woods. Our springer spaniel leaps forward into the underbrush. There's a thud off to the left followed by a fluttering. Dad bends under a large maple tree branch and half-walks-half-runs toward the sound.

A moment later, there's another shot, and another thud comes from farther off to the left, followed by the same fluttering. Dave hurries toward the duck he's just shot. I follow Dad, pushing my way through the scratchy bushes.

I scratch my arms as I push through a patch of bushes. Suddenly, I'm in a small opening in the underbrush, and right in front of me, I see a mallard flapping rapidly in circles. In an instant, Dad arrives, grasps the duck in a large sun-tanned hand and snaps its neck.

Dad dips the oars softly into the water and pulls the boat slowly forward. We pass a grove of maple trees.

T

"Dad, how do people get maple syrup out of trees?"

He smiles. "Well . . . let's see . . ." He lifts the oars out of the water and dips them in for another pull and then brings the ends over the sides of the boat, leaving the boat to slowly coast on its own.

"It can only be done when the sap is running, either fall or spring — times when the temperatures are fluxuating around freezing."

"Why?"

"This makes the sap that runs just beneath the bark flow down the trees. Okay?"

"Okay."

"So, then, people tap the trees, which means they make a hole in the bark, just a small one, and stick a hollow tube, what's called a spile, in it. That way they can get the sap to flow out of the tree. Make sense?"

"Yes."

"Then they hang a bucket over it so the end of the spile carries the sap into the bucket."

"Simple enough."

"But wait. It's still not ready. Have to boil off the excess water until it thickens into syrup."

"How did anyone ever figure this out?"

"Who knows? Hard to imagine anyone figuring out sap flows under the bark of a tree, but, I suppose someone peeled off the bark, found a sticky something underneath, tasted it, found it sweet, and, through trial and error began learning how it all worked."

"Makes sense."

"But, it's not how those who discovered it saw the world. They connected it to supernatural forces."

T

"Huh?"

"Do you believe God created the world?"

"Yes."

"Then it was God who created maple syrup."

"Okay."

"But not everyone is a Christian."

"Okay."

"And the people who discovered maple syrup weren't Christians."

"So?"

"So they believe it came from other gods."

"But those are just stories . . . not really true."

"Well . . . what's true isn't as simple as you think."

"Huh?"

He smiles. "There're a number of stories. The Indians were the ones who first discovered how to do it, and they have legends. The Chippewa believed their god; they called him Nenaw Bozhoo, purposely made it hard to get at the syrup so that they would have to work to get it and not take the gifts of nature too much for granted."

"That's a funny name. I bet you just made it up!"

"No, that's what they called him."

"Sure." I roll my eyes.

"Believe what you will."

"What are the other stories?"

"Hmm . . . well, I once heard one that a squaw named Moqua once boiled some moose meat in the sap from a maple, not realizing it would turn the sap into a sweet syrup, but it did, and her husband was so delighted with the taste he bragged to everyone that god had taught his wife how to make this delicious new food by boiling tree sap."

T

"Okay, but these are just stories." There was a time I believed Dad's stories, but I'm beginning to realize a good story isn't always the truth.

My left leg starts tingling from lack of blood so I shift to let it flow. It hurts a bit as the blood surges back, not bad, and expected.

"Well, there probably is some truth to them," he says. "But this is all I know. You remember those Ojibwa dream catchers you made in school?"

"Yeah."

"What did your teacher tell you about them?"

"She said they were called dream catchers because the Indians made them to catch dreams."

"Okay, but what else?"

"I don't know. Why?"

"Did you know they represent spider webs?"

"Yeah, the teacher said something about that."

"And that the Ojibwa hung them above the children at night to work like a spider's web and catch the demons of nightmares before they can get to the children. And then the webs hold the dangerous, frightening spirits of those nightmares until the sun comes up and burns them away. But the positive spirits of good dreams can pass through the web, slide down the feathers hanging underneath right into the children and bring good fortune."

"I don't think the teacher told us all that. I remember her saying they made them of willow and the webs are from something called nettle, and they're either round or shaped like a snowshoe."

"They help us remember our dreams." Dad smiles. "Do you believe in dreams?"

T

"What do you mean?"

"Do you believe dreams are real?"

"Sure – I have dreams all the time."

"But do you think they're real when you wake up? Do you think the people you meet in a dream are still around when you wake up?"

"No . . . Yes . . . I mean, yes – sometimes I wake up in the night and I think ghosts are around me."

"Some of the Ojibwa believed that dream catchers evaporate away as children grow up and lose the ability to believe. But others believe that they're always a part of a person's life, or at least can be, if the person retains the ability to believe. And they can help that person through the paths of life, can guide each of us – can protect us against the dangers of falling into a nightmare."

I suppose Dad is trying to tell me more than I'm grasping, but what hits me is the part about spiders – our house, my room has spiders and all kinds of insects. I live with them, but I don't like them. It's hard to think of them as being desirable. They're annoying and ugly. Besides, they're small and might crawl on me and bite or sting me while I sleep. They might even poison me. It's best not to get all caught up in these thoughts, best to find something else to think about.

"Dad, what's the story of Jonah and the whale?"

"What do you mean?"

"I was having some kind of a dream about a whale in the lake . . . and it got mixed up with Pinocchio . . . and then Jonah was talking with Pinocchio."

"You were probably just thinking about the tree-trunk-fish you saw in the lake when you fell asleep, and that got mixed with the Pinocchio movie."

T

"But, what about Jonah?"

"Well . . . what about him?"

"The story comes from the Bible . . . right?"

"Yes."

"Well, who is Jonah?"

"Okay . . . let me see . . . I don't know it very well . . . but . . . there is a chapter in the Bible titled *The Book of Jonah.* Jonah was a prophet. God sent him to . . . hmm . . . I forget the name of the place. But God sent him there to get all the people to repent."

"What does it mean to repent?"

"To admit they had sinned and ask for forgiveness."

"That seems to be the big thing in church. We're always asking God to forgive us."

Dad laughs. "Hadn't really thought about it. You still want to hear about Jonah?"

"Oh, yes, sorry."

"Jonah doesn't obey God and tries to escape across the ocean. This makes God mad, and he sends a great storm against the ship. Jonah's shipmates realize that this is no ordinary storm, and force Jonah to confess what's going on."

"How do they get him to confess?"

"I don't know. But he does, and he tells them that, if they throw him overboard, the storm will end and they will be safe. So they do. A whale swallows him, and he is inside it for three days and three nights. After this, Jonah agrees to do as God commands, and the whale vomits him onto the shore."

"That's all?"

"Well . . . Jonah goes to the city as God commands and convinces the people there to repent."

"So . . . what's the point?"

T

"I'm not the one to ask. But I remember it representing a kind of resurrection. Jonah died in the whale but was reborn because he repented and obeyed God."

"Can someone really survive in a whale for three days?"

"No. That's the point. One cannot survive death — unless God decides to create a miracle."

I lean back into the prow. So, if God decides to do it, he can create miracles. I've heard this in one way or another through the years, especially in church. I guess it's like the dreamcatcher. There's some kind of spiritual force that controls life.

It's confusing. After I think about it for a while I get frustrated and decide to find something else to think about.

It's my birthday. That's a better thought. And I've been given a new tackle box and some new plastic bobbers, and fish hooks, and fishing line. And two special knives, one a small, sharp knife to gut fish and flay them, and one a larger knife to chop off their heads and scale them. I know Mom and Dad are spending beyond their means for me.

Whatever the negatives in my life and however much I do or don't understand, this is a special day. That much I know, and that's enough. It's a chance to be out on a lake with Dad. I watch my new bobber gently bouncing on the rippling water.

I feel good.
I feel happy.
Miracles! That's what it's all about! Dad is Superman!

"Eddie," Dad says, interrupting my thoughts.

"What?" I ask in an upbeat voice, ready for another exchange of clever banter.

T

"I have something important to talk to you about," he says.

"What?" His tone doesn't feel right.

"Are you awake?"

"Sure," I say. "What is it?" An uneasy feeling comes over me.

"Last winter, when I went to the hospital." He stops.

"Yeah," I say, trying to keep the conversation on a happy plane. "I thought superstars could heal themselves."

"Eddie, be serious," he says and puts his hand on my knee.

I try to read his face. The day is losing its warmth.

"Eddie, this is important," he says softly. "This plastic bag I have to wear for my urine, not a laughing matter, right."

"No," I say. "It's not funny at all." I know he's deadly serious, but I don't want serious, not now, not today.

He looks at me for a long moment. I try not to look directly into his eyes and instead look past him, seeing two more mallards flying across the lake. They disappear over the three buckskins.

He lets the silence linger. It's as if we're having a staring contest to see who can go the longest without blinking.

The water gently rocks the boat — lap . . . lap-lap . . .

He says in a whisper, and yet it's a whisper evincing a great strength, "Eddie, I have cancer."

"That's what you said when you came home from the hospital."

"And do you know," he asks, "what cancer is?"

"A bad disease," I say and shrug my shoulder to indicate I see no reason to pursue the subject.

"How bad?" he continues, ignoring my signals.

"I don't know! You had to have an operation and now you have to wear that bag and the hospital is doing something to

T

you called chemotherapy, and it'll be a while before you get over it," I say and turn to reel in my line. The skater bugs dart back-and-forth across the crisp water.

I feel Dad's hands on my shoulders. "Eddie, look at me."

He tries to turn me, but my muscles are stiff, locked tight.

"Eddie!"

I go limp. He turns me. Takes me into his chest and holds me. I smell his skin, hear his heart, and feel his warmth, his muscles, soft and strong.

The lapping of the water and the beating of his heart rock me in a lullaby of love and safety.

"What you don't know," he whispers, "is that I probably will not get over this sickness. This is not the measles or the mumps that one gets over and forgets in a week or a month. In fact," he continues, almost more to himself than to me, "I'm probably going to get much worse rapidly." He emphasizes the final four words.

Lap . . . lap-lap . . . lap . . . bump . . . b-bump . . .

I separate . . . sit on my own . . . silent . . . still . . . .

I watch the flight of two wood ducks across the eastern horizon, half expecting to hear the bark of a twelve-gauge shotgun and see them tumbling into the water.

Lap . . . lap-lap . . .

Dad sits quietly, looking at me, giving me the time I need.

Bump . . . ba-bump . . .

Time stops.

I remember the night I'm startled out of my sleep by a loud commotion:

"Got you!"

"No! You missed!"

T

"There, take that!"

I get out of bed and walk into the hall, where I can see into the kitchen. From the kitchen it's possible to take a left into the dining room or go straight into the living room. The living room and dining room are also connected by an open wall. Thus, it's possible to run around a single wall from the kitchen into the living room, into the dining room, and back into the kitchen. And that is just what Mom and Dad are doing, squirt guns in hand.

Mom comes around the corner, right in front of me. Dad catches her and they tumble, laughing, to the kitchen floor.

I gaze at the three tall buckskins standing solemnly above the other trees.

Dad waits.

I feel his eyes on me.

What does he want?

What is he waiting for?

I can out-wait you!

You tricked me! You lied to me! You made me think this was a special day, a birthday gift!

Some gift!

He hugs me.

Time stops.

I feel the gentle rocking of the boat, hear the water lapping against it. A warm breeze blows against my back and neck.

Time eases back onto the lake.

I realize Dad has returned to his seat.

He rows the boat slowly along the shoreline. A grove of White Fir grows along the water's edge. Yesterday I walked into a similar grove in the woods to the west of the cabin and

T

was filled with the quiet dignity of them. I stood barefoot on the carpet of their fallen needles. The ground had a soft, clean feel. I looked through their branches to the blue sky above, felt a sense of God, a sense of being in a spiritual place.

Funny how some places have that sense.

It shouldn't be so, but it is. Places have a feel to them. Some feel sad, some dangerous, some happy, some calm, some filled with electricity, some filled with mystery. And, yes, some have a sacred, spiritual feel. Of course, there are literal reasons for many of these, but a sacred feel is different. It suggests there is a connection with another world, a mysterious, numinous connection with spirits one cannot see but can sense.

Dad glides the boat easily around a bend, and a swampy shoreline comes into view – patches of cattails, their cigar-shaped seed-heads rising up to eight feet above the grassy sedges, silkweed, smartweed, bulrushes, green, ribbon-like leaves of wild rice, spatterdock, dollar bonnet and white lilies. The small green flowers of a patch of mare's tail peek out from the water along the front edge.

A red-winged blackbird lands on the gray-green leaf of a duck acorn.

A noisy, energetic flock of smaller birds flits about the overhanging limbs of a basswood – chickadees, field sparrows, common grackles, juncos.

A large pignut oak leans over the marshy foliage, and then an outcrop of sandstone gives the edge of the lake a clean boarder. The distinctive gobbling of wild turkeys comes from a patch of shagbark hickory. I scan the shoreline for them but can't find them.

As we loaded the boat, Dad told me that a flock of sea hawks, also known as ospreys, has built their nests high in the

T

trees of an island on the lake, but we never see them or the nests. It's not surprising neither of us remembers to look.

The Ferris wheel at the Midway. I remember how excited I was to ride it. But, then, as it carried me higher, an inexplicable fear took hold of me. I fought against it. Rationalized it. Told myself I was locked into a seat and could not fall. Told myself thousands of people had ridden this ride without falling. Told myself I wasn't going to let myself succumb to a senseless fear. But it wouldn't let go of me.

Each time the wheel stopped to let someone on, I was forced to sit and rock gently. High above the people, thousands of tiny people in the Midway — standing in lines to purchase tickets to rides, squealing as the rides spun them in rapid circles or dropped them suddenly in a plunge toward the ground, buying cotton candy, caramelized popcorn, hot dogs, and French fries, throwing darts at balloons, and shooting and endless array of targets.

What a grand view it was. But no. Not for me. Not with this huge fear.

I was fearless. People had exclaimed again and again how fearless I am, had rolled their eyes and laughed or cautioned me. Yet, here I was, struggling to survive a fear that made no sense.

Higher and higher the ride took me.

No, no, no! This is not me! I do not like this me!

There is no way out. Nothing I can do.

I know this sickness, this cancer is serious. I've known it for some time.

But the knowing of it has been coated in a shell of belief that he's going to survive it. Always, without question — the belief has always been that he's going to survive it.

T

The dad insisting he is going to die isn't My Dad. My Dad wouldn't say such a thing. My Dad wouldn't believe such a thing. My Dad knows he will survive! The rules that apply to others don't apply to him!

No! I will not accept it!

I study him. There's a kindness in his features. I've seen movies with such stars as Cary Grant. Dad would never be mistaken for Cary Grant. Dad has a softer face. Yes, he has the rich, black hair and the fine features. He doesn't have that cleft chin, which I think is to Dad's advantage. He has a slightly rounder face, more horizontal eyes. But, though I'm not old enough to think it through, I know enough to know Dad is indeed a good looking man, a man with the kind of looks Hollywood would find suited for leading men. He also has a nice build, thin with broad shoulders. But what sets him apart is that kindness. Some people have a kindness in their features, and that's what Dad has.

Dad, my Dad, has just told me he's going to die — not someday, not as an old man with a full life behind him, but in the near future, the real future.

How is this kind? Why has he done this to me?

The truth is that I already know, somewhere inside, I know, and yet can't know, because I'm too young to believe what I know.

I'm to age rapidly.

That morning together with Dad, the day of my ninth birthday, I begin my fall into the funhouse.

Yes . . . it has been foreshadowed . . . there have been glimpses . . . moments when nightmarish images interrupt my thoughts, not long enough for me to grasp their portent, but enough to

T

leave me unsettled. There've been sounds in the silence . . . as if a door opened, letting in another world, and then quickly shut.

But this is the moment Dad gives me permission to listen.

Dad stops his rowing, picks up his rod-and-reel and flicks his line into a promising shadow in front of a large cottonwood, leaving me to my thoughts. A billowing, white, cumulus cloud passes between the sun and our boat, momentarily holding everything in a gray shadow. A dragonfly hovers over the water about ten feet from the prow of the boat. Time and eternity intersect.

Dad reels in his line and replaces the chub with a brown-and-white lure that has two little black dots painted on it to make it look like a minnow – at least that's the idea. While I watch him tie it securely on his line, I think about how idiotic the lure is – a piece of wood carefully cut, sanded, painted, and fixed with two groups of three hooks, totally fake, and yet the fish literally go for the bait, literally swallow the lie hook, line and sinker.

After he finishes tying on the lure, he flicks an accurate cast barely in front of a dead log. The lure hits the water and he gets a strike. He gives a quick jerk to set the hook. "Eddie, get the net ready."

As it turns outs, there's no rush. It takes Dad a good five minutes to work the fish close enough to the boat to land it. I wait anxiously while the battle progresses. Dad rapidly reels in the line when the fish comes toward the boat, only to grudgingly let it back out when the fish turns away. More than once I think the fish has slipped free, but Dad never loses his concentration, and the line grows shorter. Then, abruptly, the fight is over. Dad ends it with a deceptively simple pull of

T

the prize into my waiting net. I jerk the netted fish over the side of the boat and dump it next to a tackle box in the bottom. The prize is a nine-inch northern pike.

Within an hour's time Dad catches two more, each over ten inches. I don't catch a single fish, but I come close.

"Dad! A fish followed my lure right up to the boat! A big one!"

He laughs. "You should have swung your line around the prow – give him a chance to bite."

"Oh," I moan, realizing he's right.

He flashes his smile, a wide smile that creates wrinkles on the sides of sparkling eyes. People always say his smile lights up a room, and at that moment it seems to light up the entire inlet.

I laugh, even though the joke is on me.

He adjusts the plastic urine bag around his waist. Once an exceptional athlete, soon he will be unable to sit up in bed. "Well" he says, "we'd better be heading home. Mom will be wondering if we've gotten lost."

T

The Midway

Ebenezer Scrooge doesn't believe in ghosts, thinks them likely nothing more than figments of a dream, the result of a bit of bad beef in his evening stew.

Jacob Marley, such a good partner, a life based on the logic of putting the practical concerns of business first, not letting compassion weaken one's logic – Jacob wanders through Ebenezer's thoughts, those fragments of the past that get set free in dreams, irritating bits of memory, beef that won't settle in the stomach. The worldview, the rational, reasonable approach to life, each man responsible for his own well-being – Ebenezer and Jacob are good business partners, use their cold financial abilities to become wealthy. Then, Jacob dies, a pity, but not unexpected. All men must die.

Yet he lives . . . in the dreams . . . he still lives. Not because he is a daily companion for many years, at least not just that. Not because there are emotional bonds . . . certainly there is a familiarity, a routine, a way of life – the expectations of Jacob being in the office, of his look, the clothes he wears, the phrases he uses, his mannerisms. Yes, certainly it will take time for that to fade, time to get used to life without him – that is to be expected. But there's something more – a realization about Jacob, about Ebenezer's relationship with Jacob. That's what keeps waking Ebenezer in the night.

Ebenezer's childhood, his memories of a father who blames him for his mother's death in his own birth. Ebenezer knows his father hates him for it, punishes him for it, and makes no attempt to hide his contempt.

The kindness of an employer, the love of a young woman – they have touched Ebenezer, given him a taste of sentiment. But they have not been enough to get him passed his cold, protective shell.

The love and suffering of his employee's family. The heart-wrenching fate of Tiny Tim. Ebenezer refuses to consider it. Bob Cratchit is a necessary expense once Jacob dies. It's an unfortunate expense,
but the business is too large for him to handle without hiring help. That said, Ebenezer is not going to let this employee take advantage of him any more than any of those other people involved in his business relationships.

But the ghosts in his dreams will not let him alone. Why are they so persistent?

Dreams are hard to explain. Perhaps they're bits-and-pieces of the past freed during the night to wander aimlessly through the mind. Perhaps they're some form of knowing beyond the workings of the waking mind. Perhaps they're portents of things to come.

I try to sort it out. Dreams, especially nightmares, seem to be more than random thoughts or the result of an upset stomach. The mind has wandered into something so powerful people scream in their sleep, wake in a state of fear. Wandered is the wrong term. Too much of a mental pattern has come together for the randomness of wandering. Something has sparked the mind to think in images and sequences that result in terror.

T

Apparently, some even cause sleep-walking. People claim to travel into previous lives, to experience telepathy and to sense happenings beyond what the physical senses can know.

Certainly, something is going on. Scientists discuss Rapid Eye Movement (REM), when it's clear a sleeping person's eyes are doing just that. And neurologists can demonstrate through encephalograms (EEGs), computerized axial tomography (CAT), positron emission tomography (PET), and other means that a brain is active during sleep.

The disciplines of psychology and psychiatry are based on it.

In simple, real terms, people remember their dreams, especially the dramatic ones that fall under the designation of nightmares.

Some believe nightmares are visitations from exterior forces – spirits or ghosts from an invisible plane of existence. This seems unlikely, certainly not what a rational person is prone to believe. Isn't that at the center of Ebenezer's resistance?

Yet, the problem with denying this illogical reality is that, if there is no invisible plane, how can one believe in a spiritual world, a world that includes God. The Bible is filled with dreams that are just this, visitations from spiritual beings, some of them angelic, even God himself, and some demonic.

Furthermore, if one believes, these visits affect the waking world.

The night after Dad tells me the harsh truth about his cancer, I have a nightmare.

It rains.
The wind knocks the branch of a red oak against the cabin – thunk . . . thunk-thunk . . . thunk . . .

T

As I lie in my strange bed, I think about the day's fishing with Dad, relive the moment he tells me he's so sick he might die, remember the kindness in his eyes . . . his voice. I know he's trying to reassure me, tell me that it's okay.

There is an irony. While he's telling me not to worry, to put my trust in him, at the same time he's telling me he will not be there for me much longer. Or . . . I wonder . . . perhaps, he's telling me he will be there – even after he dies.

There's a knock at the cabin door. Two fishermen renting the cabin next to us have stopped by to share a beer and talk with Dad. The door slams shut the way an old screen door often does. I hear them shake off the rain and settle in the main room.

"The pikes are in the deep water, about fifty yards out from that large cliff along the north side of the lake."

"Caught two four-pound northern."

"Lake-of-the-Woods . . . they throw 'em back . . . call 'em snakes."

"Best walleye fishing in the whole damn state."

As the bits of conversation drift in-and-out of my thoughts, I think through the conversation in the boat. I try to sort out Jonah's story. We're not a family driven by religion. We usually go to church on Mom's insistence, but we seldom say grace before eating or talk much about religion. I learn the "Now I lay me down to sleep" prayer, though I seldom say it or any other prayer before going to sleep, and anyway, when I first learn that prayer, all it does is get me worried about dying before I wake, as if someone knows something I don't.

Pinocchio's song begins running through my mind. I like it, have always liked that song.

The rain falls harder. I listen to it beat against the roof.

T

Lightning flashes through the windows, followed by a dull thunder, the kind that starts as a muffled, tentative murmur, pauses, then returns as a loud boom.

I remember Dad telling me that thunder is thought by some to be the sound made by the gods when they're bowling. I try to picture the gods bowling on the clouds. I think about the days I lie on the dock and imagine clouds turning into various scenes, but I can't picture a group of gods bowling. I decide the noise sounds more like cannons going off underwater, and as I fell asleep, I get it mixed up with the tree trunk beneath the water I momentarily thought was a large fish.

The fish, that huge fish lurking in the shadows . . .
I look through the murky water, sense he's near.
The thunder . . . the booming thunder . . .

I see the first of the explosions, brilliant yellow-white-orange-and-red flashes immediately enveloped in thick clouds of gray-black smoke and dirt, surrounded by millions of bubbles. Between each flash, the smoke and bubbles and fire dissipate enough for me to see the fish with the dull black back, dirty white underbelly and golden eyes – shinny, golden eyes.

I crouch behind a large rock at the bottom of the lake, hoping the eyes will not notice me. The explosions so shake the water that I can barely see my hands.

It swims closer . . . and closer . . .

Each time it reappears, its eyes are larger, ever larger.

I crouch as much into the rock as I can, trying to reveal as little of my head as possible. But I need to see, need to expose enough of me to see where it's at.

Soon, it's close enough for me to see its glowing eye is as big as all of me! It must see me!

T

The fish is hit square, and everything is chaos. I close my eyes and cling to the back of the rock as a shockwave washes over me, threatening to take me with it.

I feel the scales and guts against my skin, the insistent pull of the water. I dig my feet into the muddy sand and lean into the rock.

I lose consciousness.

I'm sitting high on the Ferris Wheel above a huge fair.

The dramatic change and the height make me dizzy. Were it not for a metal bar, I would likely fall to my death.

Other than a strange black cloud in the distance, the sky is a friendly light blue.

Below me, thousands of tiny people walk about the large field filled with rides and tents. I see a sign I can read. My God! It hits me! I'm looking down on the Midway at the Minnesota State Fair!

The Ferris-Wheel has stopped and my seat gently sways back-and-forth. I fight my fear and force myself to look over the edge.

Five large clusters of multicolored balloons move steadily among the crowd as the balloon men sell their wares. The bark of the ticket salesman for the Freak Show rises intermittently above the general noise:

"Jojo Jones, the boy raised by the spider monkeys of the Amazon . . . the thick skin of the Rhinoceros Lady . . ."

Other voices rise above and then quickly merge back into the noise:

"Professor Matthew Marmeloduke . . . mathematical genius . . ."

T

"Little Johnny Rebel . . . away from home . . . five years old .
. ." "Ladies and Gentlemen . . . Dr. Magic's world famous . . .
only fifty cents . . ."

"Madame Naomi, world renowned psychic . . . reads the Tarot
. . ."

Every time the Tilt-a-Whirl starts up, its speakers blare out
Elvis Presley singing "Hound Dog," the Mad Copter has
Tennessee Ernie Ford singing "Sixteen Tons," and the Alpine
Slide has Bill Haley singing "Rock Around the Clock." My
own ride has Judy Garland singing "Over the Rainbow."

A girl of about sixteen looks up from the ticket booth directly
below me. She's wearing a light blue shirt that has "Toto, this
doesn't look like Kansas anymore" printed across the chest.

Every few minutes, a roar comes from the grandstands where
fair goers are watching the drag races. The drone of the cars
becomes a roar then fades.

The black cloud to the west stretches across more and more of
the horizon as it approaches. Though I sense something strange
about it, I think it must be a storm cloud. What else can it be?

A storm is coming in. I hear the rumble of thunder.

Its approach gains speed. No! Not good! I can't be caught
high on the Ferris-Wheel when a storm hits!

I curl as far as I can into the corner of my seat and peer over
the top edge. Why isn't the Ferris-Wheel moving, taking me
down! It needs to hurry! The clouds are nearly to the Midway!

But wait! It's not clouds at all. It's a flock of birds, large
birds! What?!

No . . . I'm wrong.

It's not birds.

It's some kind of flying animal!

Pterodactyls?

T

No . . .

What!?

Flying monkeys!!! It's a huge flock of flying monkeys!!!

The world abruptly goes from day to night, as if some supernatural being flicked a switch and turned off the sun.

At the same instant, the music of a calliope signals the arrival of the night world of the Midway, with its anarchy of flashing colors and discordant sounds.

It's too late.

I'm stuck high in the Ferris-Wheel, my seat held in place by but a few weak bolts!

I fear falling, but have to know what's happening, so I force myself to look down.

The flying monkeys dive into the crowd, grasping children and yanking them into the sky.

Frightened screams fill the air.

People push, stumble and fall over each other as they scramble for shelter. Some find loose boards, folding chairs or metal poles and swing them wildly at the large monkeys.

The huge Midway rides come unhinged and careen through the mass of frightened people like crazed mechanical monsters, their colorful lights crisscrossing erratically through the mayhem.

A woman dressed as a white witch walks through the pandemonium as if immune to the danger. Her demeanor has such a presence it's hard to deny her the aura she assumes. Is she real? Perhaps a specter loosened in the night.

And equally self-assured man dressed in black watches her. He's a dark, shadowy presence. Another specter?

A man holds an open Bible and reads a passage from Revelations: "Look, he is coming with the clouds," and "every

T

eye will see him, even those who pierced him"; and all peoples on earth "will mourn because of him."

The Ferris-Wheel slows and my seat descends uneasily. I fear it will dislodge and crash into the hissing electric lines, snapping cables and collapsing tents. It jerks down . . . down . . .

It tilts, sways and threatens to tip on its side — down . . . down . . . down. Closer . . . closer . . . I pull myself over the bar and jump, bend my knees as I hit the asphalt, and roll. A sharp sting comes from my left arm as it scrapes across the hard surface, and a pain shoots up from my right ankle. I stand. Apparently nothing is broken.

What to do?

I look at the scene from the shadow of the ticket booth.

Bright, colored lights cut through angular shadows. People appear as dark forms. Some pass close enough for the lights to catch them and reveal their frightened eyes, open mouths, and cheeks streaked with tears and mascara. The noise is deafening —screams, roaring motors, clanking metal, blaring music, splintering poles and ripping canvas.

The crowded space between me and the rows of game tents briefly opens, and I dash through it to the nearest one, a booth where two boys about age ten have been knocked backward into the pennies, nickels, dimes and glass plates of a coin-throw stand, their motionless bodies now tangled with broken glass, stuffed zebras, giraffes, elephants, lions and flapping red-and-white canvas.

The smell of smoke and blood mixes with that of hot dogs, ketchup, mustard, pickles, onions, frying grease, French fries, caramel apples and cotton candy.

T

I hear the bleating of a sheep. I can't see it, but I can tell it's near. I make my way around the wreckage of the coin-throw stand to get a better view. The next booth has also been brought down. A two-headed sheep has found its way into the broken frame, torn canvas, darts, balloons, stuffed animals and overturned counter. One of the sheep's heads makes the annoying sound I hear. The other nibbles at a piece of crepe paper.

I navigate to a large billboard of a giant orange superimposed with the phrase: "Are you tired, worn out, old before your time? Then wake up to the natural energy of Mr. Orange – the only true way to a long and healthy life!"

A mist of dust and smoke rises from the ground, preventing me from seeing more than a few yards.

A man and a woman appear, dressed in the style of the wealthy in the Great Gatsby.

"How do you do, my good man," the man says, removing his top-hat and bowing.

"What? Who?"

"Why, my poor, poooor boy, you must have tied your tongue in a knot when you put it on this morning," the woman says and smiles. Her eyes sparkle with mirth.

"Clowns? . . . ," I question, "Dressed like people at a ballroom dance?"

"Yes! Yes! Let us introduce ourselves. I am Mrs. Blood, and this gentleman with me is Mr. Bones. And you must be Little Boy Blue, for you surely seem to have lost your sheep, or was it goats. Oh, well, no matter. Would you care for a spot of champagne?" She holds an opened bottle out to me.

"No . . . no, no thank you."

T

"But you must! Come, come, my Little Blue Boy! Look! Look! At the bottle!" She holds it toward me, brings her face close, and whispers, "Inside! See how it sparkles, just like dancing stars in a wonderfully clear ocean! It can help you find your way." She abruptly pulls back. "Do you dance? Are you a dancer? Oh, come now, you must dance, come, come, come, you must learn to dance! It is the joy of life! To dance beneath the stars while the music of the night flows through you! Oh! Sooooo wonderful! So very, very wonderful!"

"Pinocchio!" Mr. Bones turns to Mrs. Blood. "Did you not hear him? He said his name is Pinocchio!"

"Oh, Mr. Bones, don't be ludicrous! This boy's name cannot be Pinocchio. I have received many Pinocchios in my French parlor. This is not a Pinocchio. How absurdly preposterous you do speak, my dear, dear Mr. Bones."

"But I heard it! Pinocchio — I did not make it up!"

"Yes, yes, yes, of course you heard it! You know very well just because you hear such things doesn't make them true! I assure you he did not speak that name!" Mrs. Blood begins dancing. She is a natural dancer — even in the midst of the disarray she dances as if she can hear music — a lilting rhythm.

Mr. Bones watches her with me, then puts his hand on my shoulder and pulls me close. "It's a beautiful Venetian waltz. Can you hear it? The music — the elegant Blue Danube filling the marble halls of Hofburg Palace."

Is it possible? Indeed, I believe I hear it.

"We have danced there many times. It is a beautiful palace, and the orchestra is one of Europe's best."

T

Part of the Roller-Coaster track smashes to the asphalt, breaking the spell of the dance. Mr. Bones and Mrs. Blood realize the Midway is in a state of chaos.

"Come, Cupcakes, let us leave this filthy smoke."

"Leave? No! Please don't leave!" I say.

"Oh, my poor, misled boy, no wonder you cannot find your goats," Mrs. Blood says. "Let me see . . . the haystack . . . yes . . . the little boy in the haystack."

"The sheep's in the meadow, the cow's in the corn!" Mr. Bones interjects. "Come, come, my sweet, we must be going!"

"But the goats?"

"What goats? I hate to be beastly, my dear, but we must be going! The stage is empty and the audience will riot!" He tries to grasp her hand, but she pulls it away.

"Yes, yes, the beast, yes, that's it! The beast, my sad little goat boy, the beast!" Mrs. Blood says.

"Come, Dearie," Mr. Bones says. "I do believe the poor boy's tongue will be quite tied up for some time, and we really must make our entrance."

"Oh, yes, you are so right! But he is such a lost little boy. I do wish we could bring him with us."

"Not to the Masquerade, my trifola d'Alba, not to the . . ."

They vanish midsentence.

The Zipper crashes to the pavement with such force its colored lights momentarily burn through the smog, and I glimpse the flying monkeys grasping child after child.

"No!" I scream and plunge madly into the insanity. One of the monkeys lands near me! Sees me!

I swing with all my might and hit the monkey in the face as hard as I can. He stumbles backward! Blood gushes from his mouth! I lower my shoulders and charge! Bam! Thump! I

T

tackle him and immediately straddle him between my knees!
Smack! Smack! Smack! Smack! I hit him, again and again
and again and again!

"Okay. Okay. Settle down. It's all right."
"No! No!"
"Wake up. Come on. Wake up.
"No! No! No!"
It's okay. You're having a nightmare.
I can't swing! What? What? My arms! Aah! Aah! I can't
swing! Someone is holding my arms!
"Eddie, Eddie, wake up."
"I stop swinging. What? Oh . . . oh . . . oh . . .
"It's me, it's me, see. You're having a dream. It's okay."
I wake, open my eyes. "Yes, oh, yes, yes . . . Daddy . . . oh . . .
Daddy . . ."
"Must be from sleeping in a strange bed . . . and the storm and
all. Everything's okay. See, it's all okay. I'm right here for
you."
"Oh, oh, I had a dream."
"Yes, you must have had quite a nightmare. But you're
okay. It was just a bad dream. I'll stay with you the rest of the
night. Look, I'll just sit here in this rocking chair while you
sleep. Okay? Right here. See? Now, everything's all right."
The dream. Monkeys? With huge wings, monkeys
attacking. A smell . . . gas? What was it? The cabin . . . all I
smell is the cabin, the musty cabin.
So vivid! Not one I will forget! And I don't. It returns
throughout my life, but never the same, always taking on
nuances I hadn't noticed.

T

Dad turns on the dirty-yellow light of the lamp that sits on a small table next to the rocking chair. He has not bothered to put on a shirt, and I watch his still powerful chest rise and fall peacefully — wisps of black hair, a rich tan, strong chest and shoulder muscles. Dave told me Dad had been a star football player in high school, played fullback. No way to be certain. Dave wasn't born until years later, and Dave idolized Dad, so he only ever said positive things to me about Dad. I believed him as a child. As an adult, I think he was being true to the image, maybe and maybe not to the facts.

As Dad pages through a magazine with a man catching a fish on the cover, I begin to fade. Dad is fine, looks healthy and strong. Dad won't die. How could I think that Dad would die? Dad will beat the odds. I misunderstood. He hadn't said there is no chance.

Eventually, I fall asleep.

When I wake, Dad is already up. So is Mom. She has made coffee and is busy frying eggs and bacon in the next room. Dad sits in the rocking chair as promised, sipping his coffee. I can't hear Johnny and will find out later he is still asleep.

It will be the kind of day Mom and Dad like.

Dad sees my open eyes. "Rise and shine. Mom has breakfast simmering." He gives the top of my head a tussle as he walks out of the room. I hear him waking Johnny. It takes a bit of a mental push to leave the warmth of the bed for the cool air of the room, but I throw off the blanket and sheet, and quickly pull on my T-shirt and cut-off jeans.

Breakfast is served on paper plates at the small wooden table in the main room (the only room besides the two bedrooms and small bathroom). The side facing the lake has large screened windows and a door onto a small porch.

T

Once breakfast is over, I push open the door and step into the cool morning air. The porch is beaded from the night's storm, and the yard has a few small branches scattered about from the wind, but the sun will quickly dry up the rain water, and the dew on the grass is already disappearing. I grab my fishing rod and head for the lake. The clear water reveals the mostly sandy bottom, a few rocks, an occasional patch of seaweed, and a swarm of minnows. I can see a few small sunfish settled in their sand nests, but nothing of much size. I pull the minnow pail out of the water and fasten one on my hook.

It's easy to catch the smaller crappies, perch, and sunfish, but they aren't worth keeping, so I throw them back. It keeps me busy until the rest of the family is ready.

Later that evening I gather some of the thin white bark off a dead birch tree and a sack of pine cones to take home as souvenirs. When we get home, I find my back has also gathered some wood ticks.

"Come on, Eddie," Mom calls, we're going swimming.

I reel in my line and leave the rod on the dock. It's but a short walk to the beach, little more than an "L" shaped dock jutting into a naturally sandy bottom.

There are a couple of inner tubes supplied by the resort, so take one and start jumping from the dock onto it. The idea is to land in it without tipping it over and dumping me into the water. It takes several tries, but I manage and get a happy cheer for my success.

A school of sunfish is attracted to Dad's legs. We watch them swim up and nibble at him.

T

May 17, 1960
Eddie on dock at sunset

T

Prospero's Island

William Shakespeare, yes, the magician himself, smiles.

The Tempest, it begins with the violence of the ocean, time and water coming together to tare the very fabric of the world.

Indeed, all the world is a stage, an expectant woman waiting for the artist's craft.

Gonzalo but a piece of a playwright's vision caught in a storm. Yes, to bring down the scene, the hopeless cries of a man caught in a tempest. How shall I have him wail out his fear . . . "The wills above be done!" Yet more, perhaps the agony of fate, the wished-for chance at a choice. If one must die, cannot one at least choose when and how?

But the author's will be done! Prospero banished to his island, Prospero has the books of the magician's art. Prospero stands before his cell.

And Miranda, his child, innocent, needing his words to flesh out the world, Miranda has seen the tempest and believes it is her own father's creation. And she cries out, begs the father she loves to have mercy, to make the world less frightening, and begs him to use his art to end the wild waters, for she feels for the horrible deaths of the men caught in the tempest.

But there is no reason for her to weep, for Prospero knows they are safe, washed ashore on his island.

Left of the Ticket Booth

The bough breaks
And down comes baby
Cradle and all

Dad Dies

We find it strange. They belong to our church and have three children, a boy a year or maybe two older than I, a girl a year younger, and another boy close to John's age. But we don't know them well, have never played with them outside of church gatherings.

Late afternoon, Mom packs us in the station-wagon and drops us off with a final, "Have fun!" goodbye.

It is the first time and will be the only time we ever see the inside of their house. The house is built on a small hill rising from the road, so the entrance is into a first-floor that is a walk-in basement. We enter a kitchen/office. Apparently, the father has a job as a designer and works at least partially out of the house at his large drafting desk.

"Eddie, Johnny, come here a minute," he says, picking up a jar. "I've developed a substitute for gum that won't cause cavities." He takes a small "gob" out for each of us, and we obediently chew it. I've never liked gum and find this not the enticing introduction to the evening he intends.

As soon as it seems polite, I'm ready to be done with it. Since I don't know them well, don't know the father at all, I debate whether or not to swallow it but gather up the courage to ask where to discard it.

He picks up a wastebasket and holds it towards me. "So . . . What do think? Not bad, huh?"

"Yes, it's good," I say. What else can I say?

He then goes into a discussion about how bad gum is for our teeth and how he intends to market his solution. His heart is in the right place, but his obsession adds to my already uneasy feelings.

We are led through a door into a large "play room," mainly a big empty room with some mattresses to tumble on, and we are left with the Carlson children to entertain ourselves.

Before it has even gotten dark outside, it's time for bed. They don't let their children, and thus us, stay up late. But first, they make us brush our teeth.

"Oh, your mom forgot to send along your toothbrushes," the mother says, "but that's okay. We have extras for just such an occasion." They do seem overly concerned about taking care of their teeth.

I give them credit. They are trying to be friendly, and even if it has an artificial feel about it, similar to a television sit-com, the likes of Ozzie and Harriet, Leave it to Beaver or Father Knows Best, I appreciate the effort.

That doesn't mean I'm enjoying myself. It's too goody-goody for me. Also, even in the best of environments, I'm not going to sleep well in a strange house. So, I lie awake most of the night. I can't believe the minister actually prayed for Dad to die. I remember the final fishing trip, the day on the lake when Dad said he might die. Might is bad enough, but it's not even close to praying for it.

One good thing about not being able to sleep is that I don't have any bad dreams, and after a night of debating how to handle these suggestions of Dad dying, I decide I'm going to stick with my belief he'll beat the odds.

The next morning, after, of course, we all brush our teeth, the mother calls us to a breakfast of bacon, eggs, toast and orange juice at a large table upstairs, a much more formal affair than what we do for breakfast at home.

T

After breakfast, we're sent outside to play in their backyard, which stretches to a cliff over the lake, a beautiful view. Though I have my own view over the lake, I sense how much wealthier they are than us. As much as I'm impressed that Dad seems to be able to do everything involved with building and fixing houses, I also know there is a difference in the kind of house Carlsons own.

There are some trees on one side of the yard, so, instead of playing on the nicely mowed lawn, I head into the woods, where I play army, until Mom arrives to pick us up.

Mrs. Carlson calls to me.

I come from the woods around the lakeside of the house and see Mom parked on the road below. It's curious that she has not pulled to the side of the road, but simply stopped in the middle of it. I suppose it doesn't matter, as it's a dirt road not travelled much.

They have all gathered around her.

Again, it is a scene directly out of Father Knows Best. I let the hill take me in a trot down to the gathering. At least the visit is over and I can get back to my normal routine. I hope Mom isn't going to start expecting John and me to become friends with the Carlson children.

Once I reach the road, my social concerns are forgotten. Mom is crying.

Mrs. Carlson hugs her.

Mom says, "The Funeral Home arrived early to take him away."

It hits me.

What cannot happen has.

T

The Man of the Family

"Who have we here?"

Mr. Uhlrich puts his hand on my shoulder.

"This is Eddie. His dad just died, so I'm taking him."

"Hi Eddie," the unknown man says.

"Hi."

"Are you friends with Bill?"

"Yes."

"They're in the same grade."

"Well, it's very nice to meet you."

"Thanks . . . Nice to meet you, too."

Mr. Uhlrich turns me back into the line. I hear the unknown man passing along the conversation to others as we slowly move forward.

The main reason I know Bill Uhlrich is that his family belongs to our church. The reason I'm here tonight is that the church is sponsoring this event and Bill's dad approached Mom to do this for me.

Mom has fussed me into being dressed for the event. My arms and legs have outgrown my suit coat and pants. "Don't worry," Mom says. "No one will notice." Same for the collar of my white shirt. The inside is not as white as the rest and I can't button the top button. Mom uses my navy-blue, snap-on tie to pull the collar flaps as close as she can. "There," she finishes and steps back to see what she's done. "You're such a handsome boy when you're all dressed-up!" Just yesterday she used Dad's electric hair razor to buzz cut my sun-bleached hair, so, all-in-all, I am considered "presentable" — that's the word she keeps using. I need to be "presentable."

Ever since Dad died I've needed to be presentable a good deal, one social gathering after another. But few notice me. It's as if being presentable means no one will notice.

So tonight again, I'm going to be presentable. I didn't want to go, but Mom urged me, saying it will be good for me, and after all, "Axel" is going to entertain.

The line moves forward at a steady pace and soon I'm seated at one of the tables farthest from the stage but in a good position to see the entire room. As has been the case for the recent surge of social gatherings, I don't know the sequence of activities or how I'm supposed to behave, so I patiently wait for the adults to direct me, all the time wondering why this is supposed to be a favor I need to appreciate. While the "fathers" talk, waitresses begin by filling water glasses. Another thing I've noticed about these events is that my name gets filtered into the conversations as if I'm not there.

It would seem that the only things being said about me would be sympathetic and reinforcing. I'm finding that's not how it works. The kind comments about what a good man Dad was and how Mom will have a tough go of it slide into the more exciting news they've heard that Dave has already moved out and separated from the family. They seem to know more about this than I. One whispers a suggestion they ask me, but I see two others shake their heads not to do so. Mr. Uhlrich, perhaps to cover up the discussion, turns to me and says. "Well, Eddie, I

T

guess *you're* the man of the family now. You'll have to help out your mom."

"That's right," the man across from me adds. "You're a good boy and I'm sure you'll be a great help."

I nod, not sure what to say.

I can't help but think about what little I know of it. For Dad's last birthday, Mom decides to buy him an expensive watch. Though she and everyone else continue to tell me he will recover, she has to know he is nearing the end. He likely finds it uncomfortable to even wear the watch and might not wear it much. I don't know. But it certainly is a gift of the heart, not the head. Mom is prone to spending money she doesn't have on such gifts, as she proves every Christmas. It obviously means something important to them. I suspect Dad has wanted an expensive watch, perhaps they've recently had a conversation about this, and Mom has decided it will be the perfect gift to represent her love and the unrealistic belief that the impossible will happen and he will survive. I doubt they make the connection between "time" and a "watch," but perhaps they do. It's not hard to believe it represents their love for each other and all of the hardships of cancer they've endured together.

One of the ironies of life is that tragedies are what give it depth and value, and though no one can fully know the darkness of another's mind, it isn't hard to know that this tragedy has brought them together in a deep love that dealing with the daily battles of caring for a loved one as he slowly dies does. Not only has she been his wife, friend and lover, she has been his nurse and his caretaker in all ways through the losing battle – more so then others facing similar battles because she is a nurse and has nursed him at home, caring for all of his needs.

T

After Dad dies, Dave decides that, since he is Dad's oldest boy, he should have the watch, and he takes it. When Mom finds out, she is furious. The world has reached its darkest moment for both of them. They are worn-out from the battle and now is the moment for all of their sorrow to come out. Their energy is spent. Their emotions are frayed.

Perhaps the blow-up is inevitable.

I don't know Dave's version of the story, because he separates from the family. But I hear Mom's, and I experience some of it as well. According to her, when she confronts Dave, he slams the watch on the counter and walks out. From what others tell me, he claims she kicks him out, telling him never to return. That's not unlikely. The explosive moment probably includes both him telling her he is moving out and her telling him to get out.

What I know is that he moves in with his friend, Jerry. Mom puts me in the front seat of the car and heads to Jerry's house. It's obvious that's where he has gone. Jerry is Dave's best friend, and Jerry lives with his parents by Three Points Park, so if Dave leaves the house on foot, it makes sense that's where he goes. It's possible that he tells Mom he's going there in the yelling match.

I don't know why she takes me along, though I suspect there is no special reason. She also has me walk with her to Jerry's front door. Again, I'm not sure why. She is likely operating more out of emotions than logic. Jerry's mom opens the door, and Mom says she wants to talk with Dave, wants to tell him to come back home. Jerry's mom says Dave and Jerry aren't there, even though it's easy to hear them just out of sight around the corner. This much I experience, so I know this much of the event.

T

Whether or not Dave should have gotten the watch can be debated. Taking it without asking is hard to justify. He obviously wants it, and he must believe he isn't going to get it. The only way I justify it is to put it in the context of the huge emotional strains and the fact that he is only eighteen at the time. It's clear he and Mom are not getting along as well as they might, but again, it's possible to understand the strain on both of them, and it is also the age when teenagers are breaking away from their parents, so such tensions are common even in good circumstances. Then, of course, there is the fact that Mom isn't his biological mom. I've not noticed any problems through the years, so I assume it's not serious. But this suggests there is more of a conflict than I witness.

Dave is heading to college, so in truth he's ready to move out of the house anyway. In fact, it's surprising he is still there, as he will be moving out of state to begin college in late August or early September, and this all takes place in August.

The wounds never get healed.

The following Christmas, Mom's parents claim to have gotten a letter from JoAnn and Dave that they have decided to split from the family and want nothing to do with any of us anymore.

No one bothers to explain any of it to me, so all I know is what I happen to overhear. The major argument I experience between Mom and JoAnn takes place while Dad is still alive. JoAnn babysits John and me one of the times Mom visits Dad in the hospital. JoAnn makes pancakes for supper, and John and I want more, but she has used up her batter and tells us no. When Mom picks us up, we mention it, resulting in an argument between Mom and JoAnn.

T

Good adult analysis

POV + change from

of past event.

change from

past immediacy

I cannot know how Mom and JoAnn get along through the years, but I never notice any serious problems. However, JoAnn completely separates once Dad dies, and I have the feeling that she pulls Dave to do the same. As the years go on, Dave will make a few attempts to reestablish connections with the family, but they are feeble. It's hard to know how much he realizes how seriously poor Dad's bills leave us. He has to know to some extent, as he lived in it for a time. Still, the extreme poverty following Dad's death probably escapes him, especially since he'd rather not know.

I won't realize until much later in life, how much I am affected by his absence during this time I need him. It's obvious in looking back. I needed a father figure, and he is the one I naturally turned to for that emotional need. His departure, especially in such a dramatic, negative way, confuses me and causes me to see it as a rejection, though it never occurs to him.

As the years go by, he completes his B.S at a college out of the state, where he has received a basketball scholarship, and then through his ROTC program spends two years in Germany, so he is not going to be around a great deal anyway, and when he happens to be in town, he sometimes looks me up and helps me out with a $5 bill or some such small kindness. For a time, he even helps pay my gas. Many years later, he will give me an envelope of newspaper clippings about my sports' achievements. So . . . he apparently does care about me. And yet, years go by without him bothering to contact me. So . . .

What does it mean to care?

Are there any responsibilities or requirements joined to caring about another?

T

If someone cares, should he want to keep in touch? To experience some degree of discomfort or inconvenience to help? To know? To Understand?

If so, what are the edges?

There is the famous cliché that a friend is the person who is there when times get tough.

On the other hand, there is also the cliché about friendship being a two-way street. What, after all, do I have to offer? What do I do to keep the relationship alive? Not much. If, as I'm told numerous times, I'm to take on the role of the man of the family, I should be taking my share of the responsibility.

Certainly, mere circumstance factors in. Dave is a young man moving on with his life, which means leaving the state, and eventually even living outside of the country. He has suffered the traumatic loss of his father. It is, after all, a fairly normal time for a boy to lesson ties with his parents, his family. It is what growing up is all about.

Through the lean years, I am a lost boy living a life Dave disagrees with. Eventually, I become a hippie. Dave is straight as an arrow. When I move from being a radical or at very least a liberal to a Democrat (at least for practical purposes), Dave is a strong Republican. While I hate Richard Nixon, Dave defends him. While I apply for a Conscious Objector status, Dave initiates going into the military. When Dad dies, I have an emotional breakdown and have to struggle through an extreme shyness. Dave is confident and social.

How can two people who have grown up in the same family and shared a strong bond be so different? Central to it all – why is it so hard on me that he leaves the family to pursue his life when I am but ten?

T

Mom often denies it, claiming things are fine with her two adopted children, even though JoAnn severs connections while she lives in Three Points, about a ten-minute walk away, and Dave eventually returns to Lake Minnetonka a wealthy man, proud of his membership at the Lafayette Club, and willing to make a few overtures, but not willing to make any serious move to reconnect with Mom or offer help. I suspect Dave will not allow himself to know how hard Mom has it, both during Dad's sickness and after his death, or how much it is the result of her devoting herself to Dad and being left with huge medical bills because of his sickness. Of course, it is mere speculation, and likely Dave sees it in a different light.

To make the mixture even murkier, when Dave moves to Mound and I am the one no longer living there, times I am back, mainly to visit Mom, on occasion Dave, John and I go golfing, and on even more rare occasions, Dave invites us out on his pontoon boat, even includes Mom. Once, JoAnn even joins us.

How to sort this out?

As the decades pass, I become resigned to it, see my relationship with him as a sad loss of what might have been.

It is one of the most important of the overlapping universes that do not connect. I see the world in different contexts than he does. In his vision of life, he is tremendously successful.

He has all of the qualities for success — good looks, intelligence, athletic ability, and that winning personality that comes from embracing all of the social norms. It's legitimate to consider him a golden boy, such an exceptional combination of the attributes the world admires that he can only be the leading man in a movie. He succeeds, parlaying his athletic scholarship into the fraternity world of wealthier

T

people, eventually hitting it big in computer programing and the world of the stock market.

It's nice when someone is successful, and I am happy for him, but it's sad he and I end up on opposite sides of life. When he leaves to pursue his life, I'm left without the substitute father I so desperately need.

At the time, I do not know it, cannot possibly understand the complex levels of my own psyche. Instead of realizing I need someone to be a father figure, I'm struggling with everyone telling me that I am now the one needing to be the man of the family. I take it seriously.

As I come out of my thoughts, I find the conversation has moved away from me and my family.

The waitresses are finished filling our glasses with water.

The dinner comes as several courses. After the water, the waitresses start filling the adults' coffee cups. I get a choice of pop and choose Pepsi. Baskets of bread are put in the center of the tables and we each get a salad. The main course is either baked chicken or sliced beef, in either case with mashed potatoes and corn. Before dessert comes the big event – Axel's show.

We've all seen his children's show, *Axel's Treehouse*, and even though I've gotten old for it, the mere fact he's a television star makes him an exciting presence.

The master of ceremonies announces him and he comes on stage. He's not as impressive in person as on television, but he tells a few jokes and gets some scattered laughs. Then he walks over to a basket sitting on a table.

T

"Now for the prizes! Axel has gifts for the children!" He sticks his hand into the bowl and draws out a folder paper. "Let's see here. Eddie, is it Ice?"

Me! I'm the first name drawn!

Mr. Uhlrich claps and turns to me. "It's you! Go on up!"

I make my way through the tables to the stage.

"All right," Axel says, "and you're a fine-looking boy! Here you are! A tube of Elmer's Glue!"

Axel is even less impressive up-close. His sweating face is highlighted with make-up, and it doesn't work up-close. Hmm . . . a tube of Elmer's Glue . . . ! Okay, not really much of a prize, but . . . selfish not to be happy with a gift.

I take it back to my seat.

"Pretty good, huh!" Mr. Uhlrich says.

The ceremonies continue – one boy after another getting ever better gifts. It's obvious that the gifts have been put on a continuum from the least to the best.

Then, much to everyone's surprise, my name is called again!

What?

I walk up to the stage.

"You've already gotten a gift!" Axel looks down on me in a disapproving manner.

I don't know what to do or say.

"Go on, go sit down. You only get one!" He says in a clearly condemning tone.

I make my way back to my seat, feeling crushed, both for being stuck with the much lesser gift, and for having been lectured in front of everyone as if I've done something bad.

I hear the man next to Mr. Uhlrich whisper to him, "I also put his name in to give him a better chance."

T

"Clellan Card." Mrs. October sips her Chamomile tea. "Ahh . . . hot!"

"What?" Professor Elephant responds. He delicately touches the letter "B" on his replica of the Belle of Minnetonka. It was the largest and fastest of the great steamers that carried the thousands of summer visitors to grand hotels – Ulysses S. Grant, Chester A. Arthur, William Tecumseh Sherman, and Minnesota's own empire builder, James J. Hill. Not only was it 300 feet long, but it had a fine restaurant and electricity.

"Axel's real name." Mrs. October takes a seat at the table where he's working. "So, you're determined to build yourself a bottle boat."

Professor Elephant puts down his brush. "Yes, an exact replica."

"And when it's done, you've got it all worked out to shove it through that 3" neck?"

He laughs. "Well, we'll see. So Axel's real name was Clellan Card."

"He was a radio performer and created his Axel character . . ."

"A loony Scandihoovian," Professor Elephant offers his imitation.

"Yes," Mrs. October responds. He created Axel in the late 1930s for a morning radio show on WCCO."

"That far back?"

"Yes, and then he brought it to television as Axel and His Dog in 1954."

"With Towser the dog and Tallulah the cat and Carmen the Nurse." Professor Elephant leans back in his chair and smiles.

T

"Not all at first, but they soon became the main cast. And he was so popular it was the first show to broadcast in Minnesota in color!"

"That's impressive!"

"By 1959, his show's ratings were triple those of American Bandstand!"

"His yearly performance of "'Twas the Night before Christmas is a classic!"

"Don't start!"

He laughs. "Don't worry. I can't remember it well enough. So . . . was Clellan the person like Axel the persona?"

"Does it matter?"

"Isn't that the point?"

"But . . . for Eddie . . . they were one and the same."

"At the time. But time has a way of turning on itself, so what was, what is, what will be are dishonest illusions."

"They are real."

"Depends on what reality."

"True. . . . Why does Eddie have to make it so difficult?"

"Was it his choice? That fall into the Funhouse?"

"Enough! Get back to your own silly illusion of getting that boat in a bottle with a neck it cannot pass through!"

"All things are possible in the Funhouse."

"Except getting out of it!"

"Now, how could we possibly know that?"

T

Hunting

I step over the twisting strands of rusted barbed wire from an old, mostly fallen fence winding through the wild grass, patches of fuchsia, blue Rosemary and occasional white splashes of Sunflower, but my trailing left foot catches on one, and I lose my balance. Dad's old twelve-gauge slips from my hands, hits the ground and goes off – bang!

I fall sideways into the damp weeds.

"What's that? Why the shot?" Brian's dad calls from a thicket of red oak to my left.   I roll onto my stomach and rise to my knees. My right arm stings beneath a wet sleeve. The entire left side and front of my shirt and pants are wet. "Oh . . . nothing . . . I accidentally pulled the trigger."

"Be careful!"

"Yes . . . yes . . . sorry."

How stupid of me. It's thoughtful of Brian's dad to have offered to take me hunting.

Brian McCollum and I are best friends. I suppose it's inevitable. Not only do we play sports together all the way through school, but we're both put in what are designated the "enriched" classes.

In third grade, our teacher comes up with a fun way to teach us multiplication. At least she thinks it fun, and since it's easy for me, I enjoy it. She has us all stand next to our desks. Then she calls our names in turn and asks one of the basic multiplication problems, say, what's 5 x 5, and if we get the answer correct, we get to remain standing, but if we get it wrong we have to sit down. Brian and I are always the last two standing, and her solution is to have us come to the blackboard at the front of the class to solve a more complex multiplication, say 352 x 417. We both can do this as well, and the winner depends on who manages to write the fastest, which varies with the day.

I never ask Brian, but perhaps he is able to do various levels of higher math in his head as well, squares and cubes and the even higher, say, what's the quadrangle root of 81 (3). It never occurs to the teacher or anyone else to consider this possibility, nor does it occur to me to mention it, and only in looking back do I realize it is an unusual ability.

We don't live close enough for us to interact much outside of school. However, the autumn after Dad's death, Brian and I get the okay for me to spend a Saturday afternoon at his house. Mom drops me off, promising to pick me up at 5:00. After brief introductions to his parents, Brian leads me upstairs to his bedroom, where we entertain ourselves playing Chess and Parcheesi. Just after noon his mom calls us down for lunch.

His mom has set a small table for the four of us. As we come down the stairs, his dad enters the room from an archway that appears to lead into a living-room and his mom sets a large plate of hamburgers on the last open space of the table top. The rest is filled with a plate of corn-on-the-cob, a plate of hamburger buns,

T

a bowl of potato chips, a nearly full container of milk, and the standard condiments – ketchup, mustard, pickles, Miracle Whip, butter, salt and pepper.

"Look's great, Honey," the dad says as he slides into his chair.

"Thanks, Dear. Nothing special."

"Well, Eddie," the dad says, "you all ready for hockey season to begin?"

"Yes . . ., still a bit early."

"Will be here before you know it."

"Here, Eddie," the mom says, holding the plate of buns to me. Just help yourself. We don't bother with formalities."

"Thanks," I take a bun.

"Here, Brian, take an ear of corn and pass it along to Eddie," his dad says, passing him the plate.

They are as friendly as parents can be.

Still, the debilitating shyness that descended on me when Dad died makes what is a simple gathering difficult. I push through it.

Then the inevitable happens. I pick up the quart milk carton and it slips out of my hand, banging on the floor and sending milk across the linoleum.

"It's okay, Eddie. Don't worry," his mom says and immediately heads into the kitchen for a towel to clean up the spill. His dad laughs. "Oops!"

"But Eddie never forgets," Hermine whispers and laughs softly.

"His confidence mixed with insecurity after his dad died," Pablo says.

"Yes, a curious combination," Werber adds.

"Or is it inherited?" Mr. Orange says softly.

Sophocles smiles.

T

"Predestined," Calvin says.

"Well . . .?" Mr. Orange doesn't want to let it go. "His mother has a shy side. His children are both shy, noticeably so."

"Shy? Eddie shy!" Hermine exaggerates her response. "He was always in the spotlight! Always! No one was more of a celebrity than Eddie!"

The shadowy woman next to Mr. Orange knows her man and intervenes, sliding into his left arm and bringing her soft lips across his cheek. Her warm breath moves up to his ear as she turns him toward the water. "Let it go!" It's a whisper, a caress, a loving invite, but it is a command. Yes, a command the way a woman commands.

Though we're brought together because of school and sports, other than my five-year-old birthday party, Brian never visits me at my house, and I won't visit his again for two years.

Seventh grade. Our first year at Grandview, the new Junior High. We've reached the age where it's possible to get our hunting certificates. It's announced in school. We have to attend a teaching session at the local hunting lodge. I need a .22. Fortunately, Dad's is stashed in the back of our closet.

There's not much to say about the training session. It doesn't last long. I get to shoot at some clay pigeons. I'm given my certificate.

I need a dad to take me hunting. Brian asks his, and the answer is yes.

On a Saturday, two weeks later, Brian's dad takes us hunting. We don't come on any grouse; pheasants or ducks in the woods, but his dad scares up and shoots two pheasants in a corn field. Then, just before we're about to call it a day, I see a rabbit on the edge of a row and pull the trigger – bang!

T

"I got it!" I got it!" I call. Within seconds both Brian and his dad are at my side.

"A pheasant?" his dad asks.

"A rabbit," I say.

"Well . . ," he pauses. "Alright . . . better than nothing."

So we head back to Brian's house with our game for the day, two pheasants and a rabbit.

The grey shadows of twilight turn his house and garage into the sepia colors of an old picture as we pull into his dirt driveway.

"The two of you might as well head into the house. I'll unpack the car and clean the game."

It's dark by the time Mom arrives to take me home.

"A rabbit?" Mom exclaims.

"It's in the garage. I can clean if for you if you want."

"No," Mom says.

"I'd like the fur," I say.

"No," Mom says. "Eddie, you don't need that."

"It's okay. I can do it in a jiffy." Brian's dad heads to the garage.

It's to be my last time in his house. We will continue to share classes and sports, but otherwise, our lives will wander in different directions.

I do go hunting again, but not often, and when I do I find myself mostly wondering why others enjoy it. What is it about hunting that attracts so many people, especially men?

I hear the various arguments, both the versions of how killing animals is wrong, and the justifications for it. As I tend to do with such topics, I work logically through them to develop an ethical perspective. However, what I'm more interested in here is not the ethos of it, but my personal disinterest in doing it.

T

Dad liked to go pheasant, grouse and duck hunting. He purchased Mom a double-barreled shotgun so she could join him. I got to tag along when he and Dave went hunting.

Had he lived, would I have fallen into the community's casual view of hunting local game birds? Is it likely Dad and I (and possibly Dave, John, and Mom) would have established an informal ritual of going hunting each fall? I never heard of JoAnn, or later, her husband Gordy having any interest in hunting, but perhaps, they would have also been a part of it.

There is no way to know how different life would have been, but it's hard not to believe it would have been happier. The challenge is to find a positive spin for the dramatic new direction my life has taken. That's what these memoirs are all about — the Funhouse, the Masquerade of the Mad Hatter . . . so many things to sort out.

Certainly, hunting with Brian and his dad this fall has little more to it than a child's excitement of having an adventure. I think of it as a fun thing to do. Furthermore, I've been successful enough to prove myself capable of it. And in my childish understanding of such things, I've taken home a trophy.

Dr. Marmeloduke tosses the memory back into the cardboard box. "More useless scrapes."

"Wonder why it stuck?" Mr. Bones asks, as if beginning a light song. "Why did this particular visit stay sharp and so much else surrounding it fade away?"

"Like a dream." Mrs. Blood responds.

"Things get mixed in," Dr. Marmeloduke says in a clearly dismissive manner.

"Pointless fragments," Mr. Bones says in an attempt to prevent Dr. Marmeloduke from his desired censure.

T

Mrs. Blood laughs to emphasize the intended irony. "Is it better to clean them out?"

"Eliminate the extra patches?" Mr. Bones echoes.

"Or find ways to sew them into the tapestry?" Mrs. Blood continues.

"Better to retain?" Mr. Bones says.

"Or eliminate?" Mrs. Blood adds.

"Are intelligent people the ones who can subtract the unnecessary?" Mr. Bones continues.

"Or are they the ones who remember the details?" Mrs. Blood finishes his thought.

"Does meaning come from simplicity?" Mr. Bones warms to the banter.

"Or complexity?" Mrs. Blood adds.

"Does context matter?" Mr. Bones continues.

"Okay," Dr. Marmeloduke cuts in. "Stop all this babbling! It's wrong to get stuck in a moment of time!"

"If what we are consists at least partially of our memories, our connections to our past, then what memories stick with us must both be influenced by our environment and contribute to it." Mr. Bones and Mrs. Blood laugh. They have caught Dr. Marmeloduke in their banter.

"If Eddie did not remember his embarrassment while hunting, then he would not be the same person, and since he does, then he is different than someone who would not remember it," Dr. Marmeloduke says, clearly annoyed. "Okay? Are you happy?"

"It's a tautology." Mrs. Blood says.

"Eddie remembers this because he is what he is," Mr. Bones says in a light tone.

T

"And he is what he is because he remembers this," Mrs. Blood responds.

They both laugh.

Dr. Marmeloduke silently shakes his head. "Have you noticed he remembers being good at math, embarrassing himself by spilling the milk, and the moment he embarrasses himself tripping and nearly shooting himself, perhaps also realizing how close he came to shooting himself. The final two have a strong emotion attached to them, and it's likely the first does as well. Likely that's what caused the lasting impressions."

"Think of it, my dear Duky, if he didn't remember, we would not exist, Mrs. Blood says and gives him a pointed look.

"When he lost his memory, we disappeared!" Mr. Bones adds. "Frightening, wasn't it!"

Dr. Marmeloduke has no response. Of course, they are right. When Eddie had his head injury, for a time, he lost his memories.

Mr. Bones laughs and looks at Mrs. Blood. "Would you care to dance, my dear?"

Mrs. Blood smiles. She has a beautiful smile, "I was wondering when you were going to ask?"

Mr. Bones holds out his elbow. Mrs. Blood slides her arm through it, and they walk across the entrance into the ballroom, where they are immediately caught up in a waltz. It must be admitted, they make an elegant couple swirling over the white marble floor.

The Masquerade is a moment that will return, again and again, always the same moment, yet always different.

T

Halloween

A contraction of All Hallows' Evening or All Saints' Eve, Halloween begins the three-day observance of Allhallowtide, the time in the liturgical year dedicated to remembering the dead, including saints (hallows), martyrs, and all the faithful departed.

Three Points celebrates Halloween much the same as the rest of the country. People carve pumpkins, turning them into Jack-o-lanterns, place lighted candles in them, and put them on the front porch. Adults and teens get dressed as ghosts, ghouls, goblins, witches, vampires, werewolves, Frankensteins, super-heroes, princesses, and the latest monsters and fads from movies and television, to attend parties where they bob for apples, dance to the latest "Halloween" music, and share food and drink doctored to look disgusting — eyes, worms, spiders, blood and the like.

The children do some of the same, mainly focused on costumes and the exciting trek about the neighborhood to fill up bags with candy. I make a knight custom out of an old sheet, complete with tunic, wooden sword, cardboard head-cover and shield (all painted with watercolors). Considering the crude materials and unprofessional crafting involved, it turns out well. At least I am happy with my creation, and Mom praises it.

Current restrictions on trick-or-treating are nonexistent. While parents generally take the young children at dusk, most anyone over seven goes solo or with friends. In a few years, the scares from people putting razor blades or dangerous drugs in the candy, apples and other treats will begin a reduction until each town restricts the activity to about a two-hour window before it gets dark.

The standard "tricks" consist of toilet papering trees, covering cars or house windows with eggs, and leaving bags of dog poop on porches. One of the worst is driving along a country road and smashing mailboxes with a bat.

I never get into any of the "tricks" part of Halloween. But I do race about Three Points filling my bag with candy, fruit, cookies, and even occasional coins.

This year, the weather is exactly the norm, mid-forties. There is no rain or snow. It's a perfect autumn day for trick-or-treating, much the same as last year.

We carve jack-o-lanterns, separate the seeds out of the meat of the pumpkins to salt and eat, and use the remaining to make a pumpkin pie. We bring down the box of cardboard window decorations and hang them – witches, ghosts and black cats.

Mom, as usual, stays home and hands out candy. John and I, as usual, go our separate ways. I suspect John goes with one of his friends' families, but am not sure, as I don't pay much attention. I head for Ward's Store. They always give out the biggest Hershey bar of anyone. There is no reason to expect that to be different this year.

However, the holiday holds a more important difference.

I realize it but have no way of knowing how much it will shape me. Mom puts it into a straight-forward mantra. Dad's death makes no sense. For reasons we cannot understand, God has taken him from us. Since he was a good man, he is in a better place. Through no fault of our own, we have been thrust into poverty. However, we have more important things, ethical qualities. We are good, honest, hardworking people. What's more, we love each other. That's what matters.

It's the three of us against the world.

T

Alcyone

Sometimes the ghostly reflections of sunlight off the mysteries of the moon draw me into the shadowy realm of dreams, spirits, and the surreal, half-visible truths that avoid the blinding white light of the day.

But it's a mistake to ignore the danger there, the evasive shadows that cloak enticing forces ever alert to a weakened soul that has come too soon, unprepared and vulnerable. It is the winter following Dad's death. I push my blades against the black ice of Lake Minnetonka and glide easily across the surface, alone and nearly invisible.

If a beaver, white-tailed deer, timber-wolf or coyote should wander through the shadows, it will know I'm not a threat and leave me to my thoughts. On the unlikely chance a man should be out and gaze across the lake, he'll see me as unworthy of more than a passing thought. If he's prone to such possibilities, perhaps he'll think me a specter, a phantom skating through the enigmas of the night, the shadowy presence of a dream. But I realize that's not likely, only my own imagination projected into those not likely to look for such illusive realities.

Occasional gusts of a sharp wind sting my face, giving it a ruddy color, but I am used to Minnesota weather and barely notice. It is expected, a part of the experience that would be missed were it absent.

My world of the lake on this winter night is an escape from the sun's demanding light and harsh, confusing expectations. How many times have I been told that God's will has been done? How many times that I am now the man of the family?

I need to be alone.

But there are dangers. Everyone who lives on the lake knows the dangers.

The lake must be respected.

The summer I was three, the family that lived across the street experienced the tragedy of a careless moment. Their toddler fell from the end of their dock. The noise of the rescue unit brought it to our attention. We stood in our yard and watched. I could barely see the commotion over the top of the neighbor's bank – the group of people standing at the end of the dock, the three men from the rescue vehicle dressed in identical white shirts and tan pants, one carrying some kind of

T

equipment with tubes and what looked like a swimming mask.

There would come a summer I would personally rescue Lynn from drowning not far from where I'm now skating.

Yes, I know the dangers of the lake.

And yet it has always been my home, as much a part of me as I am of it.

On impulse I swerve away from the shore toward the center that leads to other shores, other neighborhoods it would take hours to reach on land.

I slash rapidly across the ice, easily avoiding the shallow, windblown patches of snow. It is exhilarating, a rush that comes from pushing my heart and lungs and muscles to their limits. It is the closest I will ever come to a feeling of pure joy, that sense of being fully alive.

But it is a joy, a sense I realize I'm losing. I know in past winters it was more pure, more natural. I didn't think about it, didn't take the time to knowingly know it. It was what always happened in sports when everything came together, that intuitive connection of mind to body, as if I were not really telling my body what to do, but witnessing it, feeling the thrill of its natural abilities.

Now it is no longer pure, and I know it. The exciting dance driven by the innate joy of masterfully taking control of the ice surface has become a dance mixed with interludes of sorrow, as if the music beneath it has begun interweaving passages in a minor key, that third note of the chord slipping down a half step, giving the song more texture, less surface exuberance, a melancholy quality, no, not melancholy, a simple sadness, music meant to accompany a dance with sorrow, and sorrow is becoming the leading partner.

T

It confuses me. The music I knew in a major key was upbeat, happy and innocent. It was pure – the joy of being alive. Every day was filled with new discoveries, and it was all so simple, so natural. All I needed to do was to give myself to its exciting energy. But now I hear a more complex music, filled with dissonances, counterpoints and changing rhythms. How can I dance to a music I don't understand? How can I move my hips if I don't know the rhythms, or raise my arms or clap my hands or shake my shoulders? How can I strut confidently like a rooster, bold and cocky, if no one has taught me?

When I was four, I went running down our dirt road to see what the older neighbor boy was doing. He was hitting golf balls into the lake. Our cocker spaniel, just a puppy, was already by him, barking, wagging his tail, jumping about, and trying to get his teeth around one of those white balls. The boy swung his club and Skipper was dead.

I was stunned.

But it did not change my world, not the way it's changing now.

I know intuitively that my dance can't be the dance of those talented figure skaters I see on television. Those men have extraordinary athletic abilities. But those talents, that kind of dance is not me. That's the type of dance I find attractive in women – a dance of grace and beauty I could never match, nor would I want to. My dance has to be done on the edges – free form, a dance without careful choreography or caution or common sense. I don't understand it, can't explain it, but I know I only feel good when I let go of the choreography.

I scrape my blades against the ice and circle to a stop.

T

A Labrador barks from the shore – woof . . . woof-woof . . . woof.

My breath is visible and rises through the cold air. I've reached the center of the lake, or as close as I can come to it before the ice gets too thin to hold me. I raise my hands, yell as loud as I can, and listen to it fade into the distance, knowing no one can hear me. I'm free, safely surrounded on all sides by the night, standing at the center of an ice-covered lake, hidden in plain sight, and protected by nature.

But this time it isn't working. I can't feel the joy. If this is nature's sanctuary, a refuge from demands I cannot understand and questions I cannot answer, why do they still haunt me? How did they discover my secret place?

The ice rumbles, strains and cracks in dull groans, as if trapped beneath it, pushing against it were some mysterious, brooding serpent swimming ominously through the dark currents beneath me, testing the ice, threatening to ram the hard ceiling until it gives way, or . . . even more sinister, seeking an opening where it can slide stealthily above the surface and stalk me from the dark shadows along the shore – the black slits of its orange eyes studying me from behind half-open, green eyelids, a hungry, languid slime dripping from rows of teeth, and great, green wings tensed, ready to attack and drag me beneath the surface into the murky caverns of its reptilian lair, or lift me high into some huge dragon cave in mysterious mountains that rise through the clouds.

Is it my own psychic energy? My own wild imaginings?

Tonight my sanctuary includes shadowy hunters, dark spirits lurking, ever alert to weakened souls.

T

I know there are night creatures, know the shoreline surrounding the lake is filled with animals that wake when the moon appears and the sunlight world of humans sleeps.

Rather than enemies, I've sensed these creatures of the night are kindred spirits, spirits who sense I belong in their world. They know this night world is not the same as the loud, harsh, demanding world of the day. That's its attraction.

They come out at night because they know the sunlit world of man is dangerous. But they know me, have watched, and perhaps even helped me through my childhood. They are smart, can sense when even a human will not harm them.

No, I cannot believe that these animals and their spirits are threatening me. They are not the shadows that have entered my sanctuary. How could they be? They've been here all the time. No, the spirits of the animal world are not the cause of the rough chords and erratic rhythms that have found their way into my music.

It's something else.

For a time, I don't know how long because time loses its insistent progression here, I let my thoughts wander. Perhaps, if I stop thinking, perhaps it will go away, this new music, this discordant, alluring music will fade into the silence it came from.

Perhaps, if I stop thinking, perhaps I can still find my way back.

I remember JoAnn's wedding, not really the wedding, but the reception at our house that night – not a lot to it, but it was exciting for me. Mom and Dad borrow a big icebox with the red Coca-Cola logo on its sides, the kind that sits on a stand, and stock it with glass bottles of Pepsi, Orange, Grape and 7-Up. There are also two large tubs of ice to hold the dark and light brown beer bottles – Grain Belt, Hamm's, Budweiser and Stroh's. Our yard is filled with people, and I go unnoticed in the socializing taking place beneath the dim outdoor lights that have attracted the usual moths, June bugs, and flies. It's exciting, but I'm an extra, allowed to stay up after my bedtime, but meant to amuse myself, to observe but not to bother. That's okay for a while, but I grow bored, a part of me wanting not to miss the event, another part of me feeling tired. I go into the kitchen. Aha, a tin filled with homemade sugar cookies in the shape of hearts, each one covered in either a red or pink frosting. This is the thing. I take it into my little bedroom. The only light is what comes in the window, but it's enough. I sit on the floor, take all of the cookies out of the tin and stack them in neat piles. For a while I entertain myself playing with them as if they're toys, but eventually I eat all of them. They're the best cookies I ever ate, can still taste the sugar frosting and perfectly cooked dough.

But that was when I was a child and expected to act like a child. Now I'm the man of the family.

My thoughts return to the ice. Why bother reliving such events? Memories – is there no way to control them? Don't I have any voice in deciding which to keep and which to banish forever?

Are memories even real?

How are they real?

Boom! I hear the boom of the serpent against the ice, followed by a loud Crack! . . . Boom! . . . Boom-Boom! Crack!

I look towards the point, see the dark row of roughly hewn sheets of ice that have been forced up over its large rocks reaching a height above my head. The row abruptly ends at

T

the channel, the dark, watery connection to the rest of Lake Minnetonka.

I skate towards it, knowing the large sheets of ice I see are matched from the bay on the other side, creating an ice tunnel over the rocks. I've walked through it during the day and debate exploring it in the shadows of the night, though I know I'll have to be careful not to damage my state blades by stepping on exposed rocks and gravel that will be difficult to see.

As I near it, I notice the dark water of the channel where the boulders beyond the ice tunnel end and the lake surface hasn't yet frozen. It lures me from my original plan and I arc to the left.

Soon I see the thin ice that still moves with the water. I slow my pace, letting my body feel the ice beneath it. I coast to the uneasy twilight between the safe ice and open water. It's too dark to clearly see where safety and a possible watery death interact, but I feel it in my feet . . . my legs . . . all through my body. As the ice becomes less stable and begins a gentle roll on the top of the water, I know I'm at the edge. But a yard or two more and it will give way.

Is this the threshold where memories dissolve?

A light breeze touches the surface of the water, and I see the line where water is becoming ice, hear the gentle ripples caressing the emerging ice – slap . . . slap-slap . . . slap . . . slap-slap . . . slap.

During the spring thaw, I often skate or walk on the ice as it begins to break into large chunks and feel the energy and excitement of the lake waking from its winter sleep, but tonight, alone in the dark, I hear its gentle lullaby backed by the soothing sounds of the wind blowing through the trees, and

T

there is a quiet, sacred feel, a sense of witnessing a great mystery.

Just hours earlier, I get into another fight. I'm skiing on Killer Hill, a local hill where it's possible to slide or ski down and bounce over a small bank onto the ice. I've figured out how to pack snow over a makeshift frame of discarded boards and turn the bank into a small jump. It's the kind of sledding and skiing children do using cheap sleds with two thin metal runners and a crude piece of wood across the front to bend them into turns, or old wooden skis with leather straps that do not clip on but are held together with a small buckle similar to that of a belt, resulting in the frustrating, common sight of a ski accidentally escaping and gracefully making the journey down the hill by itself.

There is nothing special about the hill. It's one of those children in every small town find for their winter play. Nevertheless, it provides a brief thrill each time down, and it holds some real danger, mainly because it begins parallel to the lake and then takes a sharp turn to the right at the lake shore. If one gets going too fast and can't make the turn, a patch of cottonwood trees waits silently, and the norm is to go home bruised from collisions. Even reaching the ice isn't necessarily a sign of a successful ride, as a string of wood dock posts sticks up from the ice surface. Kevin Larson let his sled get out of control and ran into one of them, rupturing his spleen.

I compete in a pretend sporting contest, playing the roles of each of five imaginary Olympic skiers as they compete for gold.

As I'm shoving my left foot into a ski at the top, preparing for skier number three to make his last run, I hear someone call my name and turn.

T

The snowball hits me square in the face. Bob Strand and Mark Lillidahl stand across the street. They're fifteen. I'm ten. The age difference doesn't matter. The blood rushes to my head. I drop my skis and charge across the street.

Mark easily side-steps my blind flying tackle. My left shoulder brushes against his right hip, and I flip sideways into the snow. The sharp crust of the snow scratches my left forearm, but I don't notice. I'm already pushing myself up as I hit the ground.

"Calm down, Eddie!" Bob says. Mark didn't mean to hit you in the face. It was an accident. We're sorry. Okay!"

I lash out at Mark, swinging wildly. One of my punches catches him in the stomach. He reacts, hitting me in the chin with the lower palm of his right hand. I fall back into the snow.

"Listen, Eddie!" Mark says. "You calm down!"

But I'm already up, swinging.

I no longer remember Dad's funeral. I'm sure my relatives attend, but I don't remember them, don't remember the church service, though someone probably sings The Old Rugged Cross, Dad's favorite hymn. I sense more than remember Dad lowered into the ground at the small graveyard west of Mound. The minister says something over the grave. I think he includes the standard dust-to-dust phrase. The casket is lowered into the oblong dirt hole. I sense it enough to be there, but not enough to see it. I remember that it's a nice summer day, the sky is blue, and there is a light breeze.

I have a much more clear, precise memory of seeing Dad in his coffin at the undertaker's, the unreal appearance, the waxy, rosy red cheeks, his natural good looks — the fine

T

features, the wavy black hair — all enhanced to make him look like a mannequin.

I swing and catch Mark in the face. He hits me in the stomach. I double over. He shoves me into the snow.

"Mark!" Bob says in an attempt to stop the fight. He knows Mark, and he knows Mark has a temper, I suppose similar to my own. I never know, but I will later wonder if Mark also lost his father. I know his mother is still alive, and I know he has at least one much younger sister, but little more.

As I gasp for air, Bob steps between us and bends over me. "You okay?"

"Sure," I manage.

"Listen, you know Mark didn't mean to hit you in the face. You just happened to turn right into the snowball. Okay. No need to fight."

Mark speaks from behind Bob, "I'll give you one thing; you've certainly got guts!"

They leave me.

I watch them walk up the still, snow covered road until they disappear over the hill, then lie back in the snow and close my eyes. I can feel myself fading. I'm cold . . . I'm . . . falling . . . falling . . . falling . . . I struggle to breathe but the air is . . . thick . . . is . . . cold . . . is . . . is . . . water . . . I try to raise my head, reach out, stop my fall, but there's nothing to catch hold of . . . nothing to stop it. The white water becomes the world. My body falls away, a white shadow dissolving into light, white snowflakes . . . the wind scatters them . . . scatters them until they dissipate, and all I see is the white world of snow.

Then I come back. Suddenly it all makes sense! Of course! This is how it works! I lie on my back, trying to formulate it,

T

trying to keep it from fading! But it's leaving me! I know it's leaving me! No! I had it! I know, for a moment I know! But then it's gone... it's... gone.

I'm back in the snow by the road at the top of Killer's Hill. I can feel my body. It's cold. My fingers and toes sting and my face feels raw. I roll onto my stomach, push my bare hands through the snow to the solid ground beneath, force myself up, bring one knee, then one foot, then the other under me, and rise to a standing position. My entire body starts to shake. I'm freezing... yes... I've felt this before... freezing... shaking ... my whole body ... shaking ... My chin hurts. My stomach is bruised and throbs. I'm... disjointed... I'm... at odds... at odds with ... with ... everything. Adrenalin surges through me. It's wrong! It's unfair! Unfair! Why? Why? Why?

Mark and Bob have long since disappeared. What can I do? I scream out my madness, again and again. My profanity echoes down the empty street, off the snow-covered buildings and through the cold stillness of the frozen silence of my world.

I see the winter postcard splintering into sharp edges and clattering around me, so loud it's completely silent . . . so violent it's motionless . . . still . . . still and frozen . . . silent and without life.

But my anger cannot hold the vision . . . cannot freeze it and make it real. I bend down and put my hands on my knees, trying to catch my breath. The last of my profanity echoes into the smothering silence.

Snow covers the earth in a blanket of silence. Even the air is still, an anesthetic, the empty silence of an etherized world, not real, an experiment, watched by the powers beyond, those who study me and analyze me and discard me when I've nothing more to teach them, when my soulless soul has been

T

proven to be nothing more than that of a child, ignorant and helpless, a child washed . . . cleansed . . . yet not officially baptized in the eternal waters of Lake Minnetonka.

I feel exposed, feel as if I'm alone on a stage and the universe watches and condemns me for disturbing its majestic silence with my vulgar screams, feel I have overstepped my place.

I'm confused.

I'm embarrassed.

Now, but a few hours later, I stand alone beneath the stars. The ice gently rocks beneath me, gaining strength with each new wave that runs through it, like a newborn ever so slowly transforming from its watery womb into a rigid, air-breathing form. I listen to the graceful, lapping water at the edge of its birth, the gentle ripples caressing the new, innocent ice – slap . . . slap . . . slap-slap . . .

The burning light of the sun flows into the moon, and the moon transforms it, just as the feminine forces of the night do all of the masculine currents of the hard light of day. Yes, the light reflected off the moon is different. It is the soft, phantom light of the dream. But tonight is not a midsummer night's dream. It is the dream of the winter solstice, the moment of endings and beginnings, the moment when death turns into birth and a moment in forever becomes a moment in eternity. The moment when the dance of moonlight and moon-shadow ripples across the surface of the water, a soothing, inviting dance, the romantic waltz of lovers melting into each other, becoming one, giving birth, water to ice, ice to water, and the rhythm of the dance flows through the thin ice beneath me, calling me to join in the flow of the universe.

Hush pretty baby don't you cry,

T

You know your papa was born to die.
All my trials, Lord, soon be over.

I'm mesmerized by the gentle lullaby.

The river of Jordan is muddy and cold.
It chills the body but warns the soul.
All my trials, Lord, soon be over.

So soothing. The voice of the night, the eternal lullaby, a song to match the rhythms of the night, the ebb and flow of time . . . birth . . . death . . . birth . . . death . . . slap . . . slap-slap . . . slap.

If life were a thing that money could buy,
The rich would live and the poor would die.
All my trials, Lord, soon be over.

The beautiful voice of mother earth, the gentle, soothing voice of the great mother of all that exists – so kind, so loving, so gentle and enveloping.

I've not yet learned the science of the winter solstice, the moment of endings and beginnings when death and birth join in their elegant Viennese Waltz of moonlight and shadow across the surface of the water, their flowing, romantic dance of lovers melting into each other, becoming one, water to ice, ice to water, but I can feel the rhythm of the dance flowing through the thin ice beneath me – slap . . . slap-slap.

There is a tree in Paradise,
A tree they call the tree of life.

T

All my trials, Lord, soon be over.

It is the time, the world of the dream, and the dream comforts me with soft, seductive whispers, a soothing lullaby, as if Mom is rocking me to sleep, singing softly in perfect pitch, her voice, her heartbeat, her breathing the same rhythmic life I felt in the womb.

The womb . . . somewhere . . . deep in my cells . . . somewhere I still remember . . . must still remember . . . the warm loving world . . . the life-giving watery world . . . of the amniotic fluid. The beating of her heart — bump . . . ba-bump . . . slap . . . . slap-slap.

Can one disturb the universe? Is it possible to interrupt the ebb-and-flow of eternity, the movements of nature? Is there cosmic healing in the soothing, gentle song of the water and the wind at night? Why does it seem so innocent? So pure and clean? Why is it so seductive?

Perhaps this is what people mean when they say they've experienced God. Perhaps moonlight dancing on the water is God. Perhaps . . . why not?

I remember the night I sat on the living-room floor while Mom rocked John to sleep and sang a soft lullaby in rhythm to the gentle creak of the wood runners of the chair. The room had a dim yellow light and outside the window the night sky was black. As I listened I saw a glowing light in the shape of a baby floating in the air and thought that it was the baby Jesus. But why was he there? What did it all mean? As life went on, I would start to flesh it out, more and more . . . the three of us . . . . Mom and John and I . . . and Jesus . . . listening to Mom's soft, pure singing — slap . . . slap-slap . . . slap . . . slap-slap.

T

The answer . . . somewhere in it . . . the answer . . . I know . . . somewhere in it . . . that's where I can find the answer . . . but how . . . how am I to find it . . . what am I to do to learn the language . . . the meanings beyond my . . . limitations.

A sharp gust slaps my face, wakes me from the gentle lullaby.

What . . . what . . . no . . . I don't want to let it go . . . no . . . no . . . come back . . . but it's too late.

The moment is gone.

The moment when I touched Eden is gone.

I stand silent for a time, hoping it will return.

How does one experience the flow of the universe?

What did I do?

Why did it allow me in?

What does it all mean?

Time disappears when one enters eternity. I have no idea how long I was there.

I feel the wind on my face, the chill in my fingers, and know I have returned.

I push my stake blades against the ice and circle away from the dark water toward the safe ice.

The wind is playful and lifts the light snow on the top of the snowdrifts so it swirls like small tornado shaped spirits that frolic over the ice – airy wisps of energy. I chase one for a while until it disappears. It's a diversion while I struggle to make sense of what I experienced.

I scrape to a stop.

The stars sparkle and shimmer, as if they're the tiny, glittering bubbles of champagne nectar the gods have spilled across the night sky.

A lonely train whistle calls from the silence.

T

Train tracks cross the main road in Mound, running through an empty lot next to the Piggly Wiggly and across the street to a small train station with a platform, not for passengers but for unloading flatbeds and boxcars. In truth there is little reason for the train to stop in town at all. There are no grain towers and Tonka Toys, the only factory, is little more than an old two-story house that does its shipping by truck. My kindergarten class got to visit it, and though it was a dirty, unkempt building, it was exciting to see how the make-shift assembly line began with bare sheet metal and ended up with toy trucks.

One night, when Mom visits Dad at the hospital, she leaves John and me with JoAnn and her family, but when she picks us up there's an argument over whether JoAnn has fed us enough. It's clear JoAnn feels put-upon watching us, and Mom begins leaving us with neighborhood friends.

The next night I stay at Lenny and Vera Frahm's house. Vera is Mom's best friend — the two of them often shared morning coffee weekdays when their husbands were at work. Lenny and Vera have two sons, Bruce, six years older than I, and Keith, but a year older. The night I stay there, Bruce is absent, is with his girlfriend Janet Hiller, my nemesis who lives on Lane Three. We eat at their small kitchen table. I choke on a chicken skin at supper but am too embarrassed to let anyone know, so I hide my hard-working swallows for several minutes before I finally manage to get it down. However, I make a big hit with Mr. Frahm, because I choose kidney beans for the supper vegetable. Why I choose them, I'll never know. I have never eaten them. After supper Mr. Frahm settles into his living-room chair to watch *Gunsmoke*, his favorite show, and Keith and I are sent upstairs to entertain ourselves in Keith's bedroom. He has an erector set, so I keep myself busy building things with it on the wood floor until it's time to turn off the lights.

That night, sleeping, or rather not sleeping in a strange bed, I try to figure out death. Total nothingness. One dies. One no longer exists. Can't be. There must be something. What? Soul? I think about the ever-changing cycle of water – how a puddle of water evaporates, becoming invisible, then turns into clouds, then into rain, which results in puddles that will again evaporate – yet it is always something, always remains, always lives, only in different forms. But the soul? I can see the rain. I can touch it. I can even drink it, swallow it and make it a part of me. I can certainly hear it. And, yes, it has a smell, has a range of different smells. But the soul? What does the soul smell like?

What about Jesus and salvation? It makes no sense. Does God know my thoughts? If I can talk to him in my mind, then he must. Is he punishing me for my thoughts? My doubts? How can I stop myself from thinking? From doubting?

I dig my skates into the ice and dodge around the patches of snow, faster and faster, testing myself, imagining I'm in a competition with others to see who can best skate this course, this athletic competition. Finally, I reach the limit and my left skate blade slices too far into a patch of snow until it catches, causing me to stumble and fall to the hard ice. I'm not injured. I know how to fall.

I roll over and lie on my back – enjoying the aftermath of my exhilarating burst.

The sky spreads out above me. The stars, countless in number, powerful, impersonal forces traveling at tremendous speeds, many of them hundreds of times the size of the sun,

T

appear to be but tiny specks of light. But I don't think of them in terms of the impersonal explanations of science. I think of them more the way those people who lived before science must have thought of them.

Nights on the porch, Dad points out the Big and Little Dippers and how the bright North Star can be found by following the two stars forming the Big Dipper's end. He calls them constellations. Everyone in my neighborhood does, even my teachers, though I later learn that's not correct — they are asterisms. But the slight misuse of the language of astronomy doesn't matter. Neither Dad nor Mom nor anyone else in my world has even heard of the word asterism, nor do they bother to go very deep into why some of the constellations have more than one name, why so many of them have such strange names, and the stories behind those names. The main excitement is just finding their patterns in the night sky. And the cool thing about the Big Dipper is that it circles the North Star so that its two pointing stars always point to the North Star.

Had I known more, I would have been confused, but I haven't yet learned enough and matured enough to think through the conflicts between the explanations of science and the stories of Christianity. I accept both the science I'm being taught that the Earth orbits the Sun along with eight other planets, and the religion I'm taught that the Earth is at the center of existence, and out there, somewhere in the sky, is Heaven.

Even more so, I'm too young and provincial to understand much about how these star patterns relate to other religions. Mom tells me that most of the names of constellations come from Greek or Roman mythology and that they call the Big

New voc

T

and Little Dippers Ursa Major and Ursa Minor, which she says mean Big Bear and Little Bear. When I respond that they don't look like bears, she says the Greeks and Romans had stories to go along with the constellations, but she can't remember them and suggests I find a book about them in the school library.

One of Dad's friends says that the Mi'kmaq of Canada also call them bears. He says they see the Big Dipper as Celestial Bear and the three stars of its handle as hunters chasing it. In the autumn, the hunters kill the bear and its blood falls from the sky to color the leaves. In the late fall, Celestial Bear can be seen on the northern horizon about to go into hibernation for the winter.

I try to get him to tell me more, but he says that's all he knows.

The spring after Dad first tells me he has cancer, Mom finds lumps in her breast and the doctor thinks that she might also have cancer. When she goes in for surgery to remove and test the lumps, I stay with Bob Strand's parents, Barney and Gladys. Barney is a character. Mom and John and I still laugh about the night he's sitting in his lawn chair, sipping a beer while reading the evening news, and he decides that our latest cocker spaniel named Skipper, who as usual is lying on the lawn next to him, has died. He has Gladys call to give us the bad news. John is really upset, as he's the closest to Skipper. Mom gets her shoes on and is just going out the door to fetch the dead dog home when the phone rings again. This time it's Barney. Gladys has refused to call us back. Our poor, dead Skipper has just gotten up and walked away.

The night I stay with them, Barney drinks beer and jokes throughout the supper and the entire evening. He is truly

T

funny, and I can't help but laugh. Then, just before I go to bed, he puts his arm around me and tells me what a good boy I am and how I'll be able to make it in the world no matter what happens. It surprises me. What a nice thing for him to say.

It's never occurred to me that he has any thoughts about me beyond an occasional annoyance over me traipsing over his new lawn or having a Frisbee land on his roof or a Whiffle ball bounce off his window.

The doctors operate on the wrong breast, so Mom has to go back a second time. Fortunately, the lumps are not cancerous.

I bend my legs, listening to the back points of my skate blades scratch the ice. The black sky above me has no end.

How is that possible?

I take Mom's advice, find two books about Greek and Roman myths for young people and know instantly I've struck gold.

Now, when I look into the night sky, it opens to a whole new world.

I run my fingers over the ice, feel a crease. The infinite, eternal universe covers me, an ocean of stars. An infinite, eternal ocean — I wonder how it is possible. How can space and time continue in all directions without end?

My fingers slide over the smooth ice on each side of the crack, the crease. I wonder. When it gets warm enough that the ice partially melts or the snow on top of it turns briefly to water, does the crease disappear? Then, when it freezes over, do the two large slabs of ice become one?

I try to find the creases in time and space.

One of them is the summer I stay with Frahms and Strands, the summer before the end, the summer before a new beginning; and the end and the beginning are one, a crease in time, and they are filled with anxiety

T

Dad's cancer grows rapidly worse. The doctors knock some of it out with chemotherapy, but the once strong man grows thin and weak.

He wants to come home.

Since Mom is a nurse, the doctors relent and decide he can, if a hospital bed can be found, not as simple a task as it might seem. Mom and Dad have no insurance and the cost of a new hospital bed is beyond them. Phone calls are made to anyplace that might have a used one. But even used ones are too expensive. Emotions run high.

Then, finally, a member of the church locates one for $250. I never know where the money comes from, but Dad moves back home.

He seems to get better.

Perhaps it's the answer — being in his own home with his wife and children by his beloved lake. I'm sure he's through the worst of it.

Then he gets worse.

I rub my hand across the smooth surface of the ice. I chop at it with the back point of my right skate, scattering some slivers on the surface. I pick one up, stick it in my mouth and enjoy the coolness as it melts on my tongue.

My first experience of death takes place while I'm still in the womb. Mom and Dad want children, but Mom keeps having miscarriages. She says it has something to do with having Rh negative blood. Then Mom is pregnant again, this time with twins. I'm one of them, sharing her womb with a brother. But then something happens. I'm told she falls down stairs while caring for a sick sister. My twin brother dies in the womb. Is it possible my pre-birth essence realizes what's

T

happened? Possible my genetic make-up senses, knows, and incorporates an experience of death before I'm even born?

The Milky Way flows silently through the sky, a huge river of light. I enter it – see Orion trudging through its serpent filled waters.

My own lake serpent bangs the ice beneath me – boom! . . . boom-boom!

Silence . . .

Just ahead of Orion are the beautiful Pleiades – Asterope, Merope, Electra, Maia, Taygete, and Alcyone. I know there is another, Celaeno, but I cannot see her and worry about her absence.

It's amazing. They are both alluring young women and strange, sometimes frightening creatures at the same time. Neither the young women nor their stories can be explained, but it doesn't matter. They fill the sky with a wonderful enchantment.

I experience their world, and that's far more real than any explanation.

Night after night after night.

But tonight will be different.

I lie on my back and wait for it to happen.

For a while the stars are nothing more than tiny, sparkling lights in the night sky. But I'm not worried. It always begins this way. Soon the constellations begin to take form. I watch as they morph, partially visible, then disappearing, then reappearing – seeming to be debating whether to emerge into my night sky or stay hidden in their own other world.

Asterope breaks through first. Heracles is with her, handing her a lock of hair. I know the story. He gives a lock of Medusa's

T

hair and tells her to show it above the city walls to frighten off enemy armies.

But the scene fades.

Alcyone emerges. I know her stories, know that even in their contradictions they are all true, all possible in this world.

She is the famed daughter of Aeolus, god of the wind. For a time she has a happy life. That's what those who tell her stories say. I imagine her as a child playing in the clouds beneath a warm summer sun, doing all those things young girls like to do.

She grows into a beautiful young woman and she marries Ceyx, son of Eosphoros, the Morning Star. But the two of them are brash, filled with too much pride, not as respectful of their elders as they should be, so they play at being Zeus and Hera.

Their innocence, the innocent folly of youth, brings them down. That's what the stories I've read say.

Zeus finds out and is angered at their lack of respect — even the gods cannot escape death. Even the gods must die.

When Zeus gets mad, he can be vicious. He sees to it that Ceyx dies in a violent storm at sea. And Morpheus, the always dangerous god of dreams, tricks Alcyone, telling her that her beloved Ceyx has committed suicide and convinces her to join her beloved in his watery grave.

Death . . . always death . . . in everything there is death.

Yet, of course, Alcyone still lives in the night sky. Not only that, but her new existence is far more wonderful than the one she knew before she died.

Alcyone . . . I wonder . . . do you know me? Can you watch me as I watch you? Is it possible for our worlds to intertwine? Possible for me to join you? Possible Dad is somewhere in your world?

T

It seems unlikely. Stories, after all, are not real, certainly not real in the literal, physical sense. They are *just* stories, *pretend* worlds. They only exist in the mind, and anyone thinking they exist in the *real* world is insane.

But one never knows. Perhaps one day I too will break free of the bounds of Earth and live among the stars.

Perhaps . . .

Is *that* what happens when one dies?

Dad said he was going fishing among the stars of the Milky Way.

Then it happens.

Alcyone solidifies into a brightly colored bird, a bird with a large crested head and powerful beak, a bird that lives off fish, a Kingfisher.

She dominates the sky, larger than any literal bird. Her eyes take on a shimmering clarity. And they stare straight at me! I know it for certain! She *is* looking at me! This is *not* just my imagination!

She circles . . . slowly . . . floating on the air in wide circles . . . studying me.

A bird of prey, ready to plunge . . . she circles.

Anticipating the attack . . . she circles.

Waiting for the moment . . . she circles.

Then she begins a slow descending spiral – down . . . down . . . down.

I gasp for air!

Something has happened!

I've been so focused on her, I've lost touch with myself.

But now!

Now!

Now I find my entire body has changed!

T

No!
What!
Impossible!
A fish!
A fish!
The cold ice!
Breathe!
Breathe!
Can't breathe!
Alcyone!
Alcyone!
The Kingfisher!
The Great Kingfisher!
Alcyone!
Noble! Noble! Goddess!
Daughter of the wind!
Breathe!
Aaaahhhhhhhh ... I can't breathe!
Alcyone attacking!
Attacking!
Yes! No! Yes! Ooooh ... no ... no ... please, no!
A fish!
Wak! Wak! Wak!
Wak! Wak-Wak! Wak!
Feathers!
Chestnut . . . chestnut feathers . . . swirling chestnut feathers!
Wak! Wak! Wak!
Wings ... chestnut ... wings ... Flap! Flap-Flap! Flap!
Wak! Wak! Wak-Wak!
My arms! My arms! Strike! Strike!

T

Crack! Boom! Boom! Boom-Boom!

The serpent! The serpent!

Alcyone . . . the beak . . . the hard beak!

My legs . . . kick!

Kick-kick! Kick! Kick-kick-kick! Kick!

Stuck! My leg . . . my foot . . .

Waaaaaaaaaaak! Waaaaaaaaak! Waaaaaaaaaaaak!

Crack! Boom! Boom! Boom!

Hot blood . . . hot . . . blood!

My thighs . . . my thighs . . . aaaaahhhhhh!

Moving . . . bang . . . bang . . . ooooo . . . my shoulder!

The ice . . . the air . . . I'm moving . . . moving . . . being dragged . . .

Bang . . . bang . . . bang-bang-bang . . . bang . . . bang-bang . . .

Snow . . . the snow . . .

Thump!

It stops . . . stops.

At last . . . the end.

Quiet . . . quiet and still.

Aaaaaaaaaaaaahhhhhhhhh!

Noooooooo!

Not my eyes!

My eyes! My eyes!

Help me! Someone help me!

My eyes my eyes

Aaaaaaaaaaaaaaaaaahhhhhhhhhh!

My eyes!

No! No! No!

Ooooooooooooh

T

What?

Where?

I'm alone.

The ice is hard and cold.

The night sky is still and silent.

A dog barks—woolf . . . woolf-woolf-woolf . . .

woolf woolf

woolf

woolf

woolf- woolf

woolf-woolf-woolf

T

The First Christmas

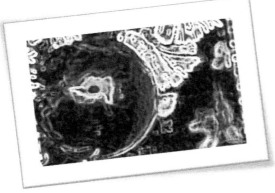

A still, crisp December morning. Other than wisps of gray smoke rising from a few chimneys and a dog barking, the frozen world sleeps as quiet as a painting. But I'm filled with energy. The night's snowfall means I can make some money shoveling the neighbors' walks.

The autumn between the hot, humid, dog-days of Dad's death and the freezing chill of winter has passed quickly, and the cold fronts sliding down from Canada have frozen the lake and land alike.

The winter of the first Christmas after Dad's death has arrived, a cold winter with a white Christmas proceeded by weeks of intermittent snow that covers the land and the lake in layers until the shoveled piles rise above the waist of a ten-year-old boy.

We all shovel until the snow becomes a landscape of rough-hewn paths leading to and from house doors to garage doors and driveways and outhouses and stacks of wood and snowplowed roads, everything edged with chunks of shoveled snow that rise above the waist of a ten-year-old boy.

It's possible in the often eerie silence to duck down and hide in the labyrinth of paths, possible to avoid the eyes and the ears and the constant sympathy of well-meaning neighbors, possible to imagine I'm a spy or a fugitive or maybe a lone soldier behind enemy lines needing to use all of my skills to avoid capture or even death. Sometimes when an enemy appears dressed in a parka or a snowsuit or a red-and-black wool lumber-jacket, all it takes is a quick duck beneath the level of the snow. But I have to be careful. The enemy is everywhere, and the frosted windows might hold spies I can't even see.

Other times I build a snow fort, stock it with snowballs and ready myself for an impending attack. Then, when the attack comes, I throw my white hand grenades at trees or posts, imagining them enemy soldiers.

Whenever it snows, my skating rink on the lake needs shoveling. So I shovel. Night after night, my shadowy figure can be seen from the street, skating behind a flat shovel held slanted to scrape the ice and send the snow cascading to the side, then turning and repeating the snow-plowing sprint back — again and again. Then my shadow discards the shovel to skate free and release its imagination, pretending it's being chased by a dozen of its neighborhood playmates, or picking up a hockey stick and pushing a puck through a team of would be defenders until it can deftly slip the black disk into a make-shift goal of two discarded car tires framing an old two-by-four.

Something has happened. I don't understand it. But the music I'm hearing fills me with dissonances and complex rhythms. I skate and I stake, night after night, all alone beneath a silent sky of pristine stars, stars that have seen other winters, stars that lure me to join them.

What has Alcyone done to me? If her attack transformed me in some way, opened a door into her world and allowed me to be a part of what I could only observe before, what does that mean? I lie on my back and enter her vast ocean of space and

T

time, the infinite, eternal, cosmic ocean that holds the answers to all of life. I try to make sense of it, try to understand a sky, a universe that has to go on forever and yet has to end, but if it does end has to have something beyond it, even if it's nothing, because nothing is something, or is it possible for nothing to be nothing. I try to understand time that has to go backward forever, has to have a beginning, yet can't because there always has to be some time previous to the beginning, a beginning before the beginning.

Sometimes, I hear The Joker laughing. I don't know it's him, but I hear the laughter, and sometimes I even catch a glimpse of him balancing on the edge of the universe.

I've thought about such things before, but not really, not with the need to push passed the simple answers, the answers that don't really answer anything. Now I need Alcyone's mythic world, that world of mysteries everyone keeps telling me I'm too young to understand. Ever since that night when she ripped my flesh and left me bleeding on the ice. Ever since that night my fresh, young skin was scarred and my warm blood melted into the cold ice.

Somewhere in the mysteries of Alcyone is the mystery of God, the all-powerful being that created everything, that all-powerful being that can't be all-powerful because he can't control everything, can't even control his once favorite angel, Satan, who is constantly doing things God tries to prevent, but can't. Even humans are doing things God doesn't want, yet apparently, he can't stop us. Why not? That makes no sense?

Is that why The Joker laughs?

The same questions, again and again, the same questions. I wondered, the night of the attack, I wondered, but they've not been answered.

T

It doesn't make sense. People say that's the point. It's beyond logic. That's what faith is all about. Humans aren't supposed to analyze it, just believe. This confuses me. Aren't humans supposed to use their minds? Isn't it good that scientists have found cures for diseases? Have learned how to build shelters and use electricity and protect humans from dangerous animals?

Besides, how can a human stop thinking? I can't help myself. Even when I want to find a mental switch to turn off, I can't do it. Does that say something bad about me?

So I skate and I wonder and I shovel and play in the snow, and I turn the cold, barren, white winter and freezing nights into a world filled with adventure and excitement and wonder.

Ever since my birth I've played in the snow, skated on the ice, and filled the cold snowy world with imaginary adventures and wondered, year after year after year, Christmas after Christmas after Christmas.

But this year is different.

Christmas will never be the same. Nothing can ever bring back what Christmas has been for the first nine years of my life.

This year, this winter, this Christmas, the snow and the cold and the nights on the ice have lost their innocence, for this is the first winter, the first Christmas after Dad's death.

"Eddie," Mom calls. It's a Saturday afternoon, the Saturday after Thanksgiving, the day we've always purchased our tree. "Eddie, I want you to get Dad's tree saw from the basement."

"Why?"

"I want to cut down our Spruce tree."

"Why?"

T

"Well," Mom says. She stops for a moment. "Well . . . I just can't go through Christmas without a tree!" She looks at me as if I should understand, but I don't.

"Why use that one?"

"There's just no way we can afford to buy one."

"But . . ."

"Eddie," Mom stops me, "we just can't come up with money for a tree."

"But, if we cut down our tree, then . . ."

"Eddie, I won't go through Christmas without a tree!"

So I shovel down into the snow, through the crusty snow on the top, through the softer snow, into the hard snow at the bottom. Though it's only 5:00 pm, it's already dark, and it's hard to hold back the branches. In the end, I toss the shovel aside, kneel into the tree and use my bare hands to sweep the snow away. Once it's cleared enough I turn to find the tree saw, but I've carelessly brushed snow over it. I shove my hands into the snow. Bang! Ouch! I hit the teeth of the saw, resulting in two cuts on the back of my right hand, nothing serious. I shake the snow off the saw, kneel under the tree branches and begin to cut into the rough bark. The saw is dull, the bark is frozen, and I can't get a good angle. But I keep at it. Even frozen, the sap gums up the blade. The metal handle is cold in my bare palm, and I know my fingers are going to hurt when I get back inside and they thaw, but it will help some to run cold water over them, and it will only last a couple of minutes. I shove my left hand into the snow to balance myself and gave the tree a push. It bends over and I can get a better angle at the final cuts.

Mom tries to charge gifts at Sears, but her card is charged to its limit and the monthly payments have not been made. She

T

tries to charge gifts at Penney's, but they've put a hold on her account. And the Ford station-wagon she drives is at the Standard station. It needs a new alternator, but there is no money.

Mrs. Haddorff knocks at our door. She has a ham and some potatoes. Yes! Such a wonderful person! We will have a Christmas dinner! A real meal! Not just the cheap, cardboard buns Mom makes with that new butter substitute, that white, greasy stuff they call margarine.

This is the same Mrs. Haddorff who has already given me another gift, a special gift, one I will not appreciate until many years later. It starts with an offer to give John free piano lessons. But John doesn't want piano lessons, free or any other way. On the other hand, I've already begun to write songs on our old piano, the one Dad cut into pieces so he could fit it through the door, down the stairs into the basement and reassemble. How badly out of key it is, but I'm untrained anyway. And so it sits in the same large room I'm now using as my bedroom, the room that still shows open spaces of dirt where Dad has dug the unfinished but useable basement room. And I've started losing myself in the piano sounds. So I eagerly replace John on Mrs. Haddorff's charity list.

And now it's December and I know that the week before Christmas I'll perform at my first piano recital, a Christmas piano recital. The songs will be simple songs, ones I've already memorized and will not forget.

But I do.

The recital takes place in a church located on the road that becomes the front entrance to Lafayette Country Club. There are only about fifty people there, mainly the other students and their parents. Mom has gotten me dressed up in her usual

T

fashion, a suitcoat and tie, my home-cut hair pushed into place and held down with her own spit.

My first song is a duet with Mrs. Haddorff's own son. He is much older and only playing it with me as a favor. She no doubt thinks it a good idea to initiate me to recitals with him there to help me out if I should get nervous. So we play *Skip to My Lou*, and it goes fine. My next song is the one I'm excited about. Mrs. Haddorff has realized that I'm bored with the standard practice exercises, but that I get excited when I'm allowed to be creative and try to figure out how to make a song fit together. So she lets me create the accompaniment to *The Star-Spangled Banner*, and I'm eager for the chance to perform it. I walk to the piano and sit. Mrs. Haddorff announces me and tells me to begin. So I do. It's great. Then it isn't.

I forget . . . half way through it, I forget.

That night I skate beneath the stars, skate through the silence, a silence broken only by the sound of my own skate-blades scrapping against the hard ice. The clear, black sky filled with stars is like a beautiful, delicate Christmas card. I skate and skate and imagine and imagine. Though the temperature is well below zero, I don't notice, not when I skate.

One day, just before dusk, I build a snowman on the ice close enough to the shore that the bank blocks the view from the road. It makes me feel safe, separated, in my own world. I place my white-with-faded-blue-strips stocking hat on the top of my snowman, count off twenty paces and begin my contest. Each contestant gets twenty throws. There are five, and I keep track of how many times each manages to knock the hat off. Soon the scenario grows and the contestants take on personalities. Each time one of them wins, he advances to the next level of

T

competition. Contest after contest, I play on, until, finally, I reach the national championship. By then, the gray dusk has long since turned into night and all I have to help me see is a bit of light from the street lamp and the natural reflection of the moonlight off the snow. Not much, but enough to continue. Besides, I'm too absorbed in my contest to notice.

It's similar to the many basketball shooting contests I've played out in my yard. Before the garage was torn down, there was an old basketball hoop bolted to a piece of plywood above the car entrance. We saved it, and I managed to nail it to the oak tree growing between the house and the street. Then I shoveled a small patch in the yard to use as my basketball court. It was wonderful. Night after night, barely able to see the hoop, I played out my shooting contests.

I decide to turn the depression left from cutting down the Christmas tree into a fort. So I dig a path from the sidewalk to it and mold the snow over the path until I have a tunnel. It's a difficult task. The snow is cold and dry, and I have to use my own body heat to warm it enough to get it to stick together. But I have all day, and it's the kind of creative activity I can get lost in and not even realize an entire day has passed. I widen the fort to about an eight-foot diameter, build up the sides so they're above my waist and make a pile of snowballs for the pretend attack.

Even in the cold winter, each day brings a new adventure.

But mostly I skate.

Then the relatives arrive, Mom's relatives, relatives to help us, to comfort us, to share their wealth with us, to bring us presents, and food.

They seldom visit, less than once a year. But here they are. They've come to a toy convention in Minneapolis, a standard

T

event for them, since they own a hardware store and stock toys. So, since they're near, they've come to visit.

It's a surprise visit! They've not let Mom know! And, since they seldom visit, it's a major moment for her.

"What a nice tree," Grandma says.

"Yes, a few decorations will make it lovely!" Uncle Jim says.

"I'll bet you and the boys had a good time picking it out!" Janice says.

Mom is too busy getting their dinner ready to reply.

"I cut it down," I say.

"You cut it down!" Uncle Jim says. "What a big boy!"

"Come and eat!" Mom calls from our little dining room.

Everyone squeezes into the dining room.

"Eddie, Johnny," Mom whispers, pushing us into to living room. "Wait until they're finished. I'll make us something later. Why don't you watch television?"

We do as asked. Our television is a large piece of furniture, covered in tan laminate, but the screen is small, and, of course, it's black-and-white. We think it delightful. We check the three channels and find one of them presenting Clement C. Moore's "'Twas the Night before Christmas." So, we're comfortably out of the way for the moment.

The relatives settle around their meal. We can hear them talking.

"Eisenhower," Grandpa says, "a Republican! Good for business!"

"Yes," Uncle Jim says. "The country prospers!"

"I hear Kennedy's running," Mom's sister Mary Ann says.

"Never get elected!" Uncle Jim says.

T

"A Catholic!" Grandpa says. "This country will never elect a Catholic!"

"Better not!" Uncle Jim emphasizes.

"What a lovely meal," Grandma says.

"Yes," says Grandpa. "That's what's great about this country. Food is plentiful."

"Look at this!" Grandma says. "Such a nice ham! And it comes all pre-prepared!"

"That's right!" Uncle Jim says. "People don't even have to prepare their food these days! It's all done for them!"

"Yeah," Grandpa says. "People are just spoiled today.

"I get so tired of reading about all those crybabies saying they don't have enough food!" Uncle Jim says.

"That's our country! People are just spoiled!" Grandpa says.

The snow falls hard that winter, and it covers the land – a white, frozen tundra.

As it turns out, Mom's promise to feed us after the relatives leave won't involve a long wait. As soon as they finish eating, they leave.

The ham is gone and so is all of the food Mrs. Haddorff has given us. But Mom has not been embarrassed. She has been able to offer her relatives a decent meal.

So we mix our Quaker Oats with water. And we sit next to the window and watch the snow fall and feel the cold air rush through the cracks. In truth the house is but a cabin, a cabin Dad has amateurishly turned into a house, and the cold air is determined to conquer it. Since some of the windows in my basement bedroom have no glass, I keep wood burning in the old, free-standing fireplace in the middle of it while snowflakes blow through the curtains and gently fall on the couch.

T

My childish hopes Mom's parents would leave us some kind of present, however slight, are not answered. Mom's thoughts they might leave her a bit of money also go unanswered. It's hard to understand. They can see we're in need, and yet they don't. It can be argued they don't realize it ... but not really.

It's even more confusing that Mom accepts their complete lack of sympathy or help. Sure, she complains about it, but apparently not to them, or ... not strong enough to them. As life goes on and I learn bits and pieces about Mom's relationship with her parents and siblings, I get vague references that there were problems going back at least to her years in college, where she purposely paid her own way, even though her parents most certainly had enough money to help. According to Mom, the only tuition they ever paid was for her final quarter, which bothered her because they used it to brag about how much they had helped her, when in truth they hadn't.

Trying to find a reason, I wonder if it has to do with the fact they wanted her to be a teacher, and after initially signing up for that curriculum and going for a short time, perhaps just one session, she decides she doesn't want that and switches to nursing instead. Is it possible that is what causes the split? Can't be.

I've heard hints of it being there before that, but never enough to draw any conclusions.

Then there is her marriage to Dad. Since he is Lutheran, they are against it. At least that's what Mom says. And as I grew older, I learn that for many at that time such a slight difference in religion is taken seriously. So that's the reason given. However, I never got the feeling anyone in the family was overly into religion. The other reason given is that Mom had lands an exceptionally good-looking man, and they are jealous. If she is on the outside already, and she surprises them by marrying a man far better than they expect, as shallow as it is, it's certainly possible they are upset. I don't know. What I do know is that there is a clear lack of concern by them for Mom. Whether or not it is nothing more than a shallow, selfish jealousy or has to do with a more serious falling out, I'll never know.

Whatever the reasons, it plays out in a curious way. Shortly before Christmas each year, Dad and Mom, and then just Mom, pack us up for the 90-minute drive to her parents' house, where we spend the night as if it's Christmas Eve. John and I always get the same presents – a pajama outfit, new underwear, woolen socks, and a magazine subscription. Mine is always Boy's Life.

When Dad is alive, I am soon put to sleep on the floor of a small upstairs bedroom no longer in use. It doesn't occur to me at the time, but now I wonder why I wasn't put to sleep in the unused bed next to me. I can hear the adults playing poker at the kitchen table as I fell asleep.

This year, as usual, a gift arrives in the mail from Grandma's sister, Auntie Moe, whose dead husband, Uncle Martin, was once in charge of U.S. Educational Exchanges with Germany. Apparently, they were and she remains extremely wealthy. She sends John a few silver dollars (because his middle name is Martin after her husband), but I get an old board game with some of the pieces missing (because mine isn't). I don't know if she sends Mom anything.

The final days before Christmas drag on forever. Slow day after slow day, the snow falls, circling, floating, dancing, covering and smothering the land.

T

And our Christmas tree, decorated with ornaments from past years, and a few new, homemade ornaments, strings of popcorn, lights from previous years, and an old white angel placed at the top, our Christmas tree stands in the corner of the living room.

Mom has charged gifts for us at Sears, nothing major, but more than she afford. And her excitement for us to open our gifts is even greater than my own. She suggests, perhaps, we can open one or two of our smaller presents before Christmas. Surprising as it seems, I want to wait. Somehow, it seems wrong to open them early.

Then it arrives, December 24, the Christmas Eve after Dad's death that it seemed would never arrive arrives.

On Christmas Eve day, Mr. Haddorff shows up with the box of apples. Later, we're surprised by a local Men's Club that shows up with a box of toys! Gifts for us! A whole laundry basket of gifts! Wow!

After they leave, we open the gifts. Toys! But . . . but . . . cheap toys, toys for young children, babies – a plastic frame with shapes for a baby to fit in pieces, a packet of three Mickey Mouse coloring books, a yellow, plastic top, one that fits on some kind of handle, so it can be wound-up and sent spinning across the floor, a bag of jacks, a stuffed monkey, and apparently by accident, a small set of play dishes.

"It's very thoughtful of them," Mom says.

Yes, I know it's thoughtful, and I know I'm being spoiled not to appreciate it . . . and yet and yet . . . .

I guess I still have some growing-up to do. The man of the family shouldn't have such childish thoughts.

And as I'm constantly told, there are children starving in India.

T

We attend the Christmas Eve service at Bethel Methodist Church, dressed in our best clothes, never mind that my suit is too small, never mind that my shoes pinch my feet, never mind that my tie is an old one of Dad's ties and that none of us knows how to tie it correctly. Mom is apparently content with it, says I look presentable.

Christmas carols are sung. Mom sings, and her voice, a voice praised by all, is close to me so I hear her above all the others. And the minister, Reverend Voll reads to us from the Bible, reads of the miracle of the birth of Jesus, reads of how the angel comes to the poor shepherds and comforts them and tells them of the miracle.

He emphasizes the key passage: "Fear not, the angel said, for, behold, I bring you good tidings of great joy, which shall be to all people. For unto you is born this day in the city of David a Savior, which is Christ the Lord."

Mom believes the story, truly believes the story, the wonderful story, and the promise it holds. And she cries. And I see her tears, and I cry. I find I often cry this winter for no real reason.

Reverend Voll continues, "Suddenly there was with the angel a multitude of the heavenly host praising God, and saying, 'Glory to God in the highest, and on earth peace, good will toward men.'"

The words flow like a beautiful light sent to melt away the ice after a cold winter. I feel the joy in his rich tenor voice and believe the words.

When I look back I know I didn't understand what I believed, was not capable of sorting out how God and Jesus and salvation worked, didn't know what it was I believed I believed. One thing I know for certain is that I didn't not

T

believe, for even if I was confused and ignorant and unable to understand God and salvation, I feared the possible punishment for not believing, for having doubts, and I feared God could read my thoughts, for it seemed somehow he could, though I wasn't sure about that either.

I remember whenever I was supposed to pray, whether it be in church or simply before a meal at home I had to fold my hands and bow my head, and I would normally peek up at those around me. They never noticed me looking at them, because they were all being obedient and usually had their eyes closed as well. This reinforced my fear that I was being bad to look up and would probably get punished by God for doing it.

In time I began to think an honest man would look God in the face, not turn his eyes away. That made it even more difficult. Shouldn't I be a man and face my judge? What, after all, did I have to hide? God could read my thoughts anyway, since he is all-knowing. So . . . the formal act of praying is stupid. And kneeling and bowing one's head seems more an act of submission than anything else. Is that what God's all about? He's on some kind of ego trip? Is he really going to zap me with a bolt of lightning for not prostrating myself to him?

One sunny afternoon, while I'm skating through the scattered patches of snow, it strikes me that Jesus was a real boy. I wonder what kind of a boy he was, wonder what it would have been like to know him, to play with him. I begin to imagine he's skating with me. I jump over one of the patches of snow, and then watch to see if he can also do it. Soon I'm imagining a competition between him and me for who can jump the largest patch of snow, and then for who can jump the most without falling. This lasts for a good hour before I tire of

T

it. I sit on the ice and chop the back of my blade into it to get myself some pieces to suck on. I wonder if Jesus was well-behaved as a child or if he did naughty things and had to be disciplined by his parents.

Christmas Day, we make our Christmas visit to Mom's parents. In some ways, it will be the same. We get similar gifts. But now instead of being put to bed upstairs I'm put to bed in the front screened-in porch. Perhaps this is simply the result of me starting to get to be too big for the cubby hole I've used in the past. Instead of poker at the kitchen table, the adults gather around a folding table in the livingroom and play Samba.

One tradition that remains is the much-praised homemade ice cream, which I'm now old enough to be assigned the job of cranking until it reaches the right consistency.

I realize a lot of things that first Christmas visit after Dad's death. The world has changed, and Christmas at Grandma's is never going to be the same, is in fact about to end. There is a lot of discussion about some letter JoAnn and Dave have written to Grandma and Grandpa saying in no uncertain terms that they no longer consider themselves a part of the family. As with so many things at the time, I'm never given the full explanation of what's going on, so I'm left to contemplate why Dave and JoAnn have made such a dramatic decision. I will never know, but it certainly suggests bad feelings and a surprisingly selfish attitude. What is that phrase about friends being there when times are tough? Guess it doesn't apply to family.

Then, when we're packing up the car the following day to leave, Grandma gets a cardboard box and fills it with various half used boxes of food or forgotten cans of soup and vegetables. While these odds-and-ends will get eaten, I'm old enough to see

T

the irony. If they realize we're so poor that we will want a half-used box of Cheerios forgotten in their pantry for months, why aren't they seriously helping us out? Is this meant to be a kind gesture or an insult? It is handled as if it is a thoughtful thing for them to do and there is no expectation that they should do more. It's all very matter-of-fact. The more I think about it, the more certain I am it is meant as a kind gesture, which only makes things more confusing.

Mom doesn't say anything on the ride home, none of us do. I know the visit singles a change, am not able to grasp what it's all about, but Dad's death has changed our relationship with Mom's family.

So the Christmas after Dad's death comes and goes.

And all that winter I skate and shovel the snow and try to understand what has happened to my world.

And I play hockey, play hockey hard. The rules of hockey are clear. It's easy to know who wins. There are leagues, peewee, midget, junior. And I'm good, the best. I score more goals than all the rest of the league added together. The league coaches get together and decide to make me a goalie to stop me. But I skate out of my goal, yes, even with a clunky goalie stick I can easily dodge through the competition all the way to the other goal and score – again and again and again. And I play all out. No fear. What is there to fear?

The snow falls, and I shovel and I grow accustomed to the cold. And I play to win. And I fight. I fight because others don't play fair. And I hate the refs because they make wrong calls and never admit their mistakes, and I get punished, but I will not be intimidated! The game has to be decided fairly! When it isn't I fight! I don't care if the entire universe gathers against me! I fight for what's right! And so I fight! And I fight! And I

T

win! And I lose! And I push — harder and longer. I never submit!

Perhaps life isn't fair. Perhaps I can't figure out the rules for life. Perhaps I can't win at life. But everything is clear in sports! And I can win at sports! And I do!

And I lose. For the losing is inherent in the winning.

The existential and the real have smashed into each other, shattering existence and splattering the me within me over a kaleidoscope of illusions, a fantastic, glittering array of random reflections, none of them real.

Memories, truths, dreams — the known skies, the means to salvation.

None of them real!

I haven't learned it, not yet. The maps of meaning and value are not absolute. There is no absolute. That lesson will take a few years, forcing its way into my determined armor, but it will continue to hit me, again and again and again, destroying all I have to save me from the abyss. My "killer instinct" will remain, but so will a terrible empathy.

Mr. Orange stands at the window and looks out the portion of glass not frosted from the cold. "How does a child face the gods?"

The woman standing next to him takes his hand in hers.

"When worlds collide . . ."

She squeezes his hand, a light squeeze.

"Emotional storms . . . neurons . . . multiplying . . . like cancer . . . synapses sputtering . . . seeking connections. . . ."

One winter day I play hockey against Keith and John, not much of a challenge because Keith isn't an athlete and John is

T

too young to be a challenge. I enjoy my easy advantage. Then Keith finally gets up enough courage to say it.

"I don't want to play with you anymore."

"Come on, why not. It's fun!"

"No it's not. I don't want to play with you anymore."

And he doesn't.

I put it all on him. What a baby. I haven't cheated. I'm simply the better player. For him to pout about it is childish. He should be giving me credit for my abilities.

"Compassion," Mr. Orange says it softly.

What does it matter if I'm good at sports, if I win at sports? Well . . . yes . . . sure it matters, but it isn't as simple as I've made it. When one person wins another loses, and it's no fun to lose. So whenever I play some sport with someone else and win, especially when I win easily and gloat about it, I'm losing in another, more important way.

I'm losing friends. I'm making others feel bad. And it doesn't just apply to sports; it applies to all of life.

Ahhhhhhhh . . . . ! This is not good!

My salvation is flawed!

There are two sets of rules! And they don't match!

I try to sort it out.

I don't want to lose, don't even want to ease off the throttle and let the contests be more even. That's dishonest! Truth is the key! Truth! If I lie then I am killing the truth!

How can a lie be the truth?

It's all becoming meaningless again!

The shattered glass, the images, they have to be real!

T

There has to be a logic . . . a solution!

People . . . friends . . . players on the other team . . . they're not my enemies.

They are humans . . . we're all humans. They didn't take my dad. They don't control life and death. They are not to blame.

If God is establishing the limits of human existence, then I can only push against those limits if I am the best of the best.

Sports have established rules. I know the rules, so I can determine the outcome. And even if I lose, I will know why. There is no unknown. I determine my fate in the game!

But it involves contests with other humans. My victories mean their defeats.

And empathy is getting in the way!

Empathy doesn't work in sports.

It's also important that others recognize my abilities. There is hubris in this, not just a pride in being good at things but a need to have others realize it.

Why does this matter?

Is this a bad quality in me?

If it's a form of conceit, then it means I am what I don't like in people.

I don't like conceited people. Conceited people refuse to face the mystery that surrounds us — hide from the terrifying darkness at the edges of the cosmos.

They don't have the guts to face God.

They are the same as those who refuse to use the essence God breathed into them, the spirit of life that turned dead clay into living flesh. They deny God's gift in the name of faith.

T

I need to be honest. My victories are not victories over God. My victories are victories *because of* the gift of life, the spirit, the mind that gives the matter of the brain life. I am me because of God. Not only did he form me out of shapeless clay, but he brought this clay to life by breathing his essence into me. It is the god within me that is fighting with the god outside of me.

It is not the mystery that surrounds us. It is the mystery that is us. Not the darkness at the edge of the cosmos, but the darkness within each human. And the darkness within is the same essence, the breath, as the darkness without.

She sees the hint of sadness in his blue eyes as he looks through the window. Gusts of wind sweep the light snow across the ice. He can barely see the boy weaving through the patches of snow . . . ten years . . . how much can he have learned . . . ten years is still but a child . . . skating through the cold, cold, cold winter day . . . alone . . . yes . . . alone on the ice . . . skating through a labyrinth of windblown patches of snow . . . driven to push his blades against the ice . . . faster . . . ever faster . . . demanding more and more . . . always demanding more . . . determined to conquer a labyrinth he has not been given the tools to navigate.

Winning is meaningless if it isn't honest. It isn't a matter of others seeing the good in me, but a matter of them judging me correctly, seeing the true me, the real me. Not the illusions.

What is good anyway?

One man's good is another man's evil.

I'm after meaning! A reason for my existence!

Is meaning relative?

T

What happens when he stumbles and hits the hard, uncaring ice?

What if he should lose consciousness?

No one will know.

There will be no one to breathe life into him and hold him and give him warmth and help him to the shore.

No one to know of his quest.

No one to save him.

I do not live up to my standards. I am not happy with me. I'm too flawed. The worst thing I can do is to fool myself. I must be brutally honest. Truth is what I'm seeking, isn't it? I'm determined. Anything that gets in the way of reality has to be confronted and eliminated.

I know people don't judge themselves honestly, because I see it. I'm not imagining it. I see it. Constantly. Whether they do it because they are not able to see their flaws or because they need to excuse or cover up their flaws, people constantly give themselves too positive a spin. If others do this, I must to be doing it as well. The best I can do to counteract my own weakness is to be overly critical. Perhaps if I demand too much, then, maybe I can find a balance in the illusions.

"What's wrong?"
"I can't follow him. The snow's getting too thick."

If I demonstrate my abilities, then I'm a bad person, because a good person will realize the importance of the feelings of others. That's far more important then who wins or loses, not only at sports but at everything in life. Being a good person is what matters, not being good at things or winning.

T

But a good person wouldn't lie, even if it was to let another win, perhaps especially to let another win.

Back-and-forth, like a pendulum that never runs down—truth and compassion, reality and illusion.

He shouldn't be out there. It's too cold.

And to make it worse, if I let others win, they brag about it. Telling me what a good person I am for allowing them their fantasies doesn't wash away the irritation of them thinking they're better than me. Should it? I don't know. Should it matter if they think less of me and my abilities because I'm purposely letting them feel better about themselves? Am I being selfish to be bothered by what they think of me? Wouldn't a truly good person rise above such feelings?

There! I see him . . . heading toward the Point . . . no . . . now he's gone . . .

I push my skates against the ice . . . lean left to avoid a patch of snow . . . a sharp cut to the right to follow a thread of ice . . . my blade hits a crack! I fall sideways! Hit an irregular blanket of snow hard with my left shoulder . . . tumble over the snow and slide on my stomach across the ice to a stop! I gasp for breath!

Being the child me has been easy. But I can't sort out how to be the adult me.

The woman turns Mr. Orange away from the window. "Let it be. The window's completely frosted over, the wind's blowing

T

the snow too hard, and he's skated too far out. He knows the lake, the ice. He'll be home soon."

One day Mark and two of his friends come down the street and see me busy improving my snow fort. It takes less than five minutes. The fort, tunnel and all, is obliterated.

Those who say history repeats itself might make that comment here, because, yet again, Mark, fifteen-year-old Mark, hits me square, this time with an ice-ball; and I charge through the snow and straight into him. This time his attempt to sidestep me doesn't work, and I land on top of him. And we fight. And we fight until I'm bleeding from my nose, and from my mouth. And I keep swinging, and I keep swinging. Again and again and again! And Mark knees on me. "Stop!" he says. "Eddie! Stop! Eddie! Stop! Eddie!" And I flail and flail and cry and cry and swing and swing and swing.

"I give you credit," he says for the second time that winter. "I've never met anyone with your guts!"

"More like stupidity!" Joey says.

Joey doesn't get it. But Mark does. Mark likes me. Mark understands.

And our Christmas tree, decorated with homemade paper ornaments, strings of popcorn we've strung together, lights from previous years, and an old white angel with some kind of gauze and a white bulb placed at the top, our Christmas tree stands in the corner of the living room from Thanksgiving through New Year's Day before we take it down and burn it in the spot where once I had my snow-fort.

And a man on television, a man on channel four, a man dressed in a thick, brown leather coat edged with a soft brown

T

fur, a man with a dark brown pipe and a dark brown hat and brown pants and brown boots, a man talks about Christmas trees. And he says:

"Christmas trees, fir trees, were used by pre-Christians as symbols of eternal life, because they're ever-green. But they were not cut down and brought fully into the house. Only a branch was brought in, a branch was enough. It was the Germans, the eighth century Germans, who began to cut down entire trees and carry them into the house."

And he says:

"There is a story . . . a story about St. Boniface, a British monk. He was preaching to a tribe of Germanic Druids near the town of Geismar, attempting to dissuade them of their belief that the oak tree was sacred, and he cut down an oak, a giant oak, to make his point. When it fell, it crushed every plant and tree in its path, except for a small fir tree. St. Boniface, ever quick to see an advantage, declared that the tree's survival was a miracle and announced that it be called the tree of the Christ Child himself!"

Outside, in the yard, in the real world, the hole I dug, the hole in the snow surrounding where once stood a fir tree, fills with new snow until only a slight depression can be seen. Our spruce tree is gone, but its death has served a purpose.

Mom has found a way to have our traditional Christmas tree, and we've decorated it, and it has helped Mom keep our Christmas alive. In spite of Dad not being there, she has continued the traditions of Christmas. In spite of there being no money or any idea how there will be any next month, Mom has found a way to make Christmas happy.

But not really.

T

And so the Christmas after Dad's death arrives and passes, a white Christmas, a Christmas where the snow rises above the waist of a ten-year-old boy.

T

Bobby Hull

On a Saturday Morning

"You look just like Bobby Hull!" Terry Holly says.

I circle back to him, shrug my shoulders and turn my hands up to indicate I have no idea who Bobby Hull is.

"Oh, yeah, I suppose you wouldn't know. He's probably the greatest hockey player of all time."

I smile. Why wouldn't I? That's high praise.

He wedges his gloves into his left armpit, takes a pack of Camels from his inner coat pocket, taps the top of it against his arm so one cigarette comes part of the way out, lifts the pack to his lips and uses them to pull out the cigarette. As he's about to put the pack back, it occurs to him to share.

I hesitate . . . then say "Thanks."

Another quick hit on the arm sends a cigarette partially out the top, and he holds it to my lips so I won't have to take off my gloves.

An exchange of cigarettes for lighter and a practiced snap result in a flame just off the end of my new experience. I suck on the unfiltered tobacco and a dry smoke fills my mouth. I don't like the taste, but I hold it over my tongue while he lights his own, then let it out.

He laughs. "I take it you're not a smoker."

"No."

"Well, that's probably a good thing. Cigs just cost you money, get your clothes smelly and burn holes in your car seats."

I take another drag, this time inhaling it, and immediately cough, catch my breath, then cough again . . . and again.

He laughs. "Hey, give you credit. It's like whiskey . . . takes a while to get used to it." He reaches out and takes the cigarette. "Here, no need to get sick."

I've skated across the clear ice through patches of snow out to the Point, dribbling my puck and pretending, as usual. This time the challenge has been to keep the puck from touching the snow. It's a normally cold Saturday morning, but the sky is clear, the light a gray-blue common on winter mornings, and there is little wind. Not paying much attention to where my game leads me, I find myself skating near the string of large rocks that make-up the final twenty yards of the Point.

I scrape to a stop. A gust of cold wind hits my exposed face. I look at the open water of the channel . . . sense the cold patch of

T

ripples over it. It's a moment of decision. I can cross the Point and skate along the other side, or make an abrupt turn back. To this point, I've not skated onto that bay, but today I decide to enlarge my world. I do my best not to step on gravel or rocks, dulling my skates more than they already are, and push off the rough ice along the opposite shore.

This bay is noticeably larger than my own. I see the island in the distance, and beyond that the shoreline of what I know are the homes and businesses of Spring Park. My breath and even the heat of my body rise as a light mist in the cold air. I turn to my right and look at the shoreline that runs from the Point along Three Points, where I see a number of boys playing hockey on a cleared rink. That's a promising way to fill up my Saturday, so I head to it.

As it turns out, Terry Holly is the one older boy among a number of younger ones. He's Bob Strand's age, another of many good hockey players living in Three Points.

He inhales both cigarettes at the same time and exhales a cloud of smoke. "Been workin' on my Imperial. Got a deal on a 392 hemi with a 4 inch bore." He stops, inhales his cigarettes, and looks at me as if expecting a response. After exhaling, he continues, "Got to cut a hole in the hood to fit it but will work with my manifold."

Terry is Bob Strand's age and like Bob has decided not to play on the high school team. Bob, I was told, because he'd rather spend his time flirting, Terry because his passion is cars. He's always working on his latest hotrod.

Since Bob lives next door and Terry lives in another part of Three Points, I get to know Bob's dad well but have few encounters with Terry's dad, one of those people who spice every sentence with a string of profanity. If one can get passed that,

T

he has a biting wit. He's more of a caricature than a real person — a cigarette in one hand, a drink in the other, disheveled and as irrelevant as one can be, spewing out sarcasm through the lens of a standup comedian.

After Terry's comparison of me with Bobby Hull, I scour the papers for a picture of him. The following week I find one in the Sunday sports, and indeed, I see the similarities.

Of course, his nose shows the signs of being broken several times. I will also end up having my nose broken endless times. I'm told it's a badge of courage. I'm not so sure of this. Am sensitive about my nose. And breaking it doesn't improve my looks.

Most hockey players also have front teeth knocked out, and though they generally wear some kind of false teeth when not playing, during their games, it's standard to see their toothless smiles.

I guess I'm lucky, because I never do have any teeth knocked out or damaged in any way. It's not because I'm careful about protecting them. Not only do I not wear the "required" mouth-guard in either hockey or football, but obviously I don't wear anything in my endless fist fights. Nevertheless, other than my one fall from a tree, I never have a serious injury. In addition to my nose, I smash my right elbow bone without even realizing it when it slams against the ice (of course, not wearing elbow pads), suffer numerous cuts to my face and head requiring stitches, and brake some finger bones hitting others' faces, but that's the extent of my injuries as I carelessly make my way from child to adult.

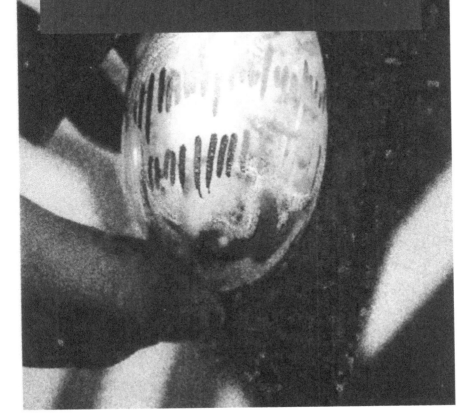

Easter

The Easter Egg Hunt at Three Points Park.

It's an established event.

No one remembers when it began or how the various customs got attached to it through the years.

It's what Americans do.

They do not know or care why an Easter Egg Hunt is a standard aspect of a holiday based on Christ's resurrection. Most of those with children, even if they're not Christian, have a similar hunt in their own homes. Many also give their children presents on Easter morning, sometimes hidden in larger baskets. The candy is often in the shape of rabbits and chickens. The eggs are boiled and dyed various colors. Some have elaborate decorations. Some are punctured and their insides emptied out. Some of these are used to make Easter Trees, similar to Christmas Trees, only much smaller and usually made from dead branches of deciduous trees or plants, rather than fir trees, and decorated with egg shells instead of equally non-Christian ornaments on Christmas trees.

The most famous of these decorated eggs are the Faberge eggs, jeweled eggs created by the House of Faberge in St. Petersburg for the Russian Tsars as Easter gifts for their wives and mothers, worth millions of dollars each.

The connection to Christianity seems broken. Christ could hardly embrace such a blatant disregard of his views about self-indulgent displays of wealth.

No one ever clarifies this for me.

Why would I challenge accepted traditions? There is no reason to ask why rabbits, eggs, candy, and a hunt are connected to Christ's resurrection. It's a part of the holiday, similar to decorating a tree, putting strings of colored lights

T

- 185 -

along the gutters, and leaving milk-and-cookies our for Santa at Christmas.

It's unchristian to challenge it.

For most of the country, including Mound, getting dressed-up and wearing Easter bonnets mainly involves women wearing more elaborate costumes, often including hats, to attend church.

Since we belong to the United Methodist Church, our church presents us with that particular version of the holiday. I don't pay much attention and am mostly lost when it comes to the details. Soon, I will go through my Confirmation, a series of weekly meetings before church service, and be taught such things – though in truth, I still don't pay much attention, and when I'm Confirmed, I know at best the general outlines. The main thing I still remember is being taught about the founder, John Westley. For the actual confirmation, we all kneel at the front of the church for a special Communion and that's it. The main thing I remember is that Jeanie Huff faints while we're a kneeling for our Kool-aide and crackers.

This Easter following Dad's death, Mom, John and I avoid the endless television shows about Jesus's life and Crucifixion. They simply bore us. For Mom, Easter might hold some comfort. I do not know. I do know that it holds nothing for John and me.

When Dad was alive, he occasionally went to church, including every Christmas and Easter. Apparently, that's the agreement he and Mom worked out. Mom still goes nearly every Sunday, taking John and me with her, and remains active in a number of the church social activities, though less so once Dad got sick and now that he is dead. This will end. I don't

T

know the exact moment, or the reasons, but she will completely separate from the church for decades.

Whatever religious meanings are attached to Easter, Mom insists on having the usual family celebration. She dyes eggs with us, hides a large Easter basket of candy and plastic toys for each of us, charges a couple of the cheap, mostly plastic, outdoor games for us to play, and finds the money to purchase and make a ham dinner for us. She has not been able to afford these minimal purchases for years, but she finds a way. Family gatherings for holidays will always mean a great deal to her.

We are excited to wake up and get our Easter baskets. After church service, we share our meal, spend about an hour trying to make the outside games work, (they don't, mostly simply break or fall apart), and end up playing Canasta and Parcheesi for most of the day.

The Easter Egg Hunt at the park takes place the day before Easter.

I don't know who organizes these events, but I'm still young enough to be excited to join the rest of the children in the mad dash to find whatever eggs, nests, and baskets of candy have been hidden about the park. Yes, I am well beyond a belief that there is a real Easter Bunny. But that doesn't mean I don't want to join in the hunt.

To top it off, there are two "big" baskets sitting on a large table in the main building, one the reward for finding a gold egg and the other for finding a silver one.

I don't think about anything beyond what I might find. Why would a child of ten consider anything more?

Seeing it through the lens of an adult looking back on his childhood, I have some of the standard nostalgia, and it does

T

seem a nice thing for a neighborhood of working-class people to do, a reason for a friendly community gathering.

As usual, the crackling loudspeakers try to keep things in order, and only partially succeed. But they succeed enough that at roughly noon, a ragamuffin group of children are gathered and told to begin.

We race from tree to tree, through the grandstands, along the edges of buildings, anywhere we might find the precious eggs and candy.

It's a chilly day, and the grass is wet with dew.

The adults are mostly staying on the hill where the park buildings, picnic tables, food and drink are located, but some are walking among us, apparently making sure there are no mishaps.

A half hour passes, and still no one has found either of the two prized eggs. It's becoming clear the children's excitement is starting to turn into frustration.

As I circle behind the storage building in back of home-plate for the third time, I see a man bend down, seem to look through the grass at the edge of the large wire backstop and move on. He looks my way briefly and smiles. It's a curious look.

I don't know what to make of it. Did he see something?

I decide to browse the line of tall grass along the backstop.

It instantly jumps out at me – the silver egg!

It seems obvious in hindsight, but at the time it doesn't occur to me. He has this egg in his pocket, waiting for the right moment to place it so I will be the one to find it.

Even though I'm the one who gains as a result, when I look back and realize what happened, I'm bothered by it. There is

T

an underlying dishonesty. All of the other children eagerly looking for the two prize eggs have been fooled.

This standard assumption that lying is okay is hard to fit into my ethos.

Of course, in a situation such as this, the motive for it is a thoughtful one.

My thoughts from winter stay with me, like the flickering flame of a candle I can't extinguish.

The longer I live, the more such things as honesty and truth melt off the candle of a pure flame. They are nothing more than the uneven wax surrounding meaning and value. They are not the wick that gives off the light.

Perhaps, it has to do with how others are affected. Do truth and honesty benefit or hurt others? If one lies for another's benefit, does that make it positive? The more I struggle with it, the more I begin to realize that even the seemingly impenetrable strands of a wick based on doing no harm start unravelling.

Love, a pure love for others. Isn't that what gets proclaimed again and again? Didn't Jesus say to love thy neighbor and even thy enemies?

Sounds good. All we need is love. The Beatles' song runs through my mind: "There's nothing you can do that can't be done / Nothing you can sing that can't be sung / Nothing you can say, but you can learn how to play the game / It's easy."

Nothing! Nothing! Nothing! What? Easy? Play the game?

How strange. It seems such a positive song, and yet it denies the possibilities, the need to do what cannot be done. That's what matters, that's the key, the human spirit that reaches beyond what it can accomplish.

T

A better song is The Impossible Dream from Don Quixote: "To dream the impossible dream / To fight the unbeatable foe / To bear with unbearable sorrow / To run where the brave dare not go / To right the unrightable wrong / To love pure and chaste from afar / To try when your arms are too weary / To reach the unreachable star."

That's the key, to connect into that part of humans that breaks through meaningless logic and reason.

"Nothing you can make that can't be made / No one you can save that can't be saved / Nothing you can do, but you can learn how to be you in time / All you need is love, all you need is love."

I like that, "you can learn how to be you in time." That's important. But why is it couched in all the negatives?

All it takes is love? What does that mean? It sounds wonderful, yet, I know it's too easy. It doesn't translate into the daily questions about what it means to love. Saying or singing it might suggest a positive approach to life, but how does one translate it into the real, literal, moment-by-moment meaning of life.

Only people looking for a mindless response to the meaning of life fall into such a meaningless abstraction. Look at the flame of the candle of love. It's not hard to realize the glorious flame of love is not a pure, white, but has layers of color.

Do these layers give it more texture, more strength, a more illuminating light — a light better suited to fighting off the dark truths of ignorance and the sadness of an empty, pointless, meaningless existence?

What happens when the wick burns away and the light goes out?

T

Is an embracement of Jesus Christ the means to salvation? Is that what is meant by the flame of truth and love? Are the illuminated beings the ones who have realized this?

Is it a realization? The realization of the god within each of us? Buddha means the awakened one. He realized exactly this. Is that what Jesus tells us, to realize the Christ within each of us? Is that what it's all about? Not a physical matter. Not an ethical matter. Not even a religious matter. A teleological truth beyond all of these.

But doesn't that deny the self?

Isn't that very awakening an awakening into the meaninglessness of life?

Doesn't faith deny reason and logic and any form of human thinking beyond what Kierkegaard famously says is a belief in the absurd? Even in the famous story of Abraham and Isaac, does it really matter that God intervenes in the last second? Yes, Abraham exhibits ultimate faith, is expecting to be murdering his much wanted and loved son, when God allows him to desist. So . . . doesn't absolute faith mean denying any value or meaning in human existence? Abraham gives up any responsibility for his actions, performing them solely in obedience to God. He is judged completely by whether or not he is willing to obey any command without question.

Perhaps, it is possible to understand this in a different way. What, after all, is God? According to the Bible, Man is made in God's image, suggesting God has the same physical form as Man. Of course, this doesn't make sense, as the human form is not capable of God's powers. Perhaps, image is not meant to refer to physical appearance. That solves a lot of the problems.

The Bible also says that God breathed his breath into man. That opens some powerful possibilities. If God's spirit or life is in

T

Man, then references to God might include the God within. One possibility this allows is that Abraham's relation to God is an inner one, a struggle within himself. If so, then it can be claimed that Abraham (the God within him) wins out over other aspects of him in terms of not killing Isaac. If so, then Abraham is responsible for his actions, and indeed human life does or at least can have meaning and value.

Perhaps, just maybe, it is possible to both have faith in Jesus Christ and self-responsibility.

T

The Fantasticks

Mrs. Kaylor looks over the classroom to see if anyone is absent and notes it in her record book. "Quiet! Jim!" She has a commanding presence. "Now, class, I have some good news. This Friday, we get to watch a musical in the auditorium."

Whispers fill the room.

"Sharon! . . . Bob! . . ." That's all it takes. "The University of Minnesota is currently performing a musical called *The Fantasticks*, and Coca-Cola has agreed to help fund some of the costs so that they can perform at a number of schools, including ours."

It's always exciting when we get to go to the auditorium. It's a small auditorium with a small stage, as one might imagine in an elementary school, but it's large enough to hold about 100 students, and whatever the musical might be, it's an event.

Mrs. Kaylor continues, "I've never seen this musical, but the announcement I've been given says that . . . let's see here . . . it tells an allegorical story, loosely based on the play *The Romancers* by Edmond Rostand about two neighboring fathers who trick their children, Luisa and Matt, into falling in love by pretending to have a feud . . . pretending they don't like each other. The fathers hire traveling actors to stage a fake abduction . . . a . . . ah . . . kidnapping. Then Matt can pretend to heroically seem to save Luisa and end the fake feud. When the children discover the deception, they reject the arranged love match and separate. Each then gains disillusioning experiences of the real world. In other words, they have some bad experiences, seen in parallel fantasy sequences . . . so each of them is shown imagining what life will be like if they are *not* together ... and ... what they imagine, they *don't* like. They return to each other bruised but enlightened. They realize they should not have refused the original arrangement for them to marry, and they renew their vows with more maturity ... they get married."

"Sounds like a fairytale," Linda says.

"What's an allegory?" Dave asks.

Mrs. Kaylor holds up her hand to indicate we need to settle down. "An allegory is somewhat how a fairytale works. The characters are flat, which means they mainly have one trait. So they might represent greedy people or cruel people or vain people, and they're often even named for what they represent. This is what we find in a lot of fairy tales. Snow White is all good, pure as untouched, white snow. Sleeping Beauty is exactly that. Cinderella is French, and it means little cinders. So, when she is growing up, her wicked stepmother makes her clean the cinders, which are the ashes from the fireplace, and her name is meant to be an insult used by her wicked stepmother and stepsisters. Prince Valient and Prince Charming are just that. In this musical, the main characters are given more realistic names, but they still represent certain types of people. That's how an allegory works.

"So, it will be like a Disney fairytale," Mary asks more than says.

"In a way, but probably not as obvious," Mrs. Kaylor says.

"And Luisa and Matt are the princess and the prince!" Dave says, obviously proud of his insight.

"Well. They are poor, both of them are poor," Mrs. Kaylor says while she is studying the announcement. "If I'm reading this correctly," she says, "it is based on this story, but the

T

characters in the play might have different names. I'm not sure if this is the plot of the play or the story it is based on."

It's starting to get confusing. But we don't care.

It's exciting. We get to spend the entire afternoon watching a play in the theatre. Certainly better than sitting at our desks doing math.

When the big day arrives, we're marched down the hall to the auditorium. At the entrance, two young adults hand out free things from Coca-Cola — a pencil, a folder, a tablet, a bookmarker, and several flyers, all with Coca-Cola images on them.

It's noisy inside the theatre. Mrs. Kaylor and other teachers direct us to our rows of seats with the usual admonishments to settle down. Once everyone is seated, music comes from the speakers and six actors, five men and a woman, walk onto the stage and pretend they are just now preparing to do the play. They carry out a Wooden Bench and a large trunk. Then they look about to make sure everything is in place and put the finishing touches on their costumes. When the music ends, they take their places. There is a brief pause. Then, music comes from the loud speakers, and a man we later learn is named El Greco, begins to sing:

Try to remember the kind of September
When life was slow and oh, so mellow.
Try to remember the kind of September
When grass was green and grain was yellow.
Try to remember the kind of September
When you were a tender and callow fellow.
Try to remember, and if you remember,
Then follow.

T

A girl we later learn is Luisa sings:

Follow, follow, follow, follow, follow,
Follow, follow, follow, follow.

I like the melody. I'm not sure what it means, but it has the feel of inviting me into another world, much as a fairytale does with the phrase once-upon-a-time. I likely latch onto this because of the recent class discussion.

El Gallo sings several similar verses, and the other actors take turns singing the "follow" accompaniment to end each.

After the final verse, the music ends. El Gallo turns to the audience and says, "Let me tell you a few things you may want to know before we begin the play. First of all, the characters are a boy, a girl, two fathers, and a wall." He turns and motions to one of the actors.

The man performing the role of the wall steps forward and tips his hat.

This is unusual. Similar to a fairytale or a fantasy, where nonhumans take on human qualities. I know it's a form of what's called personification, standard in Disney movies. It's also unusual in that the actors are going in-and-out of their roles. I like that.

Why?

I try to sort it out. By stressing the artificial aspects, as if they should be a part of the performance, the musical emphasizes the dual realities of what it is, that the performance is putting a pattern over existence, that real existence is subjecting itself to the artificial world of the story. Even more, it highlights that humans do this. Every

T

performance does this. Every musical, every play, every song, every story is doing exactly this.

Doing exactly what?

I try to sort it out.

I know, I know, I know – I have to stop thinking and watch the play!

How do I stop thinking?

El Gallo continues his narration, "Anything else we need, we can get from this box." He and The Wall walk over to the large trunk recently placed on the stage.

El Gallo puts his hand on the trunk. "It's hard to know which is more important or how it all began. The Boy was born. The Girl was born. They grew up, went to school, became shy, read romances, studied the clouds on lazy summer afternoons, and spent more time looking at the moon than doing their homework."

Yes . . . exactly, it fits an allegory. It stresses that it fits an allegory. The boy and girl might have names, but the point being stressed is that they are meant to represent a universal boy and a universal girl. That's why the narrator calls them Boy and Girl, instead of using their names.

When he says they become shy as they grow, that hits a nerve. It's happened to me, almost overnight, and to an extreme degree. But I've not noticed it in my classmates. Is this normal? I wonder . . . is the girl and boy's shyness the same as mine?

The line about lying in the sun and looking at the clouds is exactly what I do. I wonder . . . when I lie in the sun on my raft and imagine the clouds are castles or dragons or pirate ships . . . and fill them with stories . . . is that what this boy and girl do?

T

Is that what everyone does? It doesn't seem others do. Whenever I start talking about these things, others get bored. They say they do, but they don't have much to say about it. But they must. How can they not?

The reference to the moon takes me out of summer into my winter nights, lying on the ice and entering another world filled with stories of gods and goddesses, mythic beasts and wondrous happenings.

Is this what El Gallo means? Is this what the story is about?

He continues setting up the play, leading us into Louisa's big scene, where we see her fantasizing about being a princess, very much in the mode of a standard Disney movie. The main difference here is in El Gallo's interwoven commentary, which satirizes the fantasy. He bluntly tells us that believing in such a dream is insane.

We're still elementary school students, just beginning to think about these love songs as more than abstractions. It's more the fantasy of such worlds than the reality of physical attraction.

How much do my classmates think it through? I feel the huge chasm between my real world and the world of such fantasies. I know there are people living the fantasy, famous, wealthy people – kings, queens, movie stars, politicians, athletes, lawyers, doctors, businessmen. I see them on television. I read about them.

There are some in my own town. Not as wealthy as the ones in the fantasies, but wealthy enough that I instinctively put them in that category. Somewhere in the passage between Dad and Mom learning of Dad's cancer and his death, I lose my innocence, and so does my family. While it might be claimed that Mom and Dad live the poor man's version of this fantasy,

T

his cancer poisons more than the cells of his body. They fight the darkness. But it wins. Mom remains, surrounded by it. What can she do?

She is determined not to give up the house, to the point of obsession. I don't know how she manages to hold onto it, but she does.

The old house that was not well built when it was new needs constant repairs. A woman with no training, two young boys, and no money — we take down walls and rebuild them. It's the three of us, and the house is our world.

There is love. At the same time, there isn't much real hope. It's a dark, depressing world.

As the applause subsides after her song, El Gallo steps forward, "Good. And now the boy. His story may be a wee bit briefer, because it's pretty much the same."

It is just as he says. Matt is the male version of Luisa. He takes us through the fantasy, while El Gallo continually undermines it. Eventually it rises to an emotional duet with Luisa.

This is the Disney fantasy, the wonderful love of a princess and a prince. In spite of the stream of comedic references throughout, the dream wins, and we all clap and cheer at the end of it.

Then, the play gets into the standard conflict between the practical fathers and their impractical children.

Finally, Matt rebels against his father's plan: "I will not wed by your wisdom. I will not walk neatly into a church and contract out to prolongate my race. I will not go a wedding in a too-tight suit, nor be witnessed when I take my bride."

T

Huck protests, but Matt cuts him off: "I'll marry, when I marry, in my own particular way!" He continues in this vein and finishes with a resounding "There!"

We are caught up in it. We applaud.

The conflict is in place. And the same type of scene is played between Luisa and her father, Bell.

The two fathers meet and discuss their unrealistic children, connecting the play's title directly to children, fantasticks (those who believe in fantasy), lovers, and . . . geese!

Then they discuss their pretense of having a feud specifically to get their children to fall in love, how they plan to hire a man to pretend to abduct Luisa, and then let Matt think he rescues her. They exit.

El Gallo appears, looks about for a few minutes and then is joined by two travelling actors, who are actually the two fathers, only in different costumes, which he explains with cupped hand is necessary because there are only so many actors in the company, not because they are meant to be the fathers in disguise. He persuades them to help him with the kidnapping.

That evening, Matt and Luisa sing of their love together, a song titled "Soon It's Gonna Rain." El Gallo and the actors put their plan into action and abduct Luisa. As planned, Matt rescues her and the fathers can finally end their feud together. They leave the stage.

El Gallo turns to us and wonders how long this "Happy Ending" will last, explaining that what seemed lovely by moonlight is not always the same in the glaring light of day.

There is a brief intermission, during which time, the El Greco, or, rather, the actor playing him, tells us about how Coca-Cola

T

has been kind enough to sponsor the presentation and goes through the gifts Coca-Cola has given us.

He also explains that some of the songs are being cut down or completely left off because of time constraints.

It is getting long. But something new catches our interest.

While he's making these announcements, the word is being passed that a major song got left off the first half because it's about rape. Someone's parents saw the play performed on Broadway and contacted the school because they're concerned about it.

Rape? My mind races. That doesn't fit this world. Fairytales and fantasies and musicals don't include songs about rape.

The spell is broken. I can't stop thinking about it. Rape? In my once-upon-a-time world?

The second half of the play moves quickly. It begins with the fathers squabbling over their gardens, and singing This Plum is Too Ripe.

Huck tells the children that the entire abduction was staged. Matt and Luisa are upset and soon the situation evolves into a real feud between the fathers. Matt tries to win over Luisa with a real display of strength by challenging El Gallo to a duel. When he loses, Luisa is unimpressed by his boasting and they break up.

Matt decides to leave town in search of something more exciting, singing "I Can See It." Luisa comes across El Gallo and asks him to take her on an adventure, but we soon see that both Luisa and Matt have realized that the outside world can be anything but a fantasy, and they sing "Round and Round."

El Gallo tells us that he had to hurt both Luisa and Matt so they could learn to value each other. Matt returns home and

T

finds Luisa, and they both discover that the adventure they both wanted is really with each other, singing "They Were You."

At the sight of their children's reunion, the fathers end their feud once more.

Matt and Luisa are married.

The music of the first song, "Try to Remember," comes from the speakers. El Greco walks to the side of the marriage scene, leans to us and says, "It is only through their own experiences and their own coping with reality through the world of imagination that Matt and Luisa can find true love. Too often, we are told to "be realistic," not to live our dreams. They say children need to play in order to learn the lessons of life. When it comes to watching plays, we are all children. That is the power of theatre, the embracement of the imagination, not giving up on one's dreams, but bringing one's dreams into the real world."

Then he sings, "Deep in December, it's nice to remember/The fire of September that made us mellow./Deep in December, our hearts should remember/ And follow."

That's the song that sticks with me.

After school, I try to pluck out the melody and accompanying chords on the piano. The melody is an easy one, and as I've found, if I go for standard chords I can make them fit, but I also sense that some of the chord texture isn't what I've heard. After a couple of hours, I give up on it and decide to go swimming off the raft.

Then, as I usually do, I lie on the raft and take in the sun. The song keeps running through my thoughts. I try to understand what El Gallo said at the end. We need to bring the imagination into the real world. I'm confused. We need to not

T

give up our imagination, but not escape to it. Instead, we need to bring it into the world.

Mr. Orange says, "Imagination is the enchantment of the world, not separate from it. And imagination is connected to the dream. A dream is a desire, the fulfillment of a wish. We should not give up our dreams, our desires, but we also should not escape into them."

It's too much for me. I push it aside and focus on the gently rocking raft, the lapping of the waves, and the warmth of the sun.

After a time, Mr. Orange says, "It makes sense to couch it in music. There's something about music that fits with a fantasy world . . . And a musical, a play of any sort, has a structure to it. Though Shakespeare did not mean it in the same context, might it not be a better world if indeed all the world were a stage. Would there not be a map of meaning and value? And would not each actor bring his own self to his role?"

Sometimes, I wish Mr. Orange would stop trying to get me to think about things. I know he's trying to teach me in his way, but sometimes I wish I could stop all this and just enjoy life.

When we come to school the following Monday, Mrs. Kaylor immediately announces, "I've been told that the musical as it is performed for adults has a song in it about rape and that students have found out about that and been talking. I've checked it out, and that word means something different than what is being spread around. The way it is meant in the

T

musical is that Luisa is abducted or kidnapped, not sexually raped."

Smothered laughter comes from the back of the room.

"That's enough!" Mrs. Kaylor says firmly.

I think about what Mr. Orange said on the raft while I watched the clouds transform into fantasy worlds:

"In the Fantasticks, the original feud is imaginary. But that is not enough, because it is not the lovers who test their imagination against reality, but their parents. Much as parents want to protect their children from the real world, they cannot do it. This is what happens to Huck and Bell, the well-intentioned fathers. Their best laid plans run horribly awry and create a real feud between them.

This mess is inevitable. Matt and Luisa can only find real love by coping with the real world through their own fantasies. If their parents tell them to be realistic, not to live in a fantasy world, that denies them their own mental process, their own imaginations, and thus, their own means of connecting the dream with the real. Only through fantasy and the imagination is it possible to live in reality, because these are where meaning and value are given shape and color.

This is the lesson of Romeo and Juliet, who defy their parents' idea of what is real and seek out the higher truth in their fantasy exchanges of love – beautiful, poetic exchanges of love.

A love denied in the real world of their parents' feuding families.

It is also the truth of The Fantasticks, though one is a tragedy, the other a comedy.

T

El Gallo, the mysterious narrator in The Fantasticks, is the key, the character able to take Matt and Luisa from the fancies of Romeo and Juliet to the real imagination. This is what Friar Lawrence could not understand in Romeo and Juliet, mistaking innocent desires for the power of a mature imagination.

The childhood fancies of Matt and Luisa, controlled with good intentions by their fathers, are not real imagination, which must be tested by reality. That is the true strength of imagination. It comes through reality rather than denying it.

This is the great insight of El Gallo. He manipulates events so that they understand the difference between their childhood fancies and the fantasy that opposes itself to reality by testing them. This is the key. They must first see the world as it is. Only then can they form a real love based on the love of their imaginations.

As it must be, they learn this lesson through experience. Only through suffering and sacrifice can fancy transform into imagination.

Only by being given the freedom to decide for themselves can they become real.

And the connection with love is important. Real imagination is the same as real love. For love can only exist if one truly believes in his dreams.

Matt and Luisa do need to grow up. They are foolish in the beginning because they are still children. They do not know enough about the real world to bring their dreams into it. Their fathers go to extremes to try and keep them from the harsh realities of the real world. But this is wrong. This is selfish. It denies them the chance to become adults, 'real' people who think for themselves.

T

It is the gift Satan gives Eve in the Garden of Eden, the gift God tries to deny her. It is the fruit of the Tree of the Knowledge of Good and Evil. When Eve and Adam gain this, they gain the ability to choose, to think. Knowledge is the key. Without this, life is meaningless.

Only when Eve and Adam fall from "grace" into the realm of choice can they gain the responsibility of thinking for themselves and have an existence of meaning and value.

El Gallo knows this hard truth, and he sees to it that they are wounded by the real world. This is what takes their imagination of ideal love into the real world. El Gallo sings it: "Without a hurt the heart is hollow."

When the heart is hurt, there is a choice. Either one can use the wounds of life as a reason to become bitter and closed, or one can learn from them and triumph over the impossible by refusing to give up the dream.

That is the real meaning of the song El Gallo sings, "Deep in December, it's nice to remember/The fire of September that made us mellow./Deep in December, our hearts should remember/And follow."

Make the world of the ideal the world of the real.

This is the greatest gift given to humans, the gift of fire.

T

Dark Shadow

Dark Shadow spreads his magnificent black wings and hovers barely inside of God's creation. The tips of his feathers have a luminescent red glow.

What will happen if he flies beyond the edge? Beyond existence? At least beyond existence as it is experienced in God's creation?

It is not a rigid edge, more like the ice on a lake that slowly gets thinner and thinner as it approaches open water. Then there is no more ice, only water. In this case the ice is not ice, but consists of all of God's creation, and the water is not water, but is the empty nothingness surrounding God's creation.

As Dark Shadow flies closer and closer to the edge, he finds it difficult to breath the thin air and his wings have little to float on. But there is nothing to pull him down, as gravity also grows weak, threatening to disappear completely.

He contemplates death. If he flies across the edge, then he will have died in God's creation. Will he be reborn in that existence beyond God's creation?

He knows as long as he stays in God's creation, he is a part of God's thoughts. At the same time, he knows he has his own thoughts, separate and capable of going against the other thoughts in God's creation. Is this what it means to exist?

If he should leave, God will certainly notice the loss. Will God care? Will it make God less in some way? Will God be able to easily recreate him? Will God want to recreate him? Will the loss be a gain, as if shedding a disease? Ridding himself of an unwanted force or entity?

Or is there no such thing as negative in God's creation? Do opposites merge, like two sides of the same coin? Or the transformation of the flat coin into a sphere, so opposites can no longer be distinguished?

Dark Shadow feels the edge moving further into the nothingness, its size continually expanding.

He flaps his wings and glides easily through the thin air towards the horizon.

Tempting. It is tempting.

To travel beyond the known into the unknown.

Will he lose his self-awareness?

Will he gain a more powerful awareness?

Will he finally face the sublime?

The *Mysterium Tremendum*?

T

The Morning of My Life

In the morning when the moon is at its rest
You will see me at the time I love the best
Watching rainbows play on sunlight
Pools of water iced from cold night
In the morning
'Tis the morning of my life

In the daytime I will meet you as before
You will find me waiting by the ocean floor
Building castles in the shifting sands
In a world that no one understands
In the morning
'Tis the morning of my life

In the morning of my life
The minutes take so long to drift away
Please be patient with your life
It's only morning and you're still to live your day.

Barry Gibb
1965

The Morning of My Life

When Miracles are still possible

A Scar

I run up the street from the lake
I've found a tooled smooth, ½ inch thick wood rod about three feet long
One end retains the flat crosscut of a saw, but the other has splintered.
I see Mom standing on the porch and call to her, "Mommy! Mommy! Look
what I found!"
I reach the sidewalk and turn towards the house
The flat end of the stick hits the gravel
The jagged end jams against my stomach right of my belly button
"AAAAAAAHHHHHHHHHHHH!!!!!!!!"
The rod wedges between the road and me
The sharp, splintered end pierces my skin
It stops me
All I know is the pain
The rod now sticks out from me
I run to Mom
She runs to me
It's good she's a nurse
I still have the scar
And the memory

JoAnn's Bicycle

In the 1950s, Schwinn bicycles are large and heavy, and the brakes are applied by pushing backwards on the peddles, not by levers on the handles.

JoAnn's bicycle is 28 inches. Dave's is only 26. But Dave's bike has the standard male bar from the seat to the handles, whereas, JoAnn's doesn't. So I can ride her bike before my legs are long enough to ride Dave's. Her handlebars are too high for me, but I can manage. It doesn't occur to me at the time, but I must have been a curious sight with my hands level with my head and my head barely bobbing above the center of the bars.

I've seen boys on television attach playing cards to the wheel frames with clothes pins so that the cards make a noise when the spokes hit them. It isn't as easy as it seems. I find that the angle has to be right. But I keep at it until it works. Now, I have a bike that makes a rapid flapping noise, like a machine gun when I get the bike up to enough speed.

For a while, I'm excited to ride up and down the dirt road along the side of our yard, but one morning I decide to venture over the hill and see if I can manage the thrill of going down the larger hill on the other side.

It's a big, heavy bike, but I have enough strength to power it up the hill. Mr. Porter sees me from his porch and comes out into his yard. "Eddie, don't ride that bike! Take it back to your yard, right now!"

His commands come too late. I've already started down the other side, and I'm busy trying to manage the sudden increase in speed and the need to switch from pushing the peddles forward to pushing them backwards. I've been practicing and I've taught myself how to do it. But I've not had to do it against the natural pull forward of a hill of this size.

The cross-street where I catch the bus has some dangers, and I know I need to slow way down to be sure no cars are coming. The bike wobbles when I do this, but I balance it. I don't come to a complete stop, because I worry I'll tip, but I slow enough to check both ways before I ease off the brakes and pick up speed for the rest of the hill.

Almost immediately, the speed is too fast for me.

I concentrate, adjusting for each new bump as I bounce over the uneven road.

If I try to stop or even start pushing on the brakes at this speed, I know I'll crash, so I hang on and focus on keeping the handlebars pointing forward . . . waiting for the inevitable.

But then I reach the bottom and the road begins rising. I continue to concentrate on keeping myself centered and the handlebars pointed straight. The bike rapidly slows. The original problems of balancing while going too fast are almost immediately replaced by the similar problems from going too slow.

Again, I manage to stay upright, and soon I'm peddling along at a safe speed.

What a rush!

I'm going to want to do that again!

But at the moment, I'm deciding I can ride all the way up Lane Five to Ward's Store. The rest of the way is fairly level. I've made it through the main challenge. Besides, I have a dime, and that can buy a big Hershey's Bar.

It's not far, but it takes me a while. There is no hurry. This is an adventure and I enjoy myself in the realization that

T

I've found a new way to venture beyond my boundaries. I pass a woman filling a children's swimming pool and she waves. Soon I pass the cross-street where the bus picks up the blonde girl I watch run for the bus.

This is great. A bicycle goes so much faster than walking or even running.

Then an Irish Setter comes barking after me. I'm okay with it, except he runs up to the side of the bike, and I worry I'll tip. I don't know how to get him to back-off. I shout, "Go away! Stop it!" That only encourages him.

I know I can't outrace him, so I slowdown. Maybe I can stop the bike and shoo him away. I slow it and wobble toward the side of the road.

He bumps my leg.

Nothing to do but fall.

I've fallen a number of times, and this is no different. I roll quickly out so the bike doesn't land on me. It's a good thing I'm wearing jeans and a shirt, or I'd have gotten more bruised than I do. As it turns out, all I get is a slight scrape on the palm of my left hand. My shirt gets a patch of grass stains, which I don't even notice. I do notice the weeds and grass that stick to my sweating arms. That's annoying and I do my best to brush them off.

The bike has also had this experience a number of times, and this is one of the softer crashes. It hits the soft dirt and grass along the side of the road, instead of the rough gravel and stones that would have given it a few scratches. Not that it matters much. JoAnn long ago forgot about her bike, so she'll not care what happens to it, and it's all banged up anyway.

T

The dog hasn't gotten hurt at all. In fact, he seems quite content, wagging his tail and watching as I pick myself up. At least he's stopped his barking.

This might be enough for others to turn back, but I can see the back and side of Ward's not far away, and I'm not discouraged at all. I'm not even mad at the dog, who obviously expects me to pet him before I worry about the bike, but once I do, he leaves me to get at whatever it is I want to do, and once I've managed to pull the bike upright and start peddling, he wanders away, apparently content that he has both conquered me and made me his friend.

It's funny. Mr. Porter's commands made me mad, even though he could have supported them by saying he was concerned for my safety, and the dog's actions don't, even though I might have been seriously hurt.

Ward's Store is a small convenience store backed by a bar at the corner of Lane Five and Three Points Boulevard. Lane Five rises up a small hill to the main road, and Ward's has a five foot rock wall along the lane that becomes only a foot high as the lane reaches the boulevard. This wall extends two feet beyond the edge of the building, and a rows of tall, thick bushes have been planted along its top, next to the store. The store front is ten feet back from the main road, so there is a small asphalt area, just large enough for a car to swing into for a brief stop.

Two older children I don't know stand in the bushes on top of the wall. The boy says, "Hey, kid, don't you think you're a bit small for that bike?"

I don't like the tone of his voice and ignore him.

"Hey, I'm talkin' to you!" He flicks his cigarette butt at me and it hits my cheek.

T

I stop the bike and step off it, letting it fall on the road.

The girl with him drops her cigarette and takes his arm. She looks briefly at me and says. "Sorry, it was an accident." Then she turns the boy and pushes him along the bushes toward the front of the store. "Come on. Leave him alone."

He doesn't resist. I watch as they make their way through the bushes and turn out of sight around the corner of the store.

I'm not sure what I was planning on doing. I'm not sure if it was an accident or not. The whole incident confuses me.

I'm also not sure where they've gone, and it might be the inside of the store, but I'm not going to let that stop me from buying my Hershey's Bar. I pick up the bike and push it the rest of the way up the hill, stirring up dust from the road as I go. It's not a large hill, only slightly more than the length of the building, so I soon reach the point where I can see over the diminishing height of the wall. No one is there.

The bike is a hard push for me, but I'm too young and stubborn to consider stopping. I don't even pause when I reach the top, but turn the handlebars in a sharp left, making a u-turn onto the edge of the main road and immediately into the store lot. The door is on the left front of the store, directly before me. I push the bike across the ten feet of dusty, cracked asphalt and lean it on the rusty pipe rail of the two-feet-high fence running above the rock wall. As usual, the weeds growing along it have caught discarded candy wrappers, cigarette packs, bottle caps and the broken glass of emptied pop and beer bottles. No one pays it much attention.

I pull the screen door open, paying no attention to the standard scraping squeak of the hinges. Upon pushing the heavy wooden door behind it, I hear the jingle of a bell above me, announcing my arrival, as the screen door slams shut.

T

The inside is dark, especially so after being in the bright sun. The small store consists of a central counter, something of an island room within the larger room. The walls of this smaller room only go half way to the ceiling, though there are posts that go all the way up. This turns the rest of the store into nothing more than a hallway between this island and the outside walls. The island, the front wall and the two side walls are crammed with groceries and other items people are likely to purchase out of convenience. While the back area of the store is not closed off, the shelves of merchandise end, and the rest of the room is clearly for use by the owners.

If I take the hall to my right and follow it around the corner to the back, I'll find a large icebox filled with bottles of pop for sale. While I'm not planning on purchasing pop, the icebox has a bottle opener on its side, and a metal box beneath it to catch the caps. I've started collecting bottle caps, and the store doesn't care if anyone wants those discarded caps, so I consider filling my pockets with them.

Just passed the icebox is a door on the side of the building to a side entrance hall. If I go left in this hallway, I pass through a door to the tavern.

At this point in my life, I've not been in the tavern, but later my curiosity will get me to briefly look inside. It is about twice the size of the store and seems even larger, since it is more open. The bar runs along the inside wall between the tavern and the store. In addition to the barstools, there are a dozen small tables with chairs, a jukebox and a pool table. I notice a couple of stuffed deer heads and a large fish on the walls. The jukebox is playing country-western music, and I suspect that's the norm. Later, an outside porch will be added to the tavern.

T

If I go right in the hallway, I exit the store through door into a gravel parking lot.

This parking lot extends to a combination gas station/auto repair shop. The doors into the repair shop are open during working hours, and a large fan sputters relief from the hot summer days. It is a working garage, filled with tools of the trade and an assortment of automobile parts in various stages of repair or ready to be hauled to the junkyard. The wall space not being used to hold cans of oil, washer fluid, and batteries is covered with old advertisements. Faded, stained, and torn, two larger ones with nearly naked women are what catch anyone's attention. There is also a Playboy on the top of a metal toolbox with a picture of Marilyn Monroe on the cover. This is a man's world, and any women needing to enter it have to accept that.

The world inside spills out onto the surrounding lot, where thin patches of tall weeds grow out of the gravel through bent fenders and axels, even though much of the ground has dark patches of spilled oil and transmission fluid.

The small office next to the garage is as unkempt as its surroundings. Its front consists of a door and a large window. The window is in serious need of a washing, perhaps past the point where it can be cleaned. The window frame, the door and the entire building need painting. Wasps circle down from a hive in the eve, and butterflies flit along the top of a row of weeds. Two old gas pumps stand guard over a driveway of gas spills that give the gravel a variegated array of browns.

It is possible the boy who hit me with his cigarette and this companion have walked to or passed this gas station. Either that, or they are in the store. Immediately upon entering, I

T

can see down the left and front halls, but I cannot see through the island to the hall with the side door.

An older woman with gray hair and glasses sits behind the counter. The large cash register is on her left and the candy is displayed on shelves directly in front of her. So I can easily walk down the hall to the left, make my purchase and leave. Or, I can quickly go a few feet to my right, peak around the corner, and confirm that no one else is in the store. I listen for a moment and decide I would hear if anyone else were there. If I decide to fill up on pop caps, I can do that after I make my purchase. So I walk to the candy. The woman looks down at me. "What can I help you with?"

Although I came knowing what I'm going to buy, now that all of the different kinds of candy are in front of me, I hesitate. The Topps bubble gum and baseball card packs are tempting. I don't like the gum, don't especially like any gum, but I have a small collection of baseball players, and it would be nice to buy some more on the chance I'll get a Mickey Mantle or Willie Mays.

The side door squeaks and bangs shut. Someone has just entered or exited the store. The woman doesn't even seem to notice. It would be easy for anyone to come in that door, steal a couple of bottles of pop or other things and walk away, but she doesn't worry because it doesn't happen.

It gets me to think that maybe I should buy a bottle of pop. It is hot out. "Sugar-free Bubble Up has a pizzazz; that is what sugar-free Bubble Up has" runs through my mind. And then I can grab a few bottle caps as well.

As I'm debating, a man appears in the hall. He's the one who came in the side-door. "Hi Jim," the woman says. "You want a pack of Camels?"

T

"Yes," he replies, trying to slide by me.

Feeling pressured to make a choice, I say, "An Almond Hershey's, please."

"You like chocolate?" Jim asks.

"Yeah." I put my dime on the counter.

"You know a chocolate bar that size would've cost $10 during the war."

"WWII?"

"Yeah. I was under old Blood and Guts when we marched across France and straight into Germany."

"Oh . . ." I know almost nothing about WWII.

"He was a real bastard," Jim continues.

The woman slides my candy bar across the counter and picks up the dime. "Yeah, I didn't hear much about the generals dying. Just sat behind their desks, looked over a bunch of maps, and sent thousands of soldiers out to get killed."

"Not Patton," Jim cuts in. "He was right out there at the front. He was a prick, but I have to give him credit. He had a lot of guts."

"Yeah, well, so did my brother. Only his got spilled all over the sands of Normandy," she takes Jim's quarter and hands him his pack of Camels.

He immediately breaks the plastic and rips open the top. "Lotta men died." He pulls out a cigarette, taps the end against the counter top and sticks it in his mouth.

"Yeah, lotta men died. Real men died because some bigwigs decided to send a bunch of poor men out to get shot."

Jim lights his Camel, takes a deep breath and exhales. "FDR had no choice. Nazi's and Japs would be running the world if we hadn't stopped 'em."

"Well, Commies are gonna blow-up the entire world any day."

"Can't blame that on Patton. He wanted to go straight through Germany and get rid of Stalin when we had the chance."

"Okay, you've got yer memories. I've got mine. Enjoy your smoke."

"Someone hits you, ya gotta hit 'em back. Otherwise, he'll just keep hitting you."

I slide beneath his arm and make my way out the door.

Dad didn't fight in the war. Mom said he had a double hernia and was not allowed to join the service. They never talked much about the war or other political matters. But everyone was worried about the build-up of nuclear weapons. There were constant television announcements explaining how we should create and stock our bomb shelters, though no one in our neighborhood did. We had test drills at school. An alarm would go off, and we would all immediately crouch under our desks. Then an announcement over the loud speakers would explain that we needed to do this and wait there until our teacher told us it was okay to stand.

We were also told that a Senator McCarthy was leading a fight against Communists. They're all around us. Even people we've known all our lives might be Communists, so we need to watch for signs, and if we suspect anyone, we need to alert authorities.

I wonder about the woman in the store. The man was a soldier under Patton, and he wanted to continue the fight. But the woman didn't. That sounded like she didn't want to kill the Communists. Why wouldn't she?

T

I'm not paying much attention as I push my Hershey's Bar in my back pocket and push JoAnn's bike out onto the asphalt.

I put my feet on the peddles, planning on making a quick turn onto the dirt road and heading home. Wow! On asphalt it rides much smoother and faster! The trip home is forgotten as I coast straight down the middle of the road!

While I recognize the houses from the many times I've passed them in our car or on the school bus, I don't know who lives in most of them. I know which children get off when the bus stops at the corners, but I don't know which house they run to.

Within minutes, I reach the lane leading to Al Carlson's house. It occurs to me I might peddle up the lane and see if any of the children are home, but decide I'd rather ride to where the road crosses through the swamp. Maybe there will be some turtles crossing or I can muck about in the edge of the lake. I've often seen it from the rowboat and on occasion pushed into the bulrushes and other swamp plants, but never pushed all the way to the road. And I've never been in the swamp on the other side of the road.

It's amazing how a bike can open up the world! It's time to move beyond the few blocks surrounding my house, the small park I walk to.

I wonder if JoAnn rode this same bike down the main road all the way to the end of Three Points. She must have. She would have been older. The bike is meant for someone older. Does that mean she didn't expand her world until she was older?

It's hard to imagine her riding a bike. But it is her bike, so she must have ridden it. Did she also like the feel of going down a hill fast? Did she have to fend off dogs? Did older children throw cigarette butts at her? Did she like Hershey's Bars?

T

I know she wasn't into baseball cards. And she might never have been to the garage/gas station. No one in my family has much interest in cars. I wonder if she would have felt intimidated by the male atmosphere of the garage, those nude posters. I doubt it. She has a strong personality and is not one likely to be bothered by such things. Did she ever go into the tavern behind the store? She probably did at some point. But it probably didn't amount to much more than my brief peek through the door. I doubt she would have found the country-western music any more attractive than I. The mounted deer heads and large fish wouldn't have mattered any more to her than to me. Nor would the pool table have meant much.

Did she play in the swamp when she was my age or at any age? Probably not. Girls don't like playing in swamps. Girls don't like turtles and frogs and snakes, though I suspect she wouldn't have been overly squeamish about them. She must have done some fishing, though I suspect not much.

Did she meet adults at Ward's Store who talked about Europe? What did she think about WWII and nuclear bombs and Commies when she was my age, whatever age she first rode her bike all the way to the swamp, or at any stage of her life?

I swing the bike around a gradual curve, and the swamp comes into view. I see the two beaver dens in Jenning's Bay and the Spanish style cottage half-hidden by the small hill where the land pushes into the swamp. As I reach the point where the road and swamp come together, I push back on the peddles and ease the bike off the asphalt. A redwing blackbird watches me from a bulrush, as I step from the bike onto the edge of the road. I grasshopper hits my leg and sticks. I reach down and brush it off. I can see a large Snapping Turtle on the road. These can be dangerous, and this one has a shell at least a foot in diameter. I

T

run over the hot tar until I get about five feet from it. The rough, nearly black shell has patches of moss growing on it. Its long tail with prehistoric, saw-teeth projections stretches into the weeds.

Its large head with a large mouth wide open moves from side to side. I know it has powerful jaws and a long neck that can suddenly lung forward.

It moves slowly forward. The tail completely comes out of the weeds. Almost daily, turtles get run over making this passage. Powerful jaws and hard shell are no match for an automobile.

While I want to help it make its journey across this human world it doesn't understand, and I know the way to do so is to grasp it firmly from the back on both sides of its shell, I also know the dangers of any kind of mistake. I slowly circle around to the back. It's going to be heavy.

It doesn't turn its head to follow my movements. But I don't know if that means anything.

The mossy shell is going to be slippery. If I should drop it, I might crack its shell or even worse it might find a way to latch onto me. It's unfortunate I can't make it understand I'm trying to help it. I've noticed humans often can't even understand that. But then, I've also noticed animals often understand such things better than humans.

I bend, grab the shell as tightly as I can, and hold it away from my body as I begin a dash across the street. It is heavy and slippery and I know it's going to slip out any second.

While the actual time it takes can't be more than a few seconds, the feel of time expands as if I'm caught in a slow-motion cinema moment. My fingers are throbbing. How can I

T

force them to stay clamped? My back aches from the awkward bend holding the turtle away from my body.

Half the way . . . two-thirds of the way . . . three fourths of the way . . .

I make it.

But the task isn't over. The next challenge is to set it down carefully. Just like the bike, once I get it moving fast, I have to bring it to a stop without crashing, only here I don't have the space for a gradual decrease.

It doesn't go so well. I stop my run, trying to I lean forward at the same moment, so I can reach the ground and set the turtle down gently, but I ask too much of myself and fall on top of it! Instincts take over. I am off that turtle and sitting on my butt on the hot tar before I have time to think. The turtle seems to have experienced a similar instinctual reaction. I see it quickly disappear into the weeds.

I'll bet JoAnn never had an experience like this.

It's enough for me to put my swamp adventure behind me. I walk back to the bike. By now, I've gotten close enough to the intersection where Three Points begins that I want to make it all of the way, so I climb on the bike and turn it towards the exit. Now the road climbs up a small hill and then descends down a sharper one to the exit. The climb up the hill is work, and I'm sweating by the time I reach the summit. Now, I can coast down. And this will be the fastest down ride yet.

But as thoughts do, a new one strikes me. As I near the bottom of the hill, where is turns slightly, a boy in my class gets off the bus and walks up his driveway. I no longer remember his name, but at the moment it strikes me a good idea to bike up his driveway and see if he's home.

T

It's a dirt driveway up a steep hill that circles through a woods to the house, not an easy bike ride, but with the energy of youth I make it. His house is as old and rundown as the rest of ours. It is on a hill and is surrounded by woods, so that's a plus. However, the yard is even more littered than the norm. A combination of innocence and boldness takes me to the door.

His mother answers. I ask if he's home, but before she answers, he is there, greeting me. I can't say I notice it, but I expect she is confused by this unexpected visit. If she has much say in it, she doesn't bother to use it. Instead, she is friendly, invites me in, and he leads me to their back-porch, a large screened-in porch filled as littered as the yard. We begin playing as if it's a natural, normal thing to do.

One thing does hit me consciously, and I still remember it. I am struck by how simple it is to expand my world. What I never thought to do until today, I'm doing, It's almost too easy.

His mother soon comes out with a pitcher of grape Kool-Aide and some peanut-butter cookies.

We play for hours, but then the afternoon begins turning to evening, and his mother tells me it's time for me to head home. My parents will be worried. Yes, she's right. Time has passed. An entire day has passed.

I've forgotten about my determination to make it to the beginning of Three Points. In the way children tend to think, I'm in the moment, and I need to get home as quickly as I can.

The initial ride down the gravel driveway is the most difficult part of the journey, and in my rush, I fall, sliding over the gravel and into the wooded ditch on the side of it. My pants get ripped and my thigh gets scraped, but I don't notice. It's hard to pull the bike back onto the driveway, but I'm driven by my realization of being gone too long. I yank the

T

handles and yank again until the weeds give way and the bike follows me onto the dirt. I'm immediately on the peddles, dirty and sweaty and focused.

I come off the driveway onto the asphalt. A loud honk nearly causes me to fall. I've pulled in front of a car. The man in it isn't happy and swears at me as he passes.

I nearly fall, but manage to keep the bike moving forward just fast enough to stay upright.

I push against the peddles, forcing the bike forward. It's made more difficult because I'm heading up the hill. But I focus, keep the handlebars in a rigid straight position and put all of my energy into each downward thrust. I begin to gain enough speed that I'm no longer in danger of tipping. After about twenty hard earned yards up, I reach the top, that moment of balance, when everything seems to stop for an instant. Then the bike crosses over and begins to pull me forward. I push backward on the peddles, meeting the new challenge of not going so fast I lose control, then begin easing off the brakes, until I'm coasting quickly down the other side, past the mostly hidden Spanish house. In seconds, the swamp and lake open up on both sides. I coast about half way across the swamp before the impetus from the hill loses its energy and I need to begin peddling. I'm not paying attention to the surroundings this time. My adventure has played out, and I want to get back to my home. I peddle around a curve, passed lanes one, two, three and four.

The sun has nearly set. I know Ward's store is just ahead, but I can only see it as a shadow. I push towards it. A sharp left on Lane Five takes me down the hill passed the store. Mom and Dad are going to be upset. I don't notice being tired, but peddle as hard as I can.

T

Then the inevitable happens. I hit a bump in the road and the bike careens out of my control. I let go of the handle bars and manage to roll clear of the bike. All-in-all, I'm lucky, suffering only a scrape on my left arm. And the bike doesn't suffer any major damage. Since it is already old and banged-up, the new scratches aren't going to be noticed.

I don't stop to think things through. I grab the bike, mount it and push the peddles to get it moving. No dogs or people are out at the moment, so I'm able to race home without interruption.

Finally, I get to the last hill, and push against the peddles to get the bike up it. At the top, I can see Mr. Porter standing in his yard. Fearing he'll yell at me, as he normally does, I look away from him. Good, he must be busy and I'm able to bypass him without a word. I've crossed the final gate. No need to peddle anymore. I coast down the small hill and into my yard.

I'm sure I'll get a mild reprimand from Mom and Dad, but nothing serious. And it was worth it. I'm not certain what it all means, but I sense I've opened myself to a larger world.

T

The Bus Stop

My first day of school. The adventure begins.

Knowing my excitement, Mom spends much of the morning doing her best to keep me distracted by playing Canasta. It really needs more than two players, but that's okay. I've been playing with Mom and her friends for some time and am good at it. I like being good at things, but today I can't keep my eyes off the clock.

"Let's go, let's go!"

"We'll be early. Let's play one more game."

"We won't have time!"

"If we don't finish, we can finish it when you get home."

Finally, she's ready to give in and walk me to the bus stop.

My brand new, Davy Crockett, coonskin cap covers my white-blonde crew cut, and its fake striped raccoon tail dangles down to the back of my matching Davy Crockett shirt with the long fringes on the sleeves. Mom says it's too hot a shirt to wear for summer, but I don't care, and she's willing to let me have my way on my first day.

Mom smiles and laughs as she walks me up Lane Five. The bus stop is not far, just passed Strand's aunt and uncle's house, Strand's house, the empty cottage halfway up the small hill, Porter's house at the top, and then partway back down the hill to where Woodland Road comes down a steep hill from Lane Six and crosses it.

While Lane Five continues to descend for another twenty yards, Woodland Road levels off at the intersection and continues passed the row of our neighborhood mailboxes half way to Lane Four and then all the way to Lane One. Lane One is little more than a driveway into a house surrounded by swamp, the "point" of Woodland Point, one of the three points that make up Three Points.

At the top of the hill Mom lets me run the final ten yards myself and walks onto Porter's large lawn that forms a small hill above the lane the rest of the way to the corner. Linda's mother is already sitting there, coffee in hand.

This will be the only year they do this. It's also the only year school is a half day, afternoons. The next year, I'll be meeting the bus before 8:00 am, and there will be children from first through sixth grade.

Whenever we get heavy rain, the dirt roads become undriveable, and we have to walk up Lane Five to and wait in the small parking lot in front of Ward's Store.

It's similar when there's a heavy snowfall, except it is cold, and it does get cold in Minnesota. Sometimes the snowfall is heavy enough for a "Snowday" – no school at all! However, depending on one's perspective, Minnesotans are prepared for both cold and snow, so it takes a heavy blizzard before the radios and televisions are given the go-ahead to make a Snowday announcement. On such days, I grab a snow-shovel and start knocking on neighbors' doors. The pay is small, but at my age, small seems large.

This corner will be the bus stop where I catch the school bus for the next thirteen years. They will be the most important years of my life.

But I can't possibly imagine that today.

I'm five-years-old.

Today is my first day of kindergarten.

T

Mom sits on the grassy hill of Porter's lawn with Marge, sipping coffee that's no longer hot and casually watching me to make sure I don't get too wild.

I am wound-up, so there is a steady stream of warnings, "Eddie! . . . Don't throw stones! . . . Leave Linda alone! . . . Stop running, you'll fall and rip your pants!"

Because the house across the street has a small garage at the intersection, we cannot see the bus coming down the hill until it's almost on top of us. Our moms know this, and so, without really thinking about it, they listen for its droning motor.

It's not long before they hear it. It stops on the top of hill, just out of sight. "Hurry! Get in in line! Stand in line! The bus is coming! Make sure you have your lunches and rugs! Don't forget anything!"

We scramble to gather our lunch boxes and push each-other as we try to get the front spot.

The commands continue, as the moms start down the hill to take control, "Stop it . . . Settle down! . . . Stay back! . . . Watch out! You'll get run over!"

But it's a false alarm. It's not the bus. It's the milkman. We watch as he drives his small, mostly yellow truck through the bus stop. Since there are no doors or seats, I can clearly see him standing behind the wheel, dressed in a white uniform and wearing a six-sided milkman's hat. The truck has been redesigned over the years for practicality, so he can easily walk out either door to deliver the milk, cream, eggs, ice cream and butter from his ice-cooled rear compartment and return with the emptied glass bottles, payments and weekly orders.

The mothers decide to wait with us rather than walk back up the grassy hill. As expected, it's a short wait.

T

The school bus is nearly to the corner when it emerges from behind the garage and shutters to a stop. The driver cranks open the doors. I follow Linda up the bus steps, past the young woman driver, past the front seats, past the other children and settle into a window seat near the back.

The driver waves at our parents, pulls the crank to shut the doors, and turns the bus onto Lane Five.

I'm in the present and too young to think about the symbolism of what just happened, but I have literally just stepped through a door into a new world.

It begins with my first bus ride to Shirley Hills Elementary School. Halfway up Lane Five there is one final stop, where I watch a young blonde girl come running through the woods to get on. Then the bus continues the rest of the way to Wards Store and turns onto Three Points Boulevard. Since it already passed this way when it came into the peninsula, there is no need to stop now. All that remains is for it to take us to school. Three Points Boulevard ends at Commerce Boulevard, where we take a left and quickly arrive at the few stores, churches and high school that are the town of Mound. We cross the railroad tracks that run through it and take an immediate left onto Linwood Boulevard, pass along the edge of a large swamp that connects up to Lake Minnetonka, and take a right up Wilshire. A couple of blocks later we arrive at my new world.

Shirley Hills is a two-story school located next to an old Indian burial site. The town's name does come from Indian burial sites, but not this one so much as a much larger site just west of the town. In either case, the sites long ago were deserted and lost beneath the growth of trees and general foliage. Nothing about the school grounds suggests it's near a burial site. The high school nickname, Mohawks, and its logo, an

T

Indian in full feathered headdress are a natural, though, as with the burial sites, the connections are tenuous. The Mohawks are an Indian tribe from the east coast, not from Minnesota.

The school yard is a large one, surrounding all sides of the school, but stretching especially out to the right side, where the initial asphalt and gravel area along the school building, containing a standard school-yard merry-go-round, monkey bars and swing-set, transitions into a grassy field that extends some fifty yards from the school before becoming a hill falling down into a swampy area that ends at Bartlett Boulevard.

The portion of this school yard closest to the front road, the road our school bus has just taken us up to reach the school, has a softball diamond with a metal fence backstop, and between that and the road, an asphalt tennis court with surrounding fifteen-foot-high metal fences.

Directly in front of the school, next to the tennis court, is a large grassy field with a sandbox. This is where our kindergarten teacher will let us out to play. One of my kindergarten memories of these recesses is when I chase David Japs and he accidentally runs into the corner of an open window frame sticking out from the top of the window, resulting in a nasty cut above his eye.

The central entrance at the front of the school is in turn fronted by a semi-circle driveway large enough to park and unload more than a dozen buses at one time.

The left front of the school has a small grassy area, not nearly as large as that to the right, and not used for anything. Behind this, to the left of the school, is the parking lot for the teachers. This asphalt area extends around the back of the school creating an asphalt area surrounding all of the school

T

except for the front. Behind the asphalt in the back of the school is a swing-set, and behind this a small grassy hill that leads to a small woods. The main thing I remember about the hill happens in third grade, when an informal ritual gets established. As we exit the entrance onto the playground, the fifth graders come running down the small hill to attack us.

It never results in any serious injuries, and in the curious way of such things, creates more a sense of comradery between the grades than the expected fear of being bullied.

I get off the bus for my first day and follow the rest of the students through the front doors. On the right side of us is the principal's office. We're ushered into the two doors on the left, which lead into the school gym, a room consisting of a two-story basketball court, with baskets on each end, and four other baskets that can fold down from the ceiling, two on each side. At the far end of it is a small stage.

Everything is mass confusion. The adults are herding us along the walls, and the walls are bouncing back the chatter of over 200 children. As we reach our places along the walls, we're told to sit down.

A woman I later learn is the principal walks determinedly into the front of the stage. "Welcome! Welcome! Please quiet down! Quiet! Please quiet down, so we can assign you to your teachers! Miss Carson, will you please announce your class!"

This begins a slow process. The girl in front of me (I will later learn her name is Julie) rolls on her back and stretches out her legs, which pushes up her skirt and reveals her panties. I'm too young to think anything more than that she shouldn't be doing this. It's wrong for her to show her panties. I'm not sure why, but it makes other girls sitting by me giggle. A boy next

T

to me begins rubbing his black dress shoes on the floor, making thick, black lines.

Once I finally get assigned, my teacher quickly leads us out of the gym to our classroom. It's located on the front side of the building, just past the principal's office. We each have a desk. We each also have a rug for our afternoon nap. Some of the children are not completely potty-trained and have brought extra cloths in case they wet their pants during their naps.

One student, a skinny boy named Willie, has a skin disease that causes him to have permanent problems with scabs. Even more sad for him, he has some mental problems as well. However, he's always smiling. Unfortunately, what his smile often brings him in return is not so friendly. Other students immediately begin making jokes.

At the moment, I'm too busy taking in my new world and trying not to lose my Davy Crockett lunch box and coonskin hat to concern myself with the developing group dynamics.

Our teacher sits us in a circle on the floor and asks us to count as high as we can. Only three of us can count to 100. Since I've been playing Canasta and other card games, I can also add, subtract, multiply and divide, but that's not expected of me.

What is expected is that I behave. Right next to the part of the classroom where we sit to count is a closet, and it immediately becomes a frightening place, because the teacher tells us that's where we're going to be put if we misbehave.

T

Logic

It's a curious duality. My abilities at logic and math suggest a person not prone to musing about illogical, enchanted realities, or, a person sensitive to other's opinions and feelings. Yet . . . I find getting locked in a closet or punished in physical ways isn't as bad as being misjudged with no recourse.

"Eddie! You're supposed to be doing your mathematics assignment!"

"I'm done."

"Sure! Let's see it!"

I open my desk and take out the sheet.

"Really?" she says, obviously not believing.

"Yes. It's easy," I say.

"Well, I've been told you're good at math, but this is just too fast."

"Why?"

"Okay, okay, so explain this first question. Add together all of the numbers from 1 to 100."

"Well . . . I'm not sure how to explain it. It's just easy."

"Either you can explain how you did it or you cheated. So . . . if that's your response, then I'm going to have to assume you cheated."

"Okay . . . well . . . for 100, it's easy, because all I did was to add pairs of numbers. 1 plus 100 is 101. All of the pairs will equal this. So . . . I'll have 50 numbers that each equal 101. All I need to do is multiply 101 times 50, and that's 5050."

"But . . . wait . . . okay . . . let me think about this. So . . . you take the middle number between 1 and 100, and that's how many pairs you'll have. Okay. Then, you know that each pair will add up to 101. Right?

"Yes."

"Then, you multiply 101 by 50, right?"

"Yes."

"And you figured this out all by yourself?"

"It's really not that complicated."

"For someone your age, it is! I don't like cheaters!"

T

Willie

Teachers also make well intentioned mistakes about other qualities in me.

"Okay, Willie, I'm going to put you in a desk right up here. That way you'll be close to me, and you can ask me if you need any help."

"Eddie, you're going to be in the desk right behind him. He likes you, and you can help him. And the rest of you are going to stop teasing him! If I catch anyone making fun of Willie, you're going to lose your playground time! And if it continues, I'm going to contact your parents!"

Great! I think. Why is it always me?

Jesus picks up a stone. "The water is serene."

Mr. Orange bends and finds a smooth stone for himself. He runs his thumb over it, caresses the timeworn surface, so pure it has a sense of being soft. "Crystal clear. See the fish — pumpkinseed, bluegill, perch ... rock-bass."

"They say I am a fisher of men."

"Yes. And they say you walk on the water."

"They say many things."

"What of Eddie?"

"He must be what he must be." Jesus gently tosses his stone into the water and watches the circular ripples. "Each person is a center. Each person sends ripples through God's universe."

"Is it so pure?"

"Each of us is a luminary, a spirit. It can be no other way."

Mr. Orange gently casts his stone into the water and its circles began intersecting with those of Jesus' stone. "But the lake's surface is not pure. It is the texture of many centers."

"There are many truths, even more beneath the surface."

"But 'you' are the truth!"

"And I am a contradiction."

"Not if one looks 'between' the ripples."

"Within the ripples."

"It is the dance, isn't it?"

"Yes . . . and the music that gives it rhythm."

"A pattern, a texture, a meaning."

"A voice."

"In the beginning was the word."

"God's breathe on the water."

"And thus did the dance begin."

"Light and shadow."

"Always in motion."

"Look, deep in the water. Can you see?"

"The movements beneath the surface?"

"The surface is but the skin. Beneath it beats the heart and the soul, the spirit of the universe."

"God?"

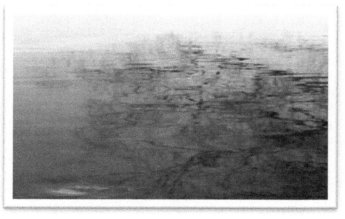

T

Lost Fish

Psychological punishments come in many forms, not all of them in school.

Keith Larson has a new rod-and-reel and is going to cast for large-mouthed bass. I have a bamboo pole with fishing line, plastic, red-and-white bobber, small lead sinker and copper hook to fish for the smaller pan fish — crappies, perch and pumpkinseed. Keith has a small tackle box with the lures he intends to use. I have my rusty coffee can of dirt and worms. Keith is understandably proud of his more expensive, fancier equipment and has us both convinced that his fishing is the important part of our experience. I'm along to witness his catch.

We walk to the beach and out on a dock just the other side of it. I kneel, dig into my can of dirt, find a night crawler and begin working it onto my hook.

Keith walks farther out on the dock. "Watch," he says.

I look up. He swings the lure behind him, then jerks it forward, casting it in an arc about twenty yards out onto the water. "See," he says. "This is how it's done."

I know how to cast and am not impressed but say nothing. Instead, I go back to getting the worm on my hook while he reels in his line.

Soon he's ready for his second cast. "Watch," he says again. "This time I'm going out farther. That's where the big ones are."

Again, I watch. By now I have my line in the water, but I really don't need to watch my bobber — I'll feel it if a fish takes the bait.

As with the first cast, his lure lands with a splash some twenty yards away, and he begins slowly reeling it in. This goes on for a while, neither of us catching anything. I'm getting bored. He's getting annoyed, finally commenting, "You're bad luck. I'm going to come back without you."

Just at that moment I feel a tug on my line. I tug back to set the hook. I can tell immediately it's a heavy fish. There is no back-and-forth reeling it in. I have but a short line on a pole. It's a simple swing up onto the dock. As long as the fish doesn't fall off over that ten feet of water, I've succeeded. Seems simple. However, larger fish often do fall off. The hook is not big enough to hold them. But this time the hook holds. I've caught a large-mouthed bass about ten inches long. "Wow!" I exclaim and quickly slip the metal prong from the stringer through its gill and out its mouth to make sure it doesn't flop or slip back into the lake. Then I work the hook loose.

"Dumb luck," Keith says, turning away and sending his longest cast yet into a patch of small ripples.

As negative as he means his comment, he is right. Barely aware of what I'm doing, I put another worm on my hook and swing it out so the bobber plops onto the surface about ten feet from the dock. This is a major catch.

I want to rush home and show Mom. There's no reason to stay. Keith is obviously unhappy and whatever I might catch from now on will be anticlimactic.

I decide to leave and am about to pull my line out of the water when I feel another tug. I automatically jerk back to

T

set the hook and lift. Even before it breaks the surface I can feel it's heavier than usual and knew I have something big.

What?! No! Can't be! Another large-mouthed bass! Even bigger than the last! "Look! Look! I did it again!" I exclaim as I swing the fish onto the dock. I quickly set the pole down so I can secure the fish with both hands. I hold it tight with my left while I bring up the chain stringer and slide a clip through its gill. Now I have it and can work the hook loose. I loop the stringer over the dock pole and drop the secured fish into the water. I don't have to think about being careful. I've grown up fishing and know better than to make a careless move and lose my catch.

I've been focused on the task, but now I smile up at Keith, expecting him to be as excited as me.

He isn't smiling and doesn't say a word. That's right, I remember. He's in a bad mood. He turns away and flings a cast as hard as he can. It's too hard. There's a technique to casting, and as with all sports, it involves timing. Brute force isn't what it takes. So instead of a longer one, his cast falls short. He immediately reels it in and casts again with the same result.

He never looks back at me but apparently he gets over his initial frustration, because he settles into a steady routine of casts in the range of his earlier ones. Since he faces the water rather than me and says nothing, I can only guess at his thoughts. But it isn't hard. I know he's mad. The joy inside me that made it difficult not to smile is matched by the anger in him.

While I want to leave, I decide it best to let him fish for a while before saying anything.

T

Neither of us catches anything over the next half hour. Then he begins to talk. "You know you're going to have to throw the bass back, don't you?"

"What do you mean?"

"Bass season hasn't even begun yet, and you need a license."

"What?"

"The season doesn't begin until next week."

"No one will even know."

"Good luck with that. They're checking all the time. If you want to get in trouble with the law, it's up to you."

He has me worried, but I'm not ready to give up my fish. "I'll take my chances. No one will ever know." No one in my entire life has ever mentioned fishing licenses or seasons when it's legal to fish on Lake Minnetonka. I think he's making all this up, but I'm too young to know for sure. Still, I'm not about to give up my prize catches.

He can see I'm going to take my chances. In a more friendly tone, he says, "Well, guess we might as well go. Nothing seems to be biting. Here, you take the poles. I'll get the fish." He hands me his rod and reel. I carry them and my pole to the shore and lean them against a tree. When I turn to walk back, I can see he's just pulled the fish out of the water and has the chain stringer in his right hand. It's a moment I'll never forget, him standing on the dock, holding the stringer with the two large bass . . . smiling.

"I'll get the worms," I say and start out onto the dock.

He turns and drops the fish into the lake! "Oops."

"What!"

"Sorry, they . . . . . slipped." He says

T

Mr. Orange

It bothers me . . . .

Mr. Orange is a quiet man . . . enigmatic . . .

Sometimes that's fine, even good.
Sometimes the sharing of silence is what I like.

Sometimes we sit or lie at the end of the dock on those hot summer days when fantasy worlds of cumulous clouds float serenely through a cerulean blue and I can hear the lullaby of the water . . . lap . . . lap . . . lap-lap . . . lap . . . lap . . . lap . . . lap-lap . . . lap . . . .

I like the heat of the sun quietly easing away the tensions in my muscles . . . the soft gusts of wind . . . .

Sometimes I close my eyes and let the warmth and the murmuring-of-the-lake lull me asleep. When that happens, I'm never sure if Mr. Orange will still be there when I wake.

Then, there are the times we explore the shoreline, pushing through patches of bulrushes, climbing over the underbrush on a steep bank, wading into the water to get past trees, and trying to keep from falling off half submerged rocks. On occasion, we catch a glimpse of a garter snake as is slithers away from us, but more often we just hear it. We also hear frogs and turtles plop into the water, and if we pause to look for them, we can see their heads poke above the surface to watch us pass. Sometimes the branches above us fill with the chatter of birds – blue jays, sparrows, titmice, finch, redwing-blackbirds . . . a seemingly endless variety.

The terrain itself is rich hodgepodge that includes more friendly stretches of sand, often mixed with small stones worn smooth, even smaller pebbles, and random strings or clumps of water plants (what we group under the vague term seaweed) that have washed ashore and are in various stages of drying and decomposing in the sun. On occasion, we encounter a dead fish, usually partially eaten and almost always attracting flies, roaches and worms.

If we pause to move a log or rock, we sometimes see salamanders darting for safety. If we stop for a moment, perhaps sit on a larger rock, and gaze over the water, we usually see a dragon fly or more hovering, hear and sometimes see fish breach the surface. If the surface is still and we look carefully, we can see the skater bugs zigzagging over the surface. Sometimes a muskrat passes some thirty feet off the shore. Sometimes mallards, wood ducks, and swans swim in-and-out of the large rocks and tall water grass, just out of our reach.

Today, we stand on the shore but twenty yards from the dock. I look at the billowing clouds floating over the point. It's too far away to make out details, but I can see small forms I know are seagulls circling above it.

"You're wrong," I say. "Time is not real. If it were real, you could touch it . . . or taste it . . . or smell or hear or see it."

I catch the hint of a smile. He isn't looking at me. He's busy brushing away the white gauze of dandelion seeds that blows against his light blue work-shirt.

T

"Tell me. Can you touch time? Is it rough? . . . Smooth? Dry? Wet? Hot? Cold? Solid? . . . Slimy?" I push my foot into the sand. "Can you feel it like I feel the wet sand sliding into the cracks of my toes?"

"Sometimes I can 'feel' it as it moves," he says, still busy brushing off his shirt. After a couple of final swipes, he looks up. "Sometimes it gets out of joint and moves in a jerky, jarring pace – a frantic rush."

He pauses. "Then again, sometimes it's annoyingly slow." He smiles, "It's moody . . . like an old friend."

"Aaaahh!" Why does he always have to get so . . . so . . . poetic? I'm not after musings about old friends. What does time have to do with an old friend? I'm not going to get sucked into that. "How about its taste?"

He tilts his head, wrinkles his brow and looks at me from under his eyelids, a visually ironic expression of the words, 'seriously . . . you're being serious'.

I ignore his look and continue, "Is it bitter? Is it sweet? . . . Does it need more salt? . . . Does it make your lips pucker-up like the sour juice of a green apple?"

"Yes," he says. "Yes, it 'does' seem bitter at times." He laughs.

I ignore his amused response. No, that's not completely true. It's more accurate to say I try to ignore it. Damn him! Why does it matter what he thinks, anyway?

"Perhaps you can also 'smell' it. Tell me, Mr. Orange. Does it 'smell' good? . . . Does it 'smell' of . . . of . . . fresh, wet earth and the clean breezes off the lake, or does it smell of . . . the damp swamp and dead, rotting carp?"

"Time is a rich bouquet of smells, a wonderful tapestry of all the smells that ever were."

T

"Not talking Hallmark card here, talking about 'real' time." I have to smile. That response came out of nowhere, a quick, clever banter to counter him.

He does seem to notice, "Oh, the smells 'are' real."

I search for more comparisons, better ones. There has to be a way to get him to take me seriously. How can I make him understand? "How about the sound of time? Tell me. Is the 'sound' of time pleasant . . . like the wind gently rustling through the trees . . . or is it filled with irritating sirens, like . . . like a police car?" These are too vague. I look over the lake. There are no boats with motors whining, but we both know the sound. "Can you hear it like the sound of an Evinrude coming across the bay?"

He laughs. "A 'rude' moment or a friendly one?"

How can I break through his causal humor? A bit louder, in a more demanding tone, "Perhaps you can 'see' time. Tell me. Is it a pretty sight? Does it drift on a blue sky like those clouds above the point, or . . . does it look like a dirty bag of someone's garbage dumped randomly along Game Farm Road? Tell me, Mr. Orange, tell me why you believe that time is real."

"Is sad the countryside is not as pure as it was but a few years ago." He bends down and picks up a flat, dark-gray stone worn smooth from centuries of caressing currents. After examining it, he skips it on a lazy trek across the water – slap . . . slap . . . slap . . . slap-slap. "We all die, Eddie."

A patch of the clouds above the channel takes on the shape of a giant dragon. Smoke in the form of wispy clouds billows out of its mouth. It seems to be surveying the lake, searching for something . . . something . . . perhaps watching the two of us, perhaps debating whether or not to float down on a summer breeze and land on the gently rippling water that flirts with

T

our naked feet, perhaps considering whether to swoop over me, grasp me in its claws and fly me into the world where dragons exist.

Then it turns and disappears into other, more distant clouds, and I know that the moment has passed.

T

Charlotte's Web

Third Grade.

In many ways, it begins the same as the previous two years, the same bus ride, assignment of teachers in the gym, and initial overview of the rules and regulations.

I like my third grade teacher.

She and one of the fifth grade teachers are friends, and they are constantly pulling pranks on each other. One day, our teacher has us go to the fifth grade classroom on the second floor when the class is at lunch and carry all of its desks into another room. Then we wait for the fifth grade teacher to return with her class. Soon we hear them coming down the hallway and going up the stairs.

We smother our laughter until they are out of range. Then we can't contain ourselves.

How long before the teacher comes bursting through our door?!

It's not long.

"Okay! What have you done with my desks?" she says and an annoyed but friendly way.

We're all laughing. The teacher shushes us.

"They're in the empty room a couple of doors down," our teacher says.

How can one not like a teacher who turns a school day into such a fun series of jokes? But it's more than this.

I still remember her reading a chapter of *Charlotte's Web* to us each day. How can one not like a teacher who does this? I don't know *Tuck Everlasting* at the time, nor is it likely I would have made the connections, but when I do read it, I also immediately make the connection of the Ferris Wheel Fern runs to ride on with Henry Fussy with Natalie Babbitt's Ferris Wheel. I will later meet and become friends with Natalie Babbitt. And I will point out to her that connection. Just as she uses the Ferris Wheel in reference to the stages of life, so does E. B. White. After all, Fern deciding she'd rather play with Henry Fussy than her childhood fantasy world of animals is clearly meant to indicate she is growing up.

The stages of life. All of us go through them. It's the natural progress of life. Stories express this wonderfully through metaphors, symbols and analogies. The four seasons in a year are a perfect match for the stages of a human life, and the death of one year giving birth to the next matches the natural continuance of life from one generation to the next.

But sometimes the natural order gets upset.

Sometimes one season isn't allowed to complete its intended time.

The stages of life.

I'm about to go through a major one.

And I'm not ready for it.

T

A Kodak Brownie 8mm

"Over here. The light needs to be behind me."

Mrs. Blood laughs. "Okay, Dearie. How about this?" She circles around and takes a pose as if mocking a wealthy woman on the beach of the Del Coronado from the 1950s. She has purposely dressed to fit the part.

Mr. Bones laughs. "Yes! Yes! Perfect! Now just hold your head back as if you're too good to bother with it all!"

Mrs. Blood looks up and to the side, but can't hold the pose. They both break down laughing.

"Come, come, Sweetie," Mr. Bones says through his laugher. "We must capture this!"

"Yes, yes," Mrs. Blood says and tries to compose herself.

It takes a few more failed efforts before they finally manage to capture the desired pose.

Then they walk into the Coronado bar, talking and laughing the whole way. Once they are seated and have ordered their drinks, Mr. Bones asks, "Darling, do you remember when Eddie's parents buy a motion picture camera?"

Mrs. Blood pauses. "Yes, I remember. Kodak comes out with the Brownie 8mm."

"Yes, that's the one. Do you remember the commercials Ozzie Nelson does for it? Points out how it has three different lenses—wide lens, normal lens, and close-up."

"Yes." She laughs. "I remember . . . the one where his two sons are playing badminton, and he demonstrates it, focusing on Ricky. Wasn't Ricky a dream!"

"Oh, stop it! You sound like one of those thirteen-year-old girls." He laughs.

The waiter returns with a bottle of champagne in a bucket of ice.

Mr. Bones greets him, "Oh! Yes! Champagne! It's the drink that brings tiny bubbles to all of life! Here . . . please . . . please . . . set it over here." As he directs the waiter, he continues the memory of the commercial, "And then some announcer's voice gives the purchasing price." Just $6 down, and less than $60 total."

"Yes," Mrs. Blood says. "Eddie's parents are quite proud of it."

"Take pictures of JoAnn's band trip to Canada."

"Bad pictures! Mainly just bad pictures of the scenery as his Mom rides the bus. She has volunteered to be a chaperone."

"Eddie still remembers selling magazines for the school to earn money so the band can make the trip."

"All of the students in all of the grades."

"Yes, yes, yes. Remember, it's a competition, and students get prizes if they sell enough subscriptions?"

Mr. Bones picks up a cracker and scoops up a full bite of caviar. "Beluga! My favorite!" He scoops another and eats it. "Eddie's mom subscribes to Better Homes and Gardens and Life"

Mrs. Blood brings her champagne to her lips but hesitates taking a sip. "Do like those little bubbles. They tickle!" She lets the bubbles do just that and giggles, then continues the conversation. "That's what makes it all work. Parents feel they 'have' to buy subscriptions."

"Remember, Eddie's parents take motion pictures of the following Christmas."

"Yes, oh, yes, what a mess. They can't figure out the lighting."

T

"Such poor photography."

"Well, what do you expect? They don't know what they're doing. Have no idea how to make the lighting work."

"It's especially difficult indoors."

"Bright lights needed to be set from the correct angle."

"And, of course, the instructions are impossible to sort out."

Mrs. Blood laughs. "Isn't that always the case. Well, it's okay. They don't let it get them down."

"Most of the footage is too poor to be of much use."

"Yes, Dear, they have more footage of glaring lights than anything else."

Mr. Blood sets down his glass. "Remember the brief footage of Gordy?"

"Looking shy and awkward."

"A nice man."

"Yes," Mrs. Blood remembers. "Hope his life went well."

"Nice men finish last!"

"Maybe not. Is that the hat from Fred Astaire's *Top Hat* movie?"

Mr. Bones picks up his Top-hat and looks at it. "No, Sweetie, a duplicate."

"Remember the amazingly clear footage they took of a large Red Headed Woodpecker busy driving his beak into a tree in the yard."

"Yes, in terms of the quality of the picture, it was the best they took."

"And I can still hear its beak hitting the tree."

"Yes, that's what alerted them to him being there."

"And the footage of John, just five years old."

"Was it five?"

"Maybe four. Not important."

T

"So serious as he tries to get a litter of puppies all in a box, only to have them immediately jump out of it and bound away."

"And the footage of the final trip to the rented cabin up north."

"The most poignant of all the footage they took."

The conversation has accidentally taken a sad turn.

"Eddie's ninth birthday."

"The water so clear it's possible to see the pan fish coming up to his dad's legs as he stands waist deep at the beach."

"And they actually capture it on film."

They grow silent, remembering.

"Oh . . . sorry . . . I'm tearing up."

"I might join you," Mr. Bones says quietly.

They sit in silence and sip their champagne.

"Reels of film – fragments of a life."

"Packed away in a box and forgotten."

"Disintegrating."

"Moments tossed in a pile of boxes in the basement."

"Separated . . . scattered among the discarded heirlooms . . . becoming junk needing to be garbaged.

"The format, so exciting an innovation at the time, becoming outdated . . . to the point of being irretrievable."

"Preserved memories."

"Disintegrating until they are gone forever."

"Same as a human life." It is not intentional . . . but the moment she says it, Mrs. Blood realizes the connection. Again they pause, sip their champagne and remember.

"Lives live on in memories, all the people who were touched." Mr. Bones' eyes are distant.

T

Mrs. Blood feels his sorrow and touches his arm, "Like ripples on the surface of the water, flowing and flowing and . . . disappearing."

"The children . . . maybe the grandchildren . . . friends . . . people whose lives were changed."

"Change . . . must be . . . a definition of life." He has let the ripples take him far off shore. She can see he is floating away from her.

"A tautology . . . with birth there must be death." He says it, but his voice suggests he is mouthing words. He has disconnected from the dialogue.

"Each time the cosmos changes . . . the old cosmos ends."

"With each sunrise there must be a sunset. Each morning must bring an evening . . . each evening a morning."

"Or the universe is still and lifeless."

"The camera, the projector, the film . . . artifacts of a time gone by." Is he there now? She wonders if he's reliving it. Most likely.

"A childhood," she says. "It's a childhood. That makes it important. He needs to understand it."

Her comments reach him as distant whispers. He hears them, stores them somewhere in the corners of the huge labyrinth. Perhaps, perhaps one day he will stumble on them. He continues, "A time that only exists in the world of once-upon-a-time, the eternity of time beyond its own boundaries."

"The Underwood typewriter goes back even further, back to his mom's college days," she says, perhaps to try and bring him back, perhaps to try and bring herself back.

"To the time before Eddie was born."

"And yet to his time as well."

"Yes, still alive and part of his world."

T

"The same physical presence in two different worlds."

"Actually, in many different worlds."

"And timelines."

"All intersecting—multiple worlds intersecting."

"All existing at the same time, and yet having different extensions."

The Joker laughs.

They can't see him dancing on the edge of the universe.

But they know his laugh.

It brings them back.

"Fine," Mr. Bones says, running his finger along the rim of the champagne glass. "Fine . . . fine—so . . . Eddie's childhood . . ."

"Even before his dad dies, Eddie is finding jobs to keep himself busy."

"Sometimes helpful."

"Sometimes even paid."

Mr. Bones sighs, "Guess we'll need another bottle." He waves the waiter over. As he waits, he continues the conversation, "With a few notable exceptions, it's a community where people wander into others' yards without much concern about inappropriately intruding or trespassing."

"For the children, most of the yards and woods and swamps and lakes and streets and shoreline is legitimate for games of capture-the-flag, hide-and-go-seek, and wherever their imaginations take them."

They know they are only mouthing the same scattered phrases . . . a way to keep from thinking about it.

"And collecting rocks . . ."

T

"And pine cones."

"And picking wild flowers . . ."

"And berries."

"And capturing everything . . ."

"Butterflies . . ."

"Fireflies . . ."

"Moths . . ."

"Spiders . . ."

"Stick beetles . . ."

"Salamanders . . ."

"Frogs . . ."

"Toads . . ."

"Turtles . . ."

"Snakes . . ."

"Rabbits . . ."

They laugh.

The waiter arrives, the new bottle is ordered, and they sit in silence.

Mr. Bones says, "Forts of different types are built by clearing out the weeds and piling up branches of deadwood or even living bushes with leaves still attached."

"Yes, and there are a number of long diserted houses."

"True, some only partially built."

"Some with bricks and lumber strewn about the undergrowth."

"Great for Eddie's endless need to create. He can clear the underbrush and use the bricks to build whatever his imagination comes up with."

"A few times, the neighbors let his mom know they think he's gone too far. After all, they say, this is someone's property.

T

No one seems to know whose or why it's been abandoned for decades, but someone owns it."

"At the same time, these same neighbors find this drive in him useful."

"True, no matter how annoying he might be, he is a conscientious, hard worker."

"He most certainly does a lot of digging!"

They laugh. They've done it! Managed to work their way back to happy.

"All those basements getting dug out by hand!"

"Not sure why it gets sparked at that particular time, but family after family decides to dig out their basement."

"Not sure of the timing, but it is how poor people in their situation can improve their houses."

"True. Let's face it, their houses are little more than fishing cabins."

"Most have no plumbing."

"Outhouses instead of indoor toilets."

"Even the foundations are little more than amateurish stacks of bricks or large pieces of timber."

The waiter arrives with the new bottle and pours it into their empty glasses. They pay him little attention.

"Those wanting to improve their cabins roll up their sleeves and do what they can."

"If it costs any real money, it can't be done."

"But digging by hand doesn't cost much."

"Shovels, picks, wheelbarrows, pails."

"Eventually basement bricks, sand, mortar.

"And a steady supply of beer."

They clink their glasses. "Cheers!"

"Maybe Eddie's dad's the one who starts it."

T

"He gets his done first."

"Well . . . not finished. It's never finished."

"True . . . but the digging is, or at least most of it."

"And Eddie's already a trained digger!" Mrs. Blood giggles. "Wow, the bubbly is starting to hit me!"

"Sounds like a Dickens' novel!"

"A rural version of London's working class!"

"A Pip!"

"Or an Oliver Twist!"

They both embrace the giddy feelings caused by the champagne.

"Whatever he is, he's willing to dig, and the neighbors like a young boy willing to dig."

"Yes, diggers . . . everyone always likes diggers!"

"Like that horse in Animal Farm! What was his name?"

"Boxer."

"Yes! That's the one!"

"Boxer's not a digger!"

"Stop it! You know what I mean!"

"Bill Howell's the first. He lets Eddie help dig out his walk-in basement."

"No pay?"

"They see it as being kind enough to let Eddie dig, more in the sense of putting up with him."

"Bill's house is on a hill so the side facing the road is a full story up. All he has to do is dig straight into that dirt foundation.

"Much easier! No need to haul the dirt up from under the house!"

"Most certainly!

T

"And he has an easy solution for disposing of the dirt as well."

"He loads a wheelbarrow, pushes it a few yards down the road and dumps it into the small swamp across the street."

"By the time he's finished, he's created a path wandering through the swamp from Lane Four to Lane Three."

"Though someone else owns that property."

"Actually two separate pieces of property are involved."

"No one knows who the owners are nor cares."

"It's nice to have a path cutting through the swamp."

"Then McClouds decide to dig out their basement."

"Turn it into a drive in garage."

"Yes, since they live on the top of Lane Four, across the street from Frahms, they also have the hill coming up to their house, creating two stories on the side away from the lake."

"Where they have their driveway."

"So, as with Bill Howell, they can dig straight in."

"And they're willing to let Eddie dig whenever he feels like it."

"He likes their small shovel that can be bent at the top of the scoop and turned into a small pick-like tool to chop the clay, then bent back and fastened tight to use as a shovel."

"Gerbers even pay him to help lay sod."

"Not couched as doing him a favor."

"No, they see him as a young boy they can hire cheap to do some yardwork, rather than as one of their friends' children they can let play in their dirt."

"They would never consider letting him play in their dirt."

"Yes, it is an example of two separate classes of people. Gerbers are one of the wealthier families sprinkled about the

T

neighborhood. Their house on the lake is truly a summer house, a second house – not a fishing cabin turned into a house."

"Yes, and yet a second house that is better than most of the neighborhood's main houses."

"A different social stratum."

"Noblesse oblige."

"Doubt Gerbers think of it in such grandiose terms. They're simply looking for cheap labor."

"Eddie's too young to understand or care."

"Social status means nothing to him."

"Yes, Eddie's exploring his world, and if he gets involved with a neighbor's project, he sees it more as an adventure than a task, and if he gets paid, it's an extra – even if he is way underpaid. He has no idea what he should be paid."

"Okay . . . is this a trait . . . something that will help?"

"He does a lot of tasks on his own, some of them not what the neighbors' want."

" But he doesn't make such distinctions. He sees unorganized landscapes and he likes to organize them, give them a frame, a purpose."

"He turns abandoned lots of discarded bricks and boards into cleaned up lands with play houses and patches of woods into storied lands with tree forts. He digs shallow caves in the banks where the land rises above the lake."

"In the winter, he creates endless paths and forts and imaginary worlds through the snow, and he can always make some money shoveling sidewalks and driveways after a storm."

"It never even occurs to him that he might not be getting paid enough to make it worthwhile."

"What's he doing? What is this all about?"

"Well . . . he's giving order to chaos."

T

"Is that it? Is that the drive? Some kind of need to put an order or pattern on things?"

"Well . . . it's what he's doing."

"It's a kind of accomplishment."

"He needs to accomplish things."

"And he's doing this *before* his father gets cancer."

"Inborn?"

"Certainly seems to be," Mrs. Blood puts her right hand to her forehead. "Think I've had enough."

Mr. Bones laughs. "Well, my dear, you seem to be in your cups!"

Mrs. Blood looks up at him, her eyes bloodshot. "What does that even mean . . . in my cups?"

Mr. Bones laughs. "Don't ask me . . . maybe it means you're about to faint into your cup or glass of champagne. But . . . back to the point. How is worth to be judged. If he never even bothered to consider being underpaid, and he chose to do it, it was worth it for him. Wasn't it?"

"Maybe the neighbors were right, after all. Maybe they weren't using him, but enabling him?"

"Are you stating or asking?"

"Not sure. Do you have any aspirin? . . . Waiter!"

"What were we doing . . . oh, yes, taking pictures! Yes! Just a moment. Here we are! Oh you're going to *love* this picture!"

T

Summer Theatre

As I cut across my yard for the door, I see Linda coming down the hill on Lane Four. Though her house is but one closer than Jackie's, she's my age and gets drawn into the group activities more, at least when we're still young, before her family moves out of the neighborhood.

"Eddie!" she calls.

That's unusual, and more likely to mean something negative than positive. While we interact and can get along with each other, we're more likely to engage in banter and one-upmanship than as friendly childhood playmates. After all, we're at the age where girls and boys are prone to do this. I'm reminded of a time a few years ago when she calls out to me from the same place. Keith is with me, and she brags about getting more "A" grades than both of us in school. Of course, I brag back that all by myself I get more than her.

Her house is a small one at the top of the hill she's coming down. It's on a band that rises from the left side of the road, just enough for a drive-in garage beneath it. Her backyard runs along part of Tom's back yard and then part of Strand's original back yard. I'm told her dad is an administrator in the school system, but neither know nor care enough to learn more than that. One thing I know is that he practices archery in his backyard, because I can look from my backyard and see the bales of hay he has stacked for his targets through the bushes and wire fence surrounding his yard.

"Is Keith with you?" she calls as she turns towards Strand's house, which means she's heading to connect with Carol.

"No . . . Why?"

We're putting on a play, and you and Keith can both be in it!"

"No thanks." Doesn't take any thought to know I don't want to be in another one of their plays.

"Yes! Really! You can play knights! Just pick up Keith and meet us at Janet's!"

As it turns out, I won't need to refuse or agree, as Keith is standing in his driveway and has heard the exchange. He alerts both of us to his presence.

Linda stops and turns his direction. "Hey, Keith, just go to Janet's. We'll meet you there."

As she crosses towards Carol's house, I run across Howell's yard and connect with Keith. Janet sees us from her driveway and waves us over. I'm not sure why, I suppose out of curiosity, I walk with Keith across his and Gerber's yard directly to Janet's cement driveway. The garage door is up, and she already has a card table and some folding chairs in place in front of it. As usual, she takes control. "Eddie, tie that rope from the corners of the door to those beams on the back wall. Here, Keith, you finish putting up these chairs."

Diane arrives next and is immediately put to work making the "playbills." Then Linda and Carol show up.

"Here," Janet says, and hands them their copies of the script.

When I've finished attaching the rope, I decide to make my move. "Okay, I'm heading to the beach. Keith, you coming?"

"Come on, Eddie!" Linda says. "Don't be such a stick-in-the-mud!"

"You can call me whatever you want, I'm not interested in being in another play," I say as I turn out of the driveway.

T

"Let him go," Janet says. "We don't need him. Keith can play both male roles."

Once I reach the end of the driveway, I start jogging down the road, not bothering to try and get Keith to follow. I've been through this enough times to know how it will fall out, and am not interested in going through the process.

"Be back at 5:00 to watch!" Carol calls after me.

"Okay," I call over my shoulder, raising my arm to acknowledge the invitation, as I continue toward the beach.

The beach is empty. I change plans and circle through Gerber's, Frahm's and Howell's yards back home. Mom has the ironing board set up in the kitchen, and is busy getting the wrinkles out or a basket of damp clothes. I take stock of my situation and end up deciding to go fishing.

I find the rusted coffee tin and shovel left lying in the weeds near the shed, dig up some worms, locate my bamboo pole and fish bucket, stick the can of worms in the bucket, and head to the dock. What other children are about are mostly at Janet's, so I'm left to fish in peace. I spend the rest of the afternoon catching what will end up being our supper – four crappies, six sunfish and two rock bass. I also catch two bullheads, but those get thrown back. By the time I've flayed the ones I keep and buried their guts in the same dirt I dug the worms, the afternoon is nearing the time for the performance, so I head to Janet's garage to see what's come of the day's big event.

It's deserted. Though the garage door is open, some blankets have been poorly hung over drooping clothes lines I put up to serve as a backdrop, and a card table is in place (holding a carelessly stacked pile of handmade tickets, a pair of black, dress gloves and a black-and-gold toy wand, apparently meant to be used in the performance), no one is there to perform.

T

I walk around the outside of the garage, debate knocking on Janet's back door, decide against it, and instead go to Keith's house for the answers.

As usual he has little to say. He was told to hang the blankets. While he did, Linda and Diane got into an argument about who was going to play the queen. Then Janet and Linda argued about something else, he wasn't sure just what. He was told he would be a knight. They gave him an old white sheet and told him to cut a hole in the middle of it and pull it over his head. Then they got a thick, black belt and a replica of a pirate's sword from Janet's basement. He said it took them a while to get the sheet and the belt arranged on him so they thought it looked okay and then he stuck the sword between his belt and hip, but he couldn't get it to hang right. Finally, Linda told him to just hold it in his hand. Then they gave him a copy of the scene. He had almost no lines.

"Well, that was a plus," I joke and we laugh.

"Yeah," Keith says. "It was boring and they kept getting into arguments."

"There's a reason I left!" I say.

"I know . . . my own fault," Keith says. "At any rate, they rehearsed for about an hour. But they never got very far into it. They kept stopping to talk about who should stand or walk where, and then they'd get into arguments about the dialogue."

"So what happened?" I cut in.

"Janet's mom came out to say Linda's mom called and she needed to go home. So everyone left."

While this might seem a lame ending to the day's big plans, it was standard. These plays always took on the appearance of a major project, but they seldom got performed.

T

Mom's Best Friend

Our theatrical productions, more accurately, the girls' attempts at them, tend to have stock characters. It's time for brief introductions some of the real characters in my life.

Keith's mom, Vera, is Mom's best friend, has been since before I was born and will be until Vera dies long after I've moved away.

Frahms live at the end of Lane Four. Lane Four dips down below the level of our house, as it passes by Strand's and Howell's yards, but then rises up higher before ending abruptly as a steep, twenty foot bank above the lake, more than double the height of the drop-off at the end of our lane. Frahms have a small yard on the side facing the lake that is technically public land and is crossed by the path that leads along the top of the bank. It's mostly just used by the neighborhood children, and Frahms don't seem overly bothered by people passing by their windowed porch throughout the summer.

Since the bank reaches its highest point along their yard, they have a great view of the lake, even though some of the trees from the bank and especially a large oak on the top kept it from being a completely open one. The house itself is one of the nicer ones in the neighborhood, two stories high on the lake side, and since it stands on the hill rising up from the land opposite the lake, it has a driveway cutting across the yard below it and leading into a basement garage, resulting in a three story house on that side, though most of the first floor is underground, covered by a rising lawn between the driveway and house. The front door doesn't fit the usual requirements of a front door. It has a sidewalk from the street coming across and next to the front of the house, parallel to but higher up the hill from the driveway. Three cement steps parallel to the house rise to a small cement porch, resulting in the feeling one is entering a side door. The land on this side/front of the house is lawn with a few trees down to the driveway, and then cleared down the rest of the hill, transitioning into what was once a small, swampy wood, but what has been cleared twenty yards into that and fenced off. This is kept mowed, but is always wet and muddy, and consists of weeds rather than grass. On occasion Keith and I and others play touch football there, but it doesn't get much use. It does, however, help to give the house an open view and a suggestion of it overlooking a more grandiose yard than it does.

Vera's husband Lenny has constructed a metal stairway down to a nice dock on the lake, and when I'm ten, he purchases a speed boat, something he supposedly wants, though I don't recall him ever using it. Keith's older brother Bruce uses it some before he graduates and leaves for college, but that's all the use it gets. Vera never goes out on it. Mom hopes they'll purchase a pontoon boat so she and Vera can go out on that, but they never do. In truth, I never remember Vera having anything to do with the lake.

She is a friendly, talkative person, quick to laugh, and though she seems old to me as a child, upon looking back I can see that she was a good looking woman, what people refer to as spry. Lenny is a large man, not a talker, not social. He's supposed to be good with his hands, though I never see him doing any woodworking or other handiwork. In truth, I see very little of him at all, and the main thing I remember about him is that his favorite television show is *Gunsmoke*. He must make

T

decent money, at least better than the average for our neighborhood, as he's an automobile union employee.

I don't have many more memories about Bruce than I do about Lenny. Whereas Keith takes after Lenny, Bruce takes after Vera. I believe he's six years older than me, and has no time for Keith or his friends. We're just a nuisance. Eventually he will marry Janet, and once in a while Mom will mention something about the two of them, but I have little interest.

T

Gerbers

Gerbers live next to Frahms, or, more accurately, have their summer house there. They are clearly a wealthier family than the rest of us, and their summer house, while it isn't ostentatious, is a nice house. They have a daughter about Bruce's age, but I never have any encounters with her. They do not like it that people walk across the public land between them and the lake, and they put in a small walkway to keep the public crossing as confined as possible.

One Saturday, they hire me to help lay sod.

Another day, I make myself a small fort in their wooded bank going down to the lake. As it turns out, I make it in the middle of a patch of poison ivy and suffer the consequences.

I only have one other memorable incident with them, and it suggests a separation between them and the rest of the neighborhood. One night, my raft gets loose and ends up by their dock. They claim it as theirs, something of a finders-keepers argument. The following night, I cut it loose from their dock and return it to mine. Nothing more is said.

Howells

Howells live directly behind us and suffer through the ugly basement brick wall Dad puts up to level our land. While it is mostly hidden by small trees and weeds, it is nonetheless, an eye sore.

They have older children who no longer live with them, but come to visit and enjoy the lake on summer weekends. They have a wonderful houseboat Mr. Howell built by welding airtight some old metal barrels. Unfortunately, one day he dives off the top of it and hit his head on the bottom of the lake, breaking his neck. Fortunately, he survives.

McClouds

McClouds live across the street from Frahms, just up the hill from Howells, and thus with a high view of the lake. They have their own steep stairs down to their dock, but they also have a storage shed next to the dock, the only one on our side of the bay. They are into water sports and have various speed boats, water skis and other lake toys. In fact, they are the ones who give me their large diving-board that I find a way to anchor off the end of our dock.

They also join the neighborhood fad for digging out basements, and they let me dig in theirs as much as I want.

Since their children are all about Bruce's age, I don't have much to do with them, but they are always friendly.

Strands

Barney and Gladys and their three children are certainly a part of my childhood, though not as much as might be expected. Bob is four years older than I, Carol two, and Doug a year younger.

Bob calls to me as I walk up from the lake, "Eddie, Eddie!"

"Hi, Bob."

He waves me to him. "How come you're not signed up for the hockey league?"

"Oh, forgot."

"You are playing?"

By now we've reached each other. "Yes, yes, oh yes."

"That's what I figured. Since you weren't on the list, Mark chose Nick Evanoff, but I thought you'd be playing, so I chose you."

I smile. Bob gives me a friendly punch on the shoulder and laughs. His dad's a good-looking man, and he's a good looking boy with a wonderful smile. "Mark was pissed, but, hey, that's the way it goes."

I always liked him. Not sure why he is as friendly to me as he is because I'm so much younger than he. Probably more a reflection of his personality than mine. Some people are naturally friendly . . . nice without thinking about it.

He's a good hockey player, and the way it works is that high school players coach the midget leagues, so he will coach me this year. It will be his only year. The next year, he will quit the high school team. Mark's tells me is because Bob is more interested in girls. I suspect Bob is popular. He has all of the qualities.

The next summer he comes down the steps to the dock while I'm fishing and catches me with a pun.

"Oh-oh," he says, studying my hair. "You've got up doc in your hair!"

"What's up doc?"

"I don't know Bugs Bunny! What's up?"

I groan.

One evening he sets up the latest electronic football game on the floor of his livingroom. The idea is to line-up small football players on a metal board that looks like a football field, turn on the electricity, and watch them vibrate. They have tiny plastic runners on their bases, so they will vibrate forward. A tiny plastic football is attached to one of them, and the idea is to see how far he can vibrate forward before a player from the other team bumps into him. It sounds like great fun. In reality, it doesn't work. The players do vibrate, and sort off vibrate forward, but mostly they just vibrate erratically, often fall over, and it's impossible to have any semblance of a real game. We're both disappointed, but it's thoughtful of him to think of me.

Another time, with similar results, he invites me to play a basketball board game. This game has a small basket on each end of a board about the same size as a standard game board. The board has several holes in it with spring mechanisms for each, and the idea is to put a basketball about the size of a ping-pong ball into one of the holes and use a lever to pull the launching spring beneath it to flip it at the basket. With a bit of practice, it is possible to play this game, so that alone

T

makes it better than the football game. But it's still not much fun.

One Saturday in late summer he holds up a football and calls to me from his yard. "Hey, Eddie, come on, let's play."

I make my way to him, and he leads us to the empty lot that stretches from the lawn portion of his back yard to Lane Four. He makes a tee out of the ground and sets the football up so he can kick it, then purposely tops it so it bounces off the ground into the air. I catch it and try to dodge passed him. He tags me, and we begin alternating our roles. The game is never explained.

The next thing I know it's getting too dark to see the ball.

Yet the game continues until Carol calls from the backdoor, "Bob . . . Bob . . . telephone!"

The closest Carol and I ever come to playing sports together is when I get promoted to the varsity hockey team and she's one of the cheerleaders.

Since we grow up living next door, we can't help but wander in-and-out of each other's lives, and it seems we will have played almost nightly neighborhood games together. However, she seldom joins them.

Nevertheless, we do have our moments. The first memorable incident takes place three summers before Dad dies, and is a rare one where she is the victim.

I'm fishing off my dock with my bamboo pole, and she comes down the steps with one of her friends.

"Hey, what're you doing on my dock?"

"I can be on your dock if I want!"

"No you can't. Now go away!" I turn and swing my line back for another spot on the water.

"Ooooowwww!"

T

It's Carol. I've caught my hook in her face, just above the eye.

Oh no!!!!!!

"Sorry! Sorry! Here! Here! Let me take it out!"

"No! Get away from me!"

"Here . . . here . . . let me cut the line!" I take the fish scaler from the bucket and draw it across the taught line. It snaps.

As soon as it's cut free of the pole, she runs up the stairs and doesn't stop until she's disappeared into her house.

She will repay me several times over.

Most of our encounters will be more neutral – including an afternoon at the end of her sidewalk being taught spin-the-bottle with several of her girlfriends, complete with the embarrassing kisses.

T

Girl Germs

Playing spin-the-bottle brings me to the following incident.

The summer before we tear down our garage, I build a fort on the side of it facing away from our house, in the narrow strip of land between it and her house. One day while Keith and Tom and I are inside it, practicing tying a Sailor's Knot with some clothesline, Janet calls loudly from Carol's yard, "Hey, Ta-a-om . . . Eddie . . . . We know you're in there!"

We crawl to the wall and look through the cracks. Carol, Linda, Diane and Janet are all standing on Carol's lawn.

"We have a surprise for you!" Janet says loudly.

"Sure you do! Pray tell, what can it be?" Tom responds.

"Have you ever seen a naked woman?" Janet taunts.

"Yes," Tom says.

"Sure you have," Janet says sarcastically. "I'm not talkin' 'bout yer sister!"

"What exactly are you talkin' 'bout?" Tom tries to match her tone.

"We have a challenge for you!" Janet says.

"Go away and leave us alone," Tom responds.

"Why? You afraid of girls?" Janet taunts.

"No . . . the word you want is annoyed!" Tom says.

"Well . . . if you've got the guts, we're gonna give you a chance to see us naked!" Janet says.

"Why would we want to?" Tom says back.

"You're too chicken to!" Carol taunts.

A deal gets struck. The girls will go into Carol's house, take off their panties and come out wearing just their skirts; then we will also have to "get naked."

I'm not sure about this. It's exciting, but getting naked in the middle of the day with or without girls is crossing a line I'm not sure I want to cross.

The girls go into Carol's house.

"They're wrong," Tom says. "I've seen naked women."

"When?"

"All the time," he says.

"Who?"

"Duh! My sister! Besides . . . I've seen Playboy magazines!"

The only naked women I've seen are pictures of African natives in a book we have titled People Around the World.

Keith doesn't say anything. He often doesn't, so I don't bother asking him. I'm too caught up in what's happening. What is the point of this? Why have they come up with this challenge? I'm feeling a combination of anticipation, confusion and fear.

We exit the fort and lean against the outside of it to wait.

As it turns out, the wait is short.

Carol's door squeaks open and they giggle onto the lawn.

I know I'm feeling excited because this is a risky challenge . . . but it's more than that. There's some other sensation drawing me to it.

The girls jiggle about like marionettes, not sure what to do, pretend to lift their skirts, pull their shoulder straps off their shoulders. Carol actually does the splits, but manages to keep from revealing anything. Linda turns and bends over, as if to reveal her butt, but she doesn't bend enough to show anything. Janet lifts her skirt above her knees and looks at us from under

T

her eyebrows in an attempt at a seductive pose. Diane is clearly uncomfortable and mainly stands and watches the others.

They have our attention, but we don't know anything more about this game of foreplay than they do. Whatever this challenge is supposed to accomplish, it seems to have gotten stuck.

Then Janet pushes Carol so she falls and her skirt lifts briefly above her waist.

Brief as it is, we get a full view . . . of her cutoff jeans!

"You're not naked!" I yell.

"You're cheating!" Tom adds.

"No we're not! We said we did take off our panties! We have no panties on!" Janet adds.

"Forget it!" I yell.

"Now it's your turn!" Janet says.

"No way!" I respond.

Janet initiates the charge. Tom runs into the fort. I pull Keith with me and lead him into Mom's station wagon. "Lock the doors!"

The girls split, Linda and Diane coming for Keith and me in the car. When they find we've outwitted them, they try to entice us, then try insulting us, then give up on us and join Carol and Janet, who've gone straight for Tom.

There is no lock on the fort.

My quick thinking saves Keith and me, but later, thinking about my clever escape, I wonder if I've made a mistake. Tom's suffering consists of being piled on by a bunch of girls wanting to remove his clothes. Is that punishment or . . . I'm not sure . . .

T

Wasn't many years ago I dodged through a whole group of girls trying to catch me on the playground, recess upon recess upon recess, bragging that I never once let them win, never got caught.

A couple of years after the incident in the station wagon, realizing girls have more going for them than "girl germs," it occurs to me that Carol showers in her basement beneath a curtain-less window after swimming, almost inviting me to spy on her. My hormones are raging. It's a harmless crime. Why would any boy driven by his new desires resist? Most would not only do it but brag about it in school the next day.

I think about it more than once when she and I happen to return from swimming at the same time.

But I never do it.

T

Tarzan's Loin Cloth

One day, as I walk up from my dock, I see Doug sitting on his entrance steps with a guitar. "Didn't know you played."

"I'm starting a group with a couple of guys from choir."

"Didn't even know you sing."

"Yeah."

"Sounds exciting." My comment is sincere. I've always admired people who can sing, and while I will never hear him myself, others will tell me that indeed he is quite good. He's let his hair grow long. Doesn't look so good on him, but maybe it's because I haven't seen him with long hair and I'm not expecting it. He's also let himself get a bit overweight. He doesn't have the athletic build of Bob.

"Well, I gotta get going. Meeting Jackie at the beach." Jackie lives on the corner next to Linda on Land Four. He stands.

"Goin' swimming?"

"Nah. We're playing Tarzan in the woods."

"Okay ... so ... what do you mean?"

"We made loin cloths and we fixed up one of the caves. You can join us if you want."

"No, no thanks."

Doug doesn't have the outgoing personality of the rest of his family, Jackie is overweight and stutters, and the group of children that centers the neighborhood for me is my age or older, so the two of them fall into secondary roles for me.

Also, while Doug lives next door, Jackie lives just enough off the main play area that I seldom see him. Of course, I feel sorry for him because he is overweight and stutters, but there isn't any other reason to interact with him.

When Doug invites me to join them, it strikes me as a strange, almost perverse activity to run around the woods in makeshift loin cloths, but as I think about it, I realize it's similar to the kind of pretend battles I fought in those same woods when I was but a few years younger than them. Of course, I didn't do it in a homemade loin cloth.

Looking back, I realize my dual feelings about the invitation match my state of mind, or, my states of mind. The child me has no problem playing Tarzan in the woods and finds the creative aspect of a loin cloth nothing more than that. The adult in me sees it from a different perspective. There are sexual connotations, intended or not. And I am right at the age where I'm not sure what to make of them.

T

Turtles

A dragon lives forever but not so little boys
Painted wings and giant rings make way for other toys
Puff the Magic Dragon

Lipton and Yarrow

It's a summer when it's still possible to live the fantasies of childhood and yet feel them melting away in the hot sun, like the sweet juice of a banana popsicle dissolving on the tongue until all that's left is the wooden stick, and then letting the smooth stick linger on the tongue – knowing the tasty ice is gone and yet reluctant to let the experience end.

Music flows through it like the flirting touch of a summer breeze rippling the leaves of the damaged red oak above the dock, the lullaby lapping of the water caressing the rocks along the shore, and the reassuring creak-creak-creak of the rowboat as it sleeps by the dock.

One day, years later I try to express it in a song that connects the seasons to the stages of life:

A chipmunk is playing his mandolin
Ol' bullfrog is sippin' on his bottle of gin
A hoot owl proclaims "Let the festival begin"
And so the seasons turn around again.

And you'll be my lady,
I'll be your knight in shining armor
And I'll fight ferocious dragons
To defend my lady's honor.

Come on, let's go walking in the rain
And if the sun don't shine

There's always gonna be a brighter day
So you can close your eyes
And pretend to look the other way

I'm throwing stones at your window
Won't you come out and play
You can be the queen of England
Send explorers on their way

And I'll be your captain
I'll sail the Seven Seas
Discover new countries
For you and me

The song continues through more verses, but this is the one focusing on the summer world of childhood where fantasy still rules, that time when boys still capture frogs and lizards and snakes — have frog jumping contests and delight in finding ways to use them to make girls squeal.

Today, Keith and I are after turtles.

I push my oar against the bottom of the swamp to slow the boat. Keith feels it and follows suit. We edge from the small path of water between the bulrushes into the larger opening.

There are a few rotted tree stumps rising unevenly above the surface. Not important. What I'm looking for is a trunk lying sideways, half submerged, the standard place for turtles to sleep in the sun.

Then I see it.

As expected, there are over a dozen mud turtles sunning on it, all of them six to twelve inches, perfect. I set my oar quietly in the boat and ease over the side, quietly lowering myself into the swamp until my feet hit bottom. They sink about three inches into the soft mixture of seaweed, water moss, leaves, plants, mud and twigs until they hit a solid floor. The water climbs to just above my crotch. I reach into the boat and carefully pick up the net. Everything depends on not startling them. Let them hear the normal sounds, nothing more.

Slowly . . . slowly . . . quiet . . . quiet . . . calm and steady — I swing the net across the bow and bring it into position.

They do not move. So far so good.

I walk toward them, my feet sliding through the silt. I step on a sharp rock and have to stop myself from reacting. Keith quietly pushes the boat behind me. If I get close enough before they sense danger, I'll be able to net two or three before they splash into the water. Once they hit the water, it becomes a guessing game.

In a few years, an enterprising company will buy up the swamp and nearby land and build Marina Manor, several buildings of condos with a man-made cove for their boats right where we're hunting our turtles. But at the moment, the only building on the nearby shore is a small, old Spanish looking house with a long driveway that circles behind a small knoll, nearly hiding the house from the road. The view of it is better from where we are, but trees and tall grass kept it mostly

T

hidden from all sides. I will never know if anyone lives there during my days exploring this swamp and passing by on the road. I never see any life and no one ever talks about it. The style of it doesn't match the neighborhood, but the sense it has of being an old fairytale cottage helps create a once-upon-a-time feel. In this way, not knowing who lived there is good, because I can people it with whatever my imagination wants.

This Jenning's Bay part of the lake is still mostly swamp and woods, and it's where Three Points Boulevard, the one connection with the mainland, normally floods over in the spring. Boulevard is too fancy a name for it. It's barely more than a dirt road. During the summer, it's always being crossed by turtles and frogs and lizards and ducks and other animals of the lake, swamp and woods that surround it. Red-winged Blackbirds like to perch on the bulrushes and sometimes swans float serenely just off shore.

Between us and the road, we can see the three beaver huts in the water, some twenty yards from the shore. They've been there since before I was born, but they will disappear a few years after the new condo complex goes in. About the same time the road will get built up a good four feet above the water so it will never flood again. Then contractors will turn the swamp on the other side of it into another man-made inlet, this one surrounded with upscale houses. After a few years, Seahorse Apartments will change hands and be renamed Marina Manner.

As I make my way toward the turtles, something moves in the corner of my vision. I look and see the head of a northern snake slowly winding its way through the swamp grass. I know if I leave it alone it will have no interest in me, so I turn back to my task.

T

I'm nearly to the log when a dragonfly lands on the back of one of the turtles. I worry it or one of the others might notice and feel the need for a snack, but they're apparently deep in their sun-bathed naps. A few more steps get me close enough. I slowly reach my fingers across the nearest shell. It's easy. I shove it into the net and quickly reach for another. I manage four of them before the rest are alerted and splash into the water.

Now the hunting goes slower, but nevertheless it's an easy task. They can only stay beneath the surface for a brief time before coming up for air and my net. Furthermore, even in the swamp, as long as I walked carefully and don't stir it up, the water is clear enough for me to see them under the surface, so I walk slowly about the clearing looking for the movements of their webbed feet. By the end of the afternoon, we've caught over twenty turtles, a good amount for the park turtle races and a bit of extra money for us.

I cannot know it at the time, but these innocent days with Keith are coming to an end. No, the world isn't going to change much, but I am. It's happening.

T

Magical Realism

Catching turtles with Keith has the feel of an illusion, the once-upon-a-time world of my childhood. But the other world, the strange new world after Dad's death also involves the real demands of poverty.

It's too easy to say I sometimes live in one reality and other times in the other reality. No. They are mixed, both present at the same time, and some of the things I stumble into have a curious, magical realism about them.

It's heavy.

I hit the keys with my middle fingers.

It's the old, Underwood typewriter Mom used when she was in college, packed away and nearly forgotten.

Mom comes across an ad in the newspaper, a way to make some extra money typing address labels, one cent for each label. She sends in an application and is immediately hired. Several pages of names and addresses are sent. She needs to type them onto a separate label for each.

She tries, sits at the typewriter late into the night. But she doesn't have the energy after a long day and realizes she can't keep up with the weekly quotas.

"Eddie, how would you like to make some money?"

"Always."

"You can have the money for whatever labels you type."

The ribbon is worn, but I hit each key hard, and go back and type over ones that don't come out as dark as they should.

It doesn't occur to either Mom or me to purchase a new ribbon.

In the end, it doesn't matter. The pay for the work isn't even enough for my modest expectations, another possible source of income fails its promise, and the typewriter goes back into the ever-growing piles of junk in the basement.

Mom collects S&H Green Stamps. The stamps are issued in perforated sheets with gummy backs, similar to sheets of postage stamps. Each stamp is a denomination of one, ten or fifty points. S&H also issues collector's books free. As we purchase merchandise from stores, mainly food from Piggly Wiggly or the Standard Gas station, we are given sheets of stamps and books. Each book has 24 pages, and it takes 50 points to fill a page, so each book contains 1,200 points. When the books are filled, we look in our S&H catalogue to see what we can order. It advertises itself as the largest ordering catalogue in the world.

For a while Piggy Wiggly replaces S&H with Greenbax trading stamps, which can be cashed in for discounts on groceries and merchandise that advertises the store, so the drawer has some sheets of those as well. Other stores and gas stations also issue stamps, and the drawer has sheets of Gold Bond Stamps from a major Minnesota company that can be redeemed for everything from a set of steak knives to a mink coat.

But S&H dominates the trading stamps market.

The challenge of getting enough books of stamps to get something free entices me. Mom also likes to page through their

T

catalogue. They have everything – radios, televisions, guitars, toy trucks, Barbie dolls, lawn mowers, exercise equipment, furniture and a huge selection of clothes.

One night we take our books of stamps to one of their stores. It turns out to be a large room that looks more like a warehouse than a department store. Everything about it is depressing. The lights are dim. The floor is dirty. The exciting things to buy don't look as glamorous sitting on the rows of tables as they do in the catalogue. And it hits home that the stamps aren't worth much, a tenth of a cent each. Those sheets of 25 stamps look impressive, but they're only worth 2.5 cents.

As with the labels, the fantasy doesn't match the reality.

I can't say for sure, but I have the feeling Mom also gets caught up in the possibilities. She's an adult and knows better, yet her world has to be a dark one, and people in disparate situations are prone to believing in miraculous solutions.

At the same time, it's likely she knows they won't pan out. While she applied for the typing job and she collects the stamps and looks through the sales catalogues, she doesn't go about it logically or sensibly, and she is an intelligent woman. So, it's likely another part of her is prone to dismissing it. She doesn't keep her stamps organized and they end up in careless piles of mail and bills and advertisements, more often making their way to the garbage than the catch-all drawer she designates for them.

In a practical, yet it would seem avoidable routine, Mom, John and I walk to the Piggly Wiggly with a red wagon to buy our food for the month. John is still small enough to ride much of the way to town in the wagon. On the way home, he has to walk, because the wagon has our shopping bags of food.

T

Mom still owns the Ford Station Wagon, but it's old, and she knows nothing about repairing a car. For the summer, it sits at the Standard Gas Station in Mound. I believe it's the gas pump that gets repaired. Whatever it is, Mom doesn't have the money to pay for it. Standard is not happy about this, but, other than a couple of unfriendly phone calls, nothing is done. Our transportation sits in the lot as other cars needing repair come and go.

It must be a curious sight, the three of us walking along the road with our wagon. The image doesn't fit even a small town in the early 1960s, certainly not a suburb of Minneapolis.

It is also when Mom makes buns for the month, dozens and dozens of buns. She freezes most of them, and then thaws them out as we need them. Most exciting for John and me, she always includes some cinnamon rolls.

She also takes plates of them to neighbors as a friendly gesture.

In hindsight, I realize her homemade buns are made from cheap ingredients, and though my taste buds are not sophisticated enough to worry about it, I wonder if the neighbors' find them as much of a present as intended. Certainly, her heart is in the right place, and the neighbors she shares her baking with are not likely to be picky, so perhaps it is all good. Nevertheless, even then, that wonderful tradition of bringing baked goods to the neighbors has an outdated feel about it, as if the world of Mother Goose Nursery rhymes and Brother Grimm bedtime stories has managed to slip into the real world.

These are all pieces of the puzzle that is my reality after Dad dies. As the past does, especially childhood, they have a feeling of another world, one where history cannot help but have the atmosphere of fiction.

Once upon a time, a boy lived on Lake Minnetonka . . .

T

Gladys' Laundry

Tom, Keith and I are playing in the large pile of sand in my yard.

Gladys finishes hanging her laundry and goes inside.

"Come on," Tom says, balling up some wet sand

"What?" Keith and I are both on our knees.

Tom walks towards Strands' yard, and throws his handful of sand at the sheets drying in the light wind.

"Come on! Come on!" Tom says and laughs.

Soon Keith and I are joining in on the forbidden fun. I know it's wrong and would never have initiated it. Nevertheless, I join in.

Besides the ethical stupidity of it, it is stupid in a practical sense, as Gladys almost has to see us from her kitchen window . . . and she does.

Other than Gladys, who has to rewash her laundry, Dave gets the worst of it, because he is supposed to be watching us. So Gladys and then Mom's wrath get directed at him.

I'm told to apologize, which I do.

"Eddie," Gladys asks. "Why did you do it?"

"I don't know." It is an honest response. I honestly don't know. I honestly feel guilty. And I'm honestly sorry.

"Now I have to rewash all my sheets," Gladys says. She isn't yelling at me. She's being nice about it, expressing a sincere frustration.

"I'm sorry," I say again.

"I saw the whole thing," she says. "I know Tom was the one who initiated it."

Mom cuts her off. "That's no excuse, Eddie. You can't let Tom talk you into doing things you know are wrong!"

"I know."

Neither Keith's nor Tom's parents are told. Gladys and Mom agree there is no point in pushing the matter. Neither of them are friendly with Tom's parents, and most likely feel telling them will be more of a headache than they want. Probably because they are friends with Keith's parents, they feel it is best not to cause any hassles with them either.

I'm certain I'm the only one who remembers. And I remember because I know I purposely did something that hurt another person for no reason. Just a silly, stupid thing children do. Yet, the fact I include it here proves I will feel guilty about a minor ethical sin all of my life.

I'm not sure if guilt is a good human emotion or a horrible one. I hate people who disrespect others, cannot comprehend people who enjoy hurting others, and avoid doing it even when honesty demands it.

At the same time, I'm aware that concern for hurting others' feelings also gets in the way and stops people from accomplishing good things. It has me.

T

Catching a Greased Pig

Yes, there are farms in Mound and the surrounding country. Some of my classmates live on farms, but not in Three Points, not the small world I know as a child. My world is not a world of farmers.

The only experience I have of being on a farm is the night I stay at Gordy's house when Mom needs someone to watch me while she visits Dad in the hospital, and all that does is to highlight how foreign farm life is for me. My main memory is the fantasy feel of it as I look out the second story bedroom window into the farmyard below. I almost expect to hear Debbie Reynolds singing or talking as Charlotte to Wilber and Paul Lynde's delightfully sarcastic Templeton muttering as he scrounges about for food.

Of course, farm life isn't so idyllic, but I'm not the only child at the time to embrace the illusion. When our teacher reads it to us a chapter a day, none of us is struck by the shocking first sentence, "Where's Papa going with that axe?" Quite a startling catch to begin a story, but the atmosphere of it immediately discounts any fears. Fern easily talks her dad into letting her raise the runt pig he plans to kill, and that's what registers.

This farm, this world is a safe world, a friendly world, a place where a child can grow up letting her imagination run wild and playing with animals that talk. In the real world, the runt of the litter would have been killed and discarded.

In this fantasy world, death isn't so blunt. In fact, in *this* world a child can save a pig from an unnatural, premature death.

Somewhere in the world of life on a farm, I've heard about greased pig contests, but a greased pig contest in my world is out of place.

"Yes," Keith insists.

"Let me get this straight . . . we chase after a pig that's covered in grease!"

"Yes."

"And anyone can do it?"

"Sure."

Then, for a moment, once-upon-a-time enters the real world. Yes, yes, yes – I have to keep stressing it, because it seems so out of place. But yes! It really does happen.

It has been set up to coincide with the Fourth of July festivities.

Three Points Park is filled with people. Six are busy behind the waist high counters of the new building specifically erected

T

for such gatherings. It's more of a frame with a roof and a concrete floor than a real building. The basement-brick walls only rise to the level of the counters, with metal posts continuing up to hold the roof. There are two entrances on opposite sides. Whatever tables, grills and other furniture it holds will all be removed when the event is over. At the moment it's filled with activity. Four separate grills are sizzling with brats, hot dogs, fried chicken and hamburgers. Large metal bins are overflowing with ice and bottles of Pepsi, Bubble-up, Orange, Grape and Strawberry pop. There are stacks of beer cases, mostly Hamm's and Grain Belt. And, of course, there are large pitchers of Kool-Aide, lemonade and ice tea. There are boxes of Old Dutch potato chips, bins of eggs, potato and tuna salads, baked beans and an overworked hot oil contraption for making French fries and onion rings.

Two temporary booths on the first base edge of the outfield are trying to keep up with customers. One has two older women swirling cardboard holders around the inside of a cotton candy machine and the other has three women ringing up sales of balloons, toy kazoos, summer hats, stuffed animals, Play-Doh, Frisbees, Hula-hoops, endless plastic trinkets and a full array of candy – Hersey, Mars, Clark, Nestle, Snickers, Marathon, Oh Henry, Kit Kat, Sugar Babies, Dots, Beech-Nut, Wrigley's, Chicklets, Bazooka and numerous types of sugar candy.

This is indeed a major summer gathering.

A loud, scratchy noise rasps through the general chatter. "Attention! Attention! Squeal-scrape-crackle – Attention! Attention! Greased pig contest is about to begin! Attention! All contestants come to Home Plate! The greased pig contest is about to begin!"

I'm one of the first to make my way down the hill.

T

"Please gather at home plate! The greased pig contest is about to begin! crackle . . . farm has been generous enough to donate one of their pigs! Please contact them at . . . squeal . . . if you stop by the table, we have flyers with all the information you'll need . . . ." The speaker is so flawed no one can make out the announcer providing the commercial information and thanks for community service to the farm for donating the pig. I pay little attention.

I'm focused and push my way through the groups talking, laughing and eating to the contestants gathering at home plate.

All I have on are my not so clean tee-shirt and cut-offs, probably as good of an outfit for catching a greased pig as any. Not only is the event meant to be a dirty affair, but it has rained hard the previous night, so the dirt part of the infield is muddy and the grass wet and slippery.

I don't know if there is some rule about it, but the thirty-some contestants gathering are all children. There are a few older, bigger children than I, but I am one of the older ones.

The announcer keeps up his patter, trying to entice people to either join in or watch. Those of us planning to participate mill about home plate, waiting for someone to direct us. The wooden stands begin to fill and people gather along the first base line.

A few light drops of rain hit my face. It is a humid, hot day, and a patch of dark clouds threatens a cloud burst.

Two men walk to the pitcher's mound, one of them holding a small pig. It strikes me that they look like farmers, though they aren't wearing anything different than the rest of us. Perhaps it's simply that I assume they are farmers and they have a pig.

T

"Okay," the announcer says, followed by the inevitable squeal of the microphone. "All of the contestants need to stand behind home plate. Once the starter shoots his gun and the pig is released, you are free to chase. Remember, keep it fair. No tripping or hitting or any other unfair actions toward your fellow contestants are allowed, and anyone doing such things is disqualified. May the best man win!"

The man holding the pig bends his knees, sets it on the pitcher's rubber. The other pulls the trigger. We surge forward. The pig squeals and runs towards third base.

I'm on the first base side of the contestants but quickly push my way to the third base line and scramble toward the front. The first boy to reach the pig bends down and tries to pick it up on the run, but the pig cuts sharply to the right, and the boy can't stop his momentum, tumbling in an awkward summersault to the ground. In avoiding him, the pig cuts directly in front of one of the bigger boys, who dives for it. He completely misses it, landing on his stomach and knocking the air out of his lungs. He rolls onto his back, gasping for breath. Another of the older boys stumbles trying to change direction, falling in front of two smaller boys, who tumble over him, bringing a burst of laughter from the stands.

For several minutes, the pig continues making quick cuts just as someone is about to fall on it. The audience loves it.

The younger ones, not really understanding what they're doing in the first place, become nothing more than obstacles. A few begin to cry.

Their parents or older siblings come onto the field to save them.

Then the pig sees an open space and heads toward the grassy outfield. This is what I need and I separate from the group.

T

I have the pig to myself.

Once it finds itself in the open field, it isn't sure what to do. It runs. Stops. Runs another direction. Stops.

I'm focused. When it dashes across my path, I pounce. It doesn't matter if the pig is greased and the slippery, muddy grass splashes about us. I grab the pig's hind legs in a vice grip. We slide through the grass, spraying water. As we come to a stop, I roll onto my back, taking the pig with me. That's it. Nothing to it. I stand, holding the pig firmly against my chest.

Right at the moment I do this, the small patch of threatening clouds passes overhead, and a light sun-shower begins. The rain feels good on my muddied face.

Now what?

The announcer calls out, "We have a winner! We have a winner!" The mike squeals.

I stand there, holding the pig.

"Bring it in! Bring it in, son!"

I walk with it into the infield.

The two men who released the pig congratulate me on the pitcher's mound, ask my name and lead me up the hill to the roofed, open-air building where the announcer sat behind a large folding table, speaking into the desk microphone that is the source of the constant scratchy squeaking and crackling. One of the men gives him my name, while the other tells me to stand beside the table so the announcer can announce me the winner.

None of the other contestants or audience have bothered to follow us up to the old building for the award ceremony. Once the pig was caught, they lost interest and moved on to other matters. Immediately after my victory is announced, the announcer and other men in charge also lose interest. Just like

T

that, it's over and I'm left to decide what I'm going to do with the pig I've just won.

It never occurred to me that the reward for my victory would be the pig. I carry it out of the building, away from the crowd and down the hill to a waist high, brick wall I can sit on. Fortunately, the pig became docile once I caught it. Perhaps it's worn-out from all of the excitement. That makes sense. It appears to be asleep. A pet pig? Can I raise a pet pig? Do I want to raise a pet pig?

Without thinking much, without thinking at all, I joined the contest. It was a chance to compete. I like to compete.

However, a man who lives on Lane Seven has thought about it. I look up and there he is, standing in front of me, wanting to know my plans for the pig.

"You have no use for a pig, no place to raise it. You can't have a pig in Three Points. It's against the law. Pigs have to be on a farm. I know a farmer who will buy it."

I'm an easy target and within ten minutes I've sold him the pig for $15. It solves my problem and results in an unexpected windfall. Fifteen dollars is a lot of money for me. I will soon learn from others that I've been conned. The pig is worth a good deal more.

It is not the first nor will it be the last time I get conned . . .

But . . .

I have the memory . . .

No one can take that away . . .

T

Killer Kayler

"Eddie, put away the book." It's Mrs. Kayler. As usual I'm reading instead of paying attention – this time about Louis Pasteur.

Mrs. Kayler continues, "I before e, except after c, as in receive, or when the sound is a, as in neighbor and weigh."

I pretend to listen, but my mind wanders to Pasteur's decision to inoculate the cattle against anthrax. I've had to stop reading right when Pasteur decides to go against his peers and try out his theory. I want to know if it works. It must. But that's not really the point. That's not why I'm reading about him.

When the loud speaker in the gym announced that I was in Mrs. Kayler's fifth grade class, I groaned. She had a reputation for being strict, and it didn't take a Pasteur to figure out that anyone nick-named Killer was not likely to be my favorite teacher. She looked the part—about fifty years old, heavy set, gray hair, lined face—a real battle axe. By now I know the old battle axe likes me. I can tell. No matter how many times she tells me to close my book and pay attention, she understands. More than the others, she understands. I can tell.

Epileptic Seizure

I gather up the brown mess in the large diaper and drag it to end of the crib. Then I use a damp washcloth to wipe away anything left behind and wash the butt clean. The replacement diaper is frayed, but still useable. I raise the three-year-old legs by the heels with my left hand and slide the diaper under with my right. A quick sprinkle of white baby power and I can pull the top corners of the diaper through the legs and fasten them to the back corners with safety pins. I finish by pulling the large baby-smock back over the legs.

I pick up the dirty diaper and head to the toilet to wash out as much as I can before throwing it in the laundry, but before I get there another three-year-old has an epileptic episode. "Mom! He's having a fit!"

"Quick, put in a mouth board so he doesn't bite his tongue."

I drop the diaper on the floor for the moment and rush into the bathroom medicine cabinet. In but a few seconds I have it in his mouth. Mom arrives as I finish.

"He remembers . . . the picture . . . the one that always hung in his parents' bedroom . . . no doubt on his mother's desires."

"That famous painting . . . the one in so many homes."

"Yes, the delicate features, the flowing brown hair, the mustache and beard."

"But not a halo?"

"No."

"Maybe?"

"I forget."

T

All the World is a Stage

By the time I'm in sixth grade, I have an afternoon paper route and get off the bus at Ward's Store to pick up and deliver my papers. I make little money. It's partially my own fault. The way it's set up, I buy the papers from the Minneapolis Star and Tribune, collect the money from my customers myself, and if I don't get paid by them, I still have to pay for the papers. If someone cancels, I need to cancel their paper myself, and if I don't, I again have to pay for it. In my ignorance and general belief my non-paying customers will eventually pay, I allow some to continue for months without paying. It's a lesson I never completely learn.

In junior high I get the morning paper route I want. Bruce Fraham passes it on to Bob Strand. Bob promises Bruce his younger brother Keith can have it next. Bob knows I want it and when he quits, he apologizes to me, but he feels obligated to keep his promise. As disappointed as I am, I understand. Fortunately, Keith quickly realizes he doesn't want it. Then I get it. That means I no longer ride the bus to school. Instead, I walk to school, delivering the papers and continuing out of Three Points to Grandview Junior High, saving time in the winter by walking across the ice of Jennings Bay to my customers in the Seahorse apartments.

It's eerie making those shadowy deliveries in the dark morning silence. I slip papers in squeaky screen doors with uneven edges that scrape metal against metal or drop them on wooden porches that groan under my steps. I cut through backyards, woods, and swamps and see the eyes of the night animals watching — raccoon, possum, skunk, fox, occasionally deer, often a common house cat, and always a few dogs.

In the winter, once I deliver the final paper on my side of the bay and step onto the ice, I feel a sense of relief — open space surrounds me. The shadows beneath trees and bushes and around houses might hold any number of dangers. But even in the dark, I can see any movement on the ice as soon as it gets past the shadows of the shore. Nothing can sneak up on me.

That open space isn't so friendly in terms of the weather. Even a mild breeze bites at any exposed skin. Friends say I should stick to the land. It might be cold, but it's not as cold as the open lake. Even more serious, they say, it's dangerous to be on the ice at night. It's only a matter of time before I fall through to my death.

I have the opposite view. On a clear morning I can walk across the open expanse of ice beneath a starry sky without any thoughts of human interaction. It gives me a sense of freedom. Some mornings I take a break from my walk, lie on the ice or a patch of snow, and look up at the stars. Yes . . . this is my world . . . this is where I feel safe. Even the chilling breezes have a sense of familiarity, of saying "See, nothing has changed. The world is as it should be. This is your world. This is where you belong."

As I approach the other side, I pass the two dark mounds of the beaver lodges partially covered with snow. On rare occasions, a beaver is outside of its lodge, and scurries back into

T

it. In the summer, they're likely to slap the water if caught outside, an alarm and a warning.

As I pass them, I see the shadowy Marina Manor that has replaced the mysterious Spanish cottage.

These condos are my destination. Once I reach the shore, it's easy to pull myself onto one of the docks, push a new path through freshly fallen snow, and walk across the plowed parking lot to the entrance for the first of the buildings. After fumbling to find and fit the cold metal key into the entrance lock, I push the door open, step inside and listen to it quietly click close behind me while I blow the numbing out of my fingers, slap the snow off my pants, and stamp my shoes.

Then it hits me – the soft silence, dim hall lights, quiet hum of heat rising from the vents – the sense I've entered a sleeping world where the ghostly spirits of the night and dream are about and might appear at any moment. Perhaps they're watching me, judging me. I feel I should be respectful, careful not to disturb them, similar to how I feel when I enter a church.

These spirits are not the same as those outside, the ones I join beneath the stars. Those spirits have a healthy, natural energy. They might be dangerous, but they're vigorous, rugged spirits. These are the spirits that appear as ghosts, shadows of what they once were. These spirits are closed in, as if they've been trapped in the same stale air for far too long. I've seen movies, read books, heard stories of people building over sacred burial grounds and disturbing the spirits there. At the time it doesn't occur to me that might be what I'm encountering here, but thinking back, I wonder. Is it possible the old Spanish house held spirits from generations ago, possible the land that

T

was torn-up and reshaped once was sacred, a place of passage from one world to another?

I've heard stories of ghosts. Many are lost souls, stuck between life and death, unable to live, unable to die. Most are harmless. But there are those who have turned evil. Some even find ways to enter into living souls, where they torture their new bodies and delight in spreading pain. Some say these are the followers of Satan. The Catholic Church even does exorcisms to free their victims, claiming humans are living in a world where God and Satan are in a constant battle for human souls.

That's what St. John's Revelations, the Apocalypse is all about. The time when Christ returns leading an army of angels to defeat Satan once and for all.

I drop papers in front of two doors in the lower hall and make my way to the second floor.

Whispers . . . in the silence . . . Do I hear them? Is it my imagination? Whispers . . . Perhaps just the furnace turning on or the wind outside . . .

"You are me . . . and I am you . . . and you can never escape our bond!"

Isn't that what the pig's head says to Simon? Yes . . . I think it is . . .

"Closer . . . closer . . . closer . . ."

"Dark Shadow? Is that you? Come out into the light and let me see your face."

Sometimes, when I walk alone down Three Points Boulevard, even in the middle of the afternoon, I imagine I'm being watched by invisible beings, and that all of the people I

T

interact with are put into my world to enact a type of study or theatre. Am I being tested, like a lab rat in a maze? Is all of the world I know not the real world, but a fake world put in place specifically to force me to act out different scenes? Are all of the people who interact with me in on it, purposely saying and doing things to see how I react?

Professor Elephant whispers, "Cogito ergo sum."

"How can one know?" Mr. Orange asks.

"If the assumption is that existence is established by knowing that one thinks, then everything else depends on that. In other words, nothing else can be confirmed other than that one thinks." Mrs. October interjects.

"The awareness of a physical existence through the senses cannot be proven, because the senses might be misperceiving. And any conclusions drawn from sensual perceptions might be wrong because of the false assumption at the beginning of the logic based on it." Professor Elephant adds.

"Furthermore, even if the initial assumptions are correct, the conclusions might be wrong because the thought process might be wrong. Simply thinking does not automatically establish correct thinking." Mrs. October concludes the discussion.

Obviously, I don't know any formal philosophy at that young age and don't force a logic over my imagination. There is no way to know for certain, no way to prove my thoughts either correct or wrong. Just a sense . . . just . . . feelings . . . feelings that I'm being watched and judged.

T

What if it were true? What would it mean? Would it mean I'm on stage, my entire world is a stage, I'm performing for an audience, and that audience is judging my performance.

Jaques says it, "All the world's a stage . . ."

The Mad Hatter laughs. No one can see him, but they all know his laugh. While they talk, it echoes and fades slowing into silence, as if disappearing into the vaulted ceiling of a large cathedral.

Mr. Orange looks at Naomi.

She smiles.

Mr. Orange says softly, "The Fool's journey through the Major Arcana."

"There are many stages and many journeys," she whispers.

Jaques doesn't notice and finishes, "And all the men and women merely players."

"And yet the journey is taken by the Fool," Mr. Orange whispers back.

"There are many travelers, each with unique journeys. Each thread of a tapestry is important. No two are identical, yet they all must be included for the tapestry to be truly beautiful and worthy of hanging in the great hall." Naomi whispers and winks at Mr. Orange.

The woman standing behind him digs her fingers into his shoulder. She knows both sides of this game . . . and he is easily fooled.

Jaques doesn't hear or see any of this. He has paused to give his words a chance to breathe, but now is ready to finish his lines, "They have their exits and their entrances." He knows it's necessary to pause here, but only briefly, before he concludes, "And one man in his time plays many parts."

T

There is much more to the speech Shakespeare gave him, the much quoted seven stages of life, but now is not the time. While Jaques might be but a minor character in Shakespeare's play, he is not completely the creation of Shakespeare. An actor, after all, is a man, and each actor contributes to his role. While the play and the stage and even the audience cannot be ignored, each man, even each performance by each man is influenced by that man. So the Jaques performing in this Comedy is not completely in the hands of his fate, not simply mouthing words and following his director's directions. No, not at all.

What of Eddie?

If true, if I am merely a performer on a stage, then the next step is to figure out what criteria the audience uses to evaluate me. How do I succeed? What does it mean to succeed? Performers on stage are judged. Audiences like them, hate them, cry for them, laugh at them. Critics analyze them. Debate them and disagree about them.

What are the criteria? Why cry for one performer and hate another?

Who decides?

If I am in such a complex reality or juxtaposition of realities, those in control must have abilities beyond what humans can do. Are they gods?

Or . . . is it possible, after all, possible that humans have enough power to manipulate the environment? Am I being judged by other humans?

Is this some form of paranoia? A mental sickness?

Am I delusional?

T

Do I need to disconnect, to stop this? Is it up to me to stop it? Can I simply tell myself to stop thinking it? Is it that simple? Do I have that much power?

I realize, even when it first occurs to me as a child, that my strange scenario is unlikely to be anything more than my imagination. I also know that the greatest truths I've been taught, those involving Jesus, the Virgin Mary, God and Satan, are hard to believe if I use logic and common sense. Most of the adults in my life tell me these indeed are true and I should not question them. They have trouble explaining them to me, and usually end by saying that I need to wait until I become an adult. I'm not yet old enough to understand. Or they say that these truths are beyond human abilities to explain, that we need to have faith. The adults who disagree, who say they don't believe, are dismissed and either condemned or given sympathy for the error of their thoughts.

The feeling of being watched and judged in this manner often occurs to me when I'm walking up an otherwise deserted country road. An eerie, otherworldly quality comes over the wild flora, as if nature itself has been alerted to my arrival and is choreographed to accompany and observe me. The still, red-winged blackbird perches on an old, barbed-wire fence post, studying me, as does the prairie dog, frozen like a sentinel next to the weeds on edge of the road. It's as if I've peeled off the surface layer of reality and I'm seeing a quivering, trembling, enchanted reality behind it.

T

Camp Christmas Tree

The names in this chapter are not the real names,
but the experience is a real one.

The woman puts her hand on the back of his shoulder. *"Sometimes time stands still, knowing the past is over, yet not knowing how to walk into the future."*

Mr. Orange looks across the bay and smiles. *It is a good moment, a good memory. That's what makes it so sad.*

I'm too old, have turned eleven and ten is the cutoff. But it is decided not to let a month deny me the opportunity of two free weeks of fun at a day camp. It is a generous gift from our church.

Everyday a bus picks me up and takes me to an enchanting wood with a magical lake and buildings I thought could only exist in once-upon-a-time fairytales.

It is a YMCA camp resting peacefully on the edge of Dutch Lake. It's less than five miles from where I live, but from the moment I step onto the bus each morning until the moment I step off it each afternoon, I feel as if I have entered another world, one where people are happy.

It all begins by herding us into an outdoor arena consisting of a gravel stage surrounded with rows of rough-hewn benches that form a semicircle up a natural incline. Once the counselors get us settled, most of them gather on the stage, where they continue joking and laughing with each other.

Then one steps to the front. "Okay! Everyone listen! Quiet! Everyone! . . . Welcome . . . welcome to Camp Christmas Tree! . . . Please . . . Quiet! . . . I'm Chuck! I'll be one of your counselors! . . . Quiet! Let me introduce all of the counselors and assign you to your groups!"

The rest of the counselors all motion for us to be quiet and listen.

"Jan! Jan! . . . Where are you? . . . . Jan . . . come up here!" Chuck turns to those behind him, sees her, and waves her to the front.

Jan is a large woman, not fat, but muscular. She smiles, a big smile. "Hi, everyone. Hi. Welcome!" She waves with both hands above her head and then backs into the others.

"Jan is in charge of food!" Chuck continues. "So you'll want to be nice to her!"

"Just watch Chuck! He'll show you how!" a skinny councilor with curly red hair standing behind him interjects, demonstrating with his right arm that Chuck has a belly.

"Okay, okay, funny . . .," Chuck replies. "That's Bill. He's in charge of softball and . . . what are you in charge of?"

"Long walks . . . assigning them to people I don't like!"

"Don't pay any attention to Bill; lately he's been having delusions of adequacy."

T

"Wait! Wait! He's just joking! . . . See the twinkle in his eyes! . . . Oh . . . no . . . sorry . . . my mistake . . . it's just the sun shining through the space between the ears!"

The banter continues, contributing to the sense of people having fun on a sunny summer day.

Chuck weaves in his introductory remarks. This will be the place we gather each morning for announcements before splitting into our separate groups. On occasion, our smaller groups will use it for activities, perhaps to initiate a leaf gathering trip or listen to a guest speaker tell us about the local birds, watch a craftsman stitch together a leather moccasin or learn about dream catchers.

Depending on our leader, we'll build fires in one of the large, rock lined pits directly in front of the gravel stage or in a similar pit at one of the campsites and learn how to roast hot dogs, make s'mores, cook potatoes, beans, corn-on-the-cob and the like.

"One day," Chuck, who isn't fat, despite Bill's joke, continues and points to a short, heavy counselor behind him, "Jeff will gather us all here and tell us some humorous folk tales, superstitions and riddles, including stories about cowboys cooking beans over open fires."

"It's a good thing it'll be outside," one of the other counselors says, bringing a spattering of laughs.

"Thursday afternoon, Linda takes center stage with her guitar and leads us through a singalong of folk songs — Red River Valley, Clementine, Casey Jones, She'll be Comin' Around the Mountain, This Land is Your Land, Froggy Went a Courtin', John Henry, America the Beautiful, Amazing Grace, All the Pretty Little Horses, Scarborough Fair . . ."

T

"We get the point," Billy says over him. "You've got more wind than a tornado, and you're not nearly as interesting!"

"Funny, funny . . . okay . . . okay . . . ahh . . . . . okay . . . I guess that's it." This is all it takes for the pent-up energy of the children to come rushing out. Chuck grasps the whistle hanging around his neck and blows out a loud, shrill note – triiiel! "Alright! Everyone! Settle down! Triiiel! Quiet! Please! Quiet!"

The rest of the counselors join him, calling out "quiet" and motioning downward with open palms.

It's all casual. One of them even turns it into a joke by using his left hand to suggest increasing our noise, much as a stand-up comedian will do to encourage applause.

Nevertheless, even with the mixed messages, we finally settle back onto our benches and the noise subsides. As it calms down, Chuck speaks over it, "Now we're going to assign you to your groups! Listen for your name and go to where your group leader is standing!"

The rest of the counselors space themselves along the front.

"Listen carefully, when I call your name, stand, and immediately go to your group leader," he repeats. "Most of the time you will be separated into your own groups." He begins reading off the names and pointing to where each of us should go – "Shaun, where are you, Shaun . . . you're with Sam, down at the end." He points to each in turn. "Mary, you're with Billy, over here."

It takes time for him to read through the names and we're not in the mood to sit still and be quiet. But eventually the process finds its way to the desired conclusion, and after some initial exchanges the counselors begin taking their groups to

T

wherever each is meant to begin in the scheduled rotation of activities.

As it turns out, Chuck is my group leader and since he is the one assigning groups, he calls our names last. "Gather over here," he says and leads us to the front center of the stage area. "Thirteen . . . let's see," he counts us off. "Good. Our schedule begins with swimming class. So, we need to head down to the lake and take the path to the left."

The path is nothing more than a worn trail running alongside the lake. The trees and bushes on the land side of it immediately block out the view of the main camp. The lake side of it is mostly open to the water, but there are a number of trees, bushes and a continuous hedge of tall grass. We don't need to walk far before reaching the beach. There is no sandy shoreline. Instead, a sturdy dock of rough timber posts a foot thick and 3x8 timber cross-planks extends directly from a bank two feet above the water. Tall cottonwood trees grow from the land side of the path on either side of it. Their branches extend over the path, the bank and most of the dock. The shore is covered with wild plants growing from spaces between large rocks. The water is clean and clear, and the lake floor surrounding the dock mostly sandy. The dock extends thirty feet straight out and then has a ten-foot cross-section. Two wooden ladders have been built straight down from the dock into the water, and there is a small tower built up from the left side of the cross section for jumping or diving. There is no diving board, but a wooden ladder has been built up the side of the tower, about eight feet above the water, and the top of it is a six-foot square surface.

Sally meets us there. After a friendly exchange with her, Chuck tells us she has a Life Guard Certificate and is a great

T

gal we'll all love. Then he smiles, waves, promises to catch up with us later, and heads back toward the main camp.

She is not smiling. In a firm voice, she says, "Okay, before anyone gets in the water . . . come . . . over here . . ." She motions us to a flat area of grassy land just past the beach. "Now . . . sit . . . come on . . . everyone . . . the first thing we have to do is establish the rules. Stop it! You two, sit!" She points at two of the boys who are laughing about something. Once she has us all sitting, she begins her speech. "First, is anyone afraid of the water?" She walks back and forth in front of us, observing us as she talks. "No one? Everyone is okay going in the lake? . . . No one has any problems going in a lake? . . . Okay, good. Now, there are thirteen of you and each of you must have a partner, so one of you will be my partner. Eddie . . .?"

I raise my hand.

"I'm told you're the oldest and you're a good swimmer . . . right?"

I nod.

"Good! Then you will be my partner! Now, you two . . . you two . . ." She walks through us, putting the couples together. "At first, everyone must wear life jackets."

"What?" I groan.

She turns and stares at me. "Everyone!"

Well, I think, that just ruined swimming.

I soon learn my dismay is unfounded. Once Sally sees that none of us is going to have problems being in the water, she tells us we can all remove our jackets. It's just an initial safety guard to be certain there are no extreme cases.

As it turns out, my initial negative impression of Sally is also unfounded. By the end of the class her demeanor has

completely changed, so much so that she begins talking with
me as if I'm her helper — and her commands to me switch to
requests. I know they are still to be obeyed, but the shift in how
they're stated changes everything.

When the hour set aside for swimming ends, she blows her
whistle, gathers us all on land and directs us down the path to
Jenny. Jenny is in charge of canoes. She is a slight, spry girl
with long red hair and freckles. I noticed her getting the canoes
ready while we were swimming.

As we approach her, she finishes arranging paddles in the
final canoe and greets us with a bright smile and energetic
wave. "Hi! . . . Just get with your swimming partner and form
a line along the path. I'll be right up."

Since I don't have a partner, I assume I'll again be with the
instructor and I walk to the end of the line.

She nimbly climbs the small bank, like a cat. As she takes
us in, her natural smile and sparkling amber eyes make me
happy. She has a light, airy quality. "Now . . . let's see here,"
she says as she picks up her clipboard. "That's right . . . there
are thirteen in this group . . . and . . . Eddie?" She looks up and
I raise my hand. "Okay," she smiles. "You are the oldest and
the one who will be on your own."

I smile back and nod. Yes, on my own. Good. It's obvious my
age got discussed by the counselors to my advantage.

She picks up a life jacket and tosses it to me. Not again!
But perhaps it's the same routine as for the swimming class.
Besides, she is so upbeat. Hard to believe such a friendly person
is going to be mean. She goes through the rest of the group,
making sure everyone has a partner and helping each get the
jackets properly fastened.

T

"Now . . ." she says. "Never take off your life jacket until you are safely on the land, all the way out of the water onto the land." She pauses to let this sink in. It occurs to me that she gets it to register with a smile. Most adults do it with a more threatening expression. Even so, a life jacket is going to ruin the whole experience.

She shakes her red hair and continues. "Always stay in sight of the rest of the group," pause . . . smile. "Never stand in the canoe," pause . . . smile.

My mind wanders as she continues reading the list on her clipboard. My thoughts are like those people put into lyric poems, feelings more than thoughts. I haven't felt this way for some time. The hot sun warms my muscles. The light breeze caresses my shoulder blades. The smell of the lake makes me . . . makes me . . . happy.

Then she laughs . . . for no reason . . . she laughs. "Okay, now everyone come down to the canoes." Soon she has all of us standing knee deep in water next to our canoes. She tosses her clipboard lightly onto the bank and walks into the shallow water on the opposite side of my canoe. "When you get into a canoe, be sure it is stable. Do not pull yourself in but step over the side. If you try to pull yourself in, you will tip the canoe." She lightly steps into the canoe, kneels and turns again to face us. "These canoes are meant to be paddled by kneeling on the bottom. Always immediately get into a kneeling position, like this . . . Never stand in the canoe longer than absolutely necessary," . . . smile.

"Okay . . . one at a time, get into your canoes, assume a kneeling position and pick up your paddles."

It sounds simple, but for children who have little experience on the water and even for those who have, it's more a comedy of

T

mostly inept attempts, some resulting in awkward falls into the water, the successful ones little more than awkward falls into the canoes. If not for Jenny's sunny smile and lilting laugh, it could quickly turn negative, but her happiness is infectious. She even initiates a water fight by using her paddle to splash a spray of water on Jill when Jill's head pops up from inside the canoe she has tumbled into and she yells out "Victory," raising her arms in a show of success.

Somehow the ensuing splashes of water, laughter and an overturned canoe result in everyone kneeling in proper position with paddles ready for whatever comes next. Jenny left my canoe to get everyone in place, but has returned and assumed her position. She takes a paddle and begins to demonstrate paddling techniques.

"The Forward Stroke or Cruising stroke is the most often used canoe stroke." She demonstrates it as she talks. "It is initiated by placing the blade away from the hull, at a right angle to the centerline of the canoe and drawing it straight back toward the paddler's knee. Like this. See?"

All of us try to imitate her.

"Watch me." She demonstrates it again. "Blade out, away from the canoe. At a right angle, see? Then pull it straight back." She finds it necessary to repeat her demonstration several times, and even then, many are not able to imitate it. Again, her smile and encouragement keep even those clearly confused from getting too frustrated. "Don't worry, it will come once we get out on the bay and practice it."

While I've rowed and poled various floating devices on the lake all my life, I've never been in a real canoe and only accidentally figured out techniques that work, so I find it interesting to have her name, demonstrate and explain the

T

different strokes. She goes through the Reverse stroke, what she says is also called Back Paddling, the J stroke, which rotates in the shape of a J as the normal stroke is brought toward the canoe, useful when trying to steer the canoe for docking or to prevent it from drifting. She explains and demonstrates how this can also be done more powerfully with what she calls the Goon stroke, a more forceful reverse using the back side of the paddle. She continues through a number of variations — the Pitch stroke, the Indian stroke, the Pry stroke, the Running Pry, the Push-away, the Draw, the Scull, the Sculling Draw, the Reverse Scull, the Cross-draw, the Sweep . . .

Then she stops — smiles. The time for canoeing is over. We haven't even left the shore. "Tomorrow," she says, "tomorrow we'll take our first canoe adventure."

Fortunately, as with the swimming class, my age and experience on the water show, and as it turns out will be the case for the entire experience, the counselors see me as a kind of junior counselor, a little helper who will be allowed more leeway than normal. By the end of the next day's lesson, Jenny announces that the assigned twosomes may check out canoes and that I will be allowed to take out a canoe by myself and paddle where I will. When I ask if I can remove my jacket, the answer is "No, everyone has to wear a life jacket." But as the class is being led away she pulls me aside and whispers in my ear, "Once you're out of view of the others, you can just toss it in the bottom of the canoe."

Not only is this good news, but when she tells me her cheek accidentally touches mine. The feel of her skin, her smell and the light caress of her breathe remains with me the rest of my life.

T

That afternoon and part of most days after it, I spend time paddling around the bend from the camp to where no one can see me. Even though my own lake is mostly surrounded by wooded area, it has houses and docks and the markings of the real world. This lake has nothing to break the spell. It is out of time, a world ripe for the imagination. I can believe anything I want and if I should run into a buckskin-clad frontier man or feathered Indian slipping through the foliage along the shore, it won't faze me in the least. A part of me expects it.

It's a curious thing. I know the worlds in my mind don't exist outside of it and at the same time I know they do. That isn't exactly the way to say it. The world in my mind is real, perhaps more real than the world outside of it. That's not right either. Somehow, both are real because of the other. It's that connection of the brain and the mind. Separate them and . . . .

Still . . . even years later . . . I sense what I know cannot be . . . yet is . . . It would be wonderful to go back to that lake, paddle a canoe into that forest and come to a quiet rest in the shadows near the shore . . . a quiet . . . silent . . . rest . . . and wait . . . and wait . . . until I am no longer noticed . . . wait until that other world comes alive . . . .

Unfortunately, while I'm experiencing the Camp Christmas Tree world that seems to exist outside of time, at the same time, I'm feeling the urgency of not having enough time, hearing an incessant tick . . . tick . . . tick . . . tick . . . pulling me into the future.

I don't know. Is it good that the counselors are insistent on keeping us all entertained? Is it good that Camp Christmas Tree has so many enchantments that my realization of the lack of precious time keeps breaking the spell?

T

I know I have but two five-day weeks, ten short days.

At the time I don't think it through and see the irony. I just feel it, feel the end, the loss I am about to experience. Later, I will better understand the uneasy truth I'm experiencing, the truth that living outside of time doesn't eliminate but accentuates time.

At the same time I'm experiencing the joy of a timeless world, I'm also living in the future. And the future is all tangled up with the past. I keep pushing the future aside, forcing myself to stay in the moment, but I know it's there, know the most unexpected happening will bring a wave of sorrow.

Perhaps a casual comment . . . a sound . . . an image. Perhaps nothing at all.

When it happens, I need to be alone. I need to disappear.

This is what the counselors do not like. They lecture me about it. It is the one thing they insist I cannot do.

I know. They are right. Yet, my need to be alone overpowers me. I need to disappear . . . to disappear . . . not to tell anyone anything . . . but to disappear.

On the third day, Mike and Chuck take us to the archery field. I've seen it each day as the bus drives up the entrance road, nothing more than a level clearing of sparse grasses with six stacks of three hay bales lined along one end.

The previous spring, Mom and Dad agreed to spend money they didn't have to purchase me a bow-and-arrow set, my "big" birthday gift during what turned out to be dad's final summer, and similar, though less impressive, hay bales were stacked in our yard.

T

As with each activity, the group is introduced with the stress on safety, and we are told we have to have a counselor with us if we want to do archery in the future.

"Mike is the expert, at least that's what he tells me," Chuck says.

"Funny . . . at least I can hit the target."

"We'll see."

"Okay, pay attention," Mike says, as he picks up one of the bows. "This is a traditional or recurve bow. It's the one you've all seen in the movies. Professional hunters often use what's called a compound bow. Those are more powerful and have numerous extras to help with accuracy. If any of you have fathers who do bow hunting, that's probably what they use. But for target shooting, most people use this type of recurve bow."

"Boys, pay attention!" Chuck slides around the group to the back.

"My dad has a big compound bow," Gerald says. "He kills a deer with it every fall!"

"He must be a good bowman," Chuck says. "Do you have a bow?"

"Not until I'm twelve. Then he's going to get me one just like his and take me hunting with him!"

"Yer too small and skinny," Billy says. "You couldn't even pull back the string on a big bow!"

"Okay . . . okay . . . stop it . . . ," Mike cuts in. "Listen. That's exactly what I need to explain to you. You see these tags." He grasps the tag dangling from the bow in his hand and turns it to us. These indicate what's called the draw weight for the bow they're attached to. The draw weight is how much strength you need to pull back the string, so you want a different

T

tension depending on how hard you're going to pull. That's important, so when you choose one of these bows to use you want to try ones with different weights to see what feels right for you. We have them stringed at three different weights. I'll help you with that when we're ready."

"You'll need the weakest," Billy says to Gerald.

"Shut-up! You don't even know anything about bows!" Gerald says and shoves Billy. Chuck immediately steps between them. "Okay! This stops now or you're both going to spend the rest of the morning sitting at separate tables in the craft building!"

The command stops time.

No one moves.

It only lasts a few seconds, but those seconds break the membrane of time and the eerie stillness of eternity slips in.

In an attempt to save face, Billy weakly waves away Gerald, rolling his eyes as if to say it's not worth his time, eternity disappears back through the rip, and time's normal progression returns.

Mike smiles, as if telling himself a joke about the incident, and continues his demonstration. "The other part of this is the length of the bow, which is based on what's called your draw length. Your draw length is a little less than half the span of your arms. You want a bow that is double your draw length." He demonstrates as he explains. "Our bows come in three lengths. Chuck and I will help you get the right one."

I think about my own bow. Wish I had known all this before I got it.

"It is possible to buy what's called a take-down bow. These can be taken apart and reassembled, so they can be stored, transported and serviced more easily. And you can buy

T

attachments for them to change the draw weight. We don't have those, but if you ever encounter them, now you know what they are."

I know . . . there is no way around what I know . . . I know that Mike is taking about real bows. What he is saying doesn't apply to my bow. Mine is just a toy.

Mike sets down the bow and picks up an arrow. "It's also important to use the correct arrow."

None of this applies to my special birthday present.

"Most arrows are made of either fiberglass or carbon, which keeps them relatively lightweight." He motions us to move closer to see the arrow. "These are fiberglass . . . see. The arrow weight can vary in the shaft. The heavier the arrow shaft, the deeper it will sink into a target. If you're using an arrow for target practice, you don't need the arrow to sink in very far. If you're using it for hunting, however, you do need a much heavier arrow, because it has to sink through skin, muscle and bone. Also, if you're hunting, you want arrows that have broad heads, so they stay in. As you can see, ours just have small points, because that works best for targets."

I know I've gotten stuck, know I should force myself into a different line of thought, but knowing and doing are not the same. My arrows are neither fiberglass nor carbon. They're just painted wood with some kind of cheap metal point and plastic feathers.

He steps back and points the arrow at the bales of hay stacked on the other side of the field, each of them now holding a target. "Don't just start shooting your arrows anywhere. Make sure to have a safe place. Get a target. If you plan on practicing someplace, say, your backyard as opposed to a range, then you will need to purchase a suitable target that won't

T

ruin your arrows. Targets are available at sporting goods stores. A good idea is to purchase hay bales and stack them, as we've done here."

We did get some free hay bales, and the set came with some paper bullseyes.

He sets down the arrows and picks up a piece of dark brown leather with some straps. "Buy an armguard. An armguard goes on the forearm of the arm that's holding the bow." He straps it on. "See?" He shows us his arm with it in place. "Its purpose is to protect your arm if the string hits it." He pulls back the bow string to demonstrate.

I never heard about archery arm guards, never saw any Indians on television wearing bow straps. Seems kind of a sissy thing, type of equipment wealthy pretenders would use, those femme preppies from out East.

He picks up an even smaller piece of leather. "You should also get a finger tab. A finger tab is a strap of leather that protects your fingers from the tension of the string as you pull it back." He picks up the bow and demonstrates. "Your finger tab goes on the fingers that will be drawing back your bowstring with your pointer finger above the arrow and middle and fourth below. You can also touch your thumb to your pinkie behind the string to keep them out of the way."

When I first heard we would be doing archery at the camp, I was excited, but now . . .

I watch a monarch butterfly flit by and land on a tall stalk of grass.

"Consider optional training equipment. Depending on the bow you rent or purchase, it may or may not come with

T

-

additional parts helpful for beginners, such as a sight and a clicker. A clicker especially can be useful for beginners because it makes an audible click, letting the shooter know when the arrow is drawn back to the ideal pull . . . Stand perpendicular to the target. If you are right-handed, stand with your left hip pointing toward the target. Keep your body vertical. Don't lean to one side or the other . . . Imagine that your body is aligned with a center vertical line to keep yourself straight . . . Straddle the shooting line. The shooting line is a line that marks a particular distance from the target. Stand with your feet shoulder-width apart, centering yourself over the shooting line . . . like this . . . ."

A light breeze bends the stalk of grass. The butterfly rises and lightly floats toward a small pile of logs cut for firewood. A chipmunk appears on top of one of them, looks about, jumps to the ground and scurries into a patch of nearby weeds.

"Keeping your feet firmly planted at shoulder-width also maximizes your stability as you shoot . . . see . . . Look directly at the target by turning your head toward it . . . like this. Be sure not to turn the rest of your body, which should instead remain perpendicular to the target. Keep your chest in and shoulders down, making sure not to hunch up your shoulders . . . Hold the bow with a firm yet comfortable grip. If you are right-handed, hold the bow with your left hand on the hand grip. Most recurve bows have handles, so you will know where to hold the bow."

I only remember once when Dad disciplined me. He must have disciplined me more than that once, but only once did it

T

involve a belt, which is no doubt why I remember it. I deserved a punishment, but I don't know why Dad went to this extreme. It wasn't like him.

In context, it should be remembered that using a belt on a child's butt wasn't seen as such a terrible thing to do at the time. My junior high gym teacher, Mr. Halverson, one of my favorite teachers, incorporated using a wooden paddle into his class. Every day he identified a few students who were guilty of something, mostly of simply screwing around rather than paying attention, and had them bend over for a swat in front of the class before excusing us.

On the other hand, I don't know of any parents doing it as a normal means of discipline. I do know of rare, but real, incidents of parents and teachers hitting their children and students with their fists. And I saw a rather famous incident of a student physically attacking a teacher in a school hallway.

I'm six, John three. We are in the partially dugout basement, sitting on a small pile of dirt, playing war with an old deck of cards, and we want the homemade toy trucks that have been left in the sand outside.

"Okay," I say. "We'll cut for it. If you get the highest card, then I have to get the trucks. If I get the highest card, you have to get them."

"I don't want to."

"Well, you have to if you lose! Here, draw a card!"

John draws his card, an eight of spades. "Aw, no!"

"That's not so bad. You've got about a 50/50 chance." I hand him the cards. "Okay, now you hold them out for me."

He takes them and tries to shuffle by cutting the deck in half and sliding the halves together in as much of an

T

alternating form as he can. Then he fans them out in his small hands and holds them toward me. I pull out one and turn it over, ten of hearts.

"I win. Now go and get two dump-trucks!"

"No!"

"You lost!"

"I didn't want to play!"

"Yes you did! You drew a card! Now go and get the trucks!"

"No!"

"If you don't, I'll pee on you!"

"No you won't!"

"Yes I will!"

"You'll be in trouble!"

"You better not tell!"

"I will!"

"Just get the trucks! You lost! It's fair!"

"No . . . you won't pee on me!"

"Yes I will!"

"No you won't"

"Come on! Just get the trucks!"

"No!"

In the end, I have no choice. At least I don't think I do.

John immediately tells Mom. When Dad gets home, Mom tells him, and he decides he needs to send a strong message.

I don't recall ever seeing Dad lose his temper or be violent in any way other than that spanking. However, one of Mom's favorite stories is about just that. It seems Dad's dad was at the house, visiting the two of them shorty after their marriage. He was drunk and got so obnoxious that Dad took him out in the yard, beat him up, and told him never to come back.

T

Mom must have seen it as the poor man's version of chivalry. It certainly appears Dad was standing up for her honor.

It's also clear Dad's father did not have a good relationship with the two of them. If I ever met him, it was only once. A man came out one summer to fish off our dock, and that man "might" have been my paternal grandfather. I encountered him on the edge of our driveway as he was making his way down the road to the dock.

"The thumb and index finger should turn slightly inward, while the rest of your fingers on this hand should be relaxed . . . see . . . like this. Your wrist should also be relaxed. Don't hold your bow with a death grip. This will cause inaccuracy in your shooting. Stay relaxed so that every movement will be smooth."

Dad carefully taps the tiniest of nails through the two pieces of wood. "See . . . ?" He folds the wood blade into the wood handle. It's a perfectly carved replica of a jack knife.

"Load an arrow onto your bow. You need to load the arrow by fitting the notch in the end of the arrow onto the bow string. Do this before lifting your bow and without actually drawing the string. This is called 'nocking' the arrow."

"Eddie," Mom says. "Just look straight ahead. Don't look at the camera . . . okay, now, Honey, raise the razor like you're just going to start shaving the back."

Click . . .

"It didn't flash. The bulb didn't go off."

T

Dad sets down the razor and walks over to look at the camera. He takes the bulb out and pushes it back in. "There . . . maybe it just wasn't completely lodged."

"Okay, okay," Mom says. "Eddie, just look ahead like nothing is happening."

Click/Flash!

"Wait. Let me take another just in case this one doesn't work."

"Lift the bow to shoulder height. As you lift, ensure that the arm holding the bow is straight and locked at the elbow. If your elbow is bent at all, it will be much more difficult to draw the bow. Now, keeping the elbow of your bow arm straight additionally helps to keep your arm away from the bow string as you release. See? . . .

See . . . Okay, now, pull the bowstring back. You should pull back far enough that your hand rests right under your jawbone. Your bowstring should nearly touch your face around the corner of your mouth. Check again as you draw back that you are not twisting your torso to face the target. You want to practice letting the stronger muscles in your back do most of the work as you draw the bow as opposed to your arm muscles . . . Take aim. You want to aim with your dominant eye while keeping your other eye closed. Your dominant eye is much more reliable for your aim to the target.

If your bow has a sight, use the notches in the sight to help you line up your target. Also check your aim with your eyes."

It's hilarious. John is so serious. He takes one of the puppies and carries it to the box. Then he goes back and picks up another to carry to the box, but as he does this the first pushes

T

over the side of the box and runs back. So he sets down the one he is carrying and goes after the one that escaped.

"I'm getting the camera," Mom says. "I have to get this on film." It is the new toy, the expensive toy – a camera that takes motion pictures. Mom needn't have hurried, as even a five-year-old John is not one to give up easily, so the comedy will continue for longer than necessary to capture it on film.

"Relax your fingers off the string to fire. Don't jerk the string back, or the arrow won't fly straight. Keep your release as smooth and gentle as possible, thinking of the action more like relaxing your fingers off the string as opposed to letting it go . . . Stay in position until the arrow hits the target. Once you release the string, the arrow still must accelerate off the bow, and any movement during the fraction of a second can disrupt the intended flight path of the arrow. Train yourself not to jerk or flinch by holding your position until you hear the arrow hit the target."

A horsefly circles my hair. I try to bat it away, but it immediately returns.

Dave throws me the football. I catch it and run towards him. He crouches down and grabs me as I attempt to dodge passed him. It's a chilly Saturday afternoon. The leaves have turned and the wind gusts, causing them to swirl down. He catches me around the waste and swings me up to his shoulders. "Got you!"

"Come on!" Sharon waves us toward a building. Soon she has us all at the front door. "Now . . . settle down . . . settle down . . . you have to behave in the building!" She pushes open

T

the double doors and motions us inside. "This is the Crafts Building."

It's a large room with eight long tables. Two of the walls have windows from about waist high on up, and the other two are a mixture of shelves, bulletin boards and file cabinets.

"Everyone find a seat at one of the tables . . . come on . . . stop pushing! You have to behave or we'll leave and not get to use this building!"

It takes a few minutes to get everyone seated and relatively quiet. "Now," she begins, "what you can do in here is to make things having to do with nature." She walks around the room, pointing at where various materials are storied and at a few of the saved creations of previous children as she talks. "There are all different kinds of paper, drawing pencils, watercolor paints, brushes, scissors, glue, tape, cardboard . . . even pieces of hobby wood! . . . but . . . most importantly . . . is that you will be bringing in things you collect outside, and we will show you how they can be used for all kinds of crafts!"

I feel like the proverbial child in a candy store. As I try to take it all in, I lose my concentration and miss much of what she says.

After my longest fade, her voice filters in, "One of the things I want all of you to do is to create your own scrapbook as a memento of your time here. And the first project you're going to be putting in it is a leaf tracing, a picture you make by coloring over leaves."

As she says this, she takes a piece of drawing paper and sets it on the table in front of her. Then she reaches into a small wire basket and takes out some leaves. "Now," she continues as she demonstrates, "you set a leaf on the table, bottom side up . . . then you carefully set the paper over the leaf like this . . .

T

then . . ." She turns and picks up a shoebox filled with crayons. "Then you choose a crayon." She takes a red crayon and gently rubs it over the paper. Like magic, the lines of the leaf appear on the paper and she holds it up. "See. It's called a leaf rubbing! You continue by putting other leaves under the same piece and rubbing over them with different colors until you've created your final picture." She turns and picks up a stack of examples from previous children. "See!"

I'm enchanted. Never thought of doing this . . . and some of them are amazing. I'm still thinking about what I might create while she finishes showing her examples and turns away to replace them.

When she turns back, she has a new batch of examples. "Once you've done this, I'll show you how to make leaf cuttings that you can paste together to make leaf wreaths! . . . "See" . . . .

"So . . . ," she says, "tomorrow . . . before we come in here, we'll go leaf hunting, and each of you can choose leaves you want to use."

Shortly after Dad died, the Johnson family stopped by, and the father brought me a large roll of paper from where he worked. It was great. I could unroll as much as I wanted and draw pictures or make cutouts. "It's not much," he said to Mom, "but I know Eddie likes to draw, so . . . ."

I barely register her plans for us. I'm too busy sizing up what materials are available. While it stresses crafts involving nature, building a bird feeder or bird house from sticks gathered about the camp bound together with the stocks of certain weeds or twine , I could care less if the materials are natural ones or

T

the boxes of Popsicle sticks and Elmer's glue I see on a nearby cupboard.

One day, Chuck takes us outside to the grassy field next to the sidewalk leading to the front of the main office, where he hands us off to Mike.

"Come on," Mike says, "make a semi-circle . . . over here . . . come on . . . sit on the grass."

As usual, it takes a few minutes to get the group settled, but once we're all sitting, he turns and reaches into a large, beat-up, dark brown, leather satchel sitting on the grass behind him.

As he feels about inside it, he talks, "Okay . . . ahh . . . today . . . just a minute . . . okay . . . there . . . got it . . . today . . . I'm going to show you how to make what's called a 'laid up' rope." He holds out a ball of twine.

This sounds interesting.

"Making rope is a skill that has been around for thousands of years. Once people got past vines and other natural materials for binding things, they discovered that fibers could be combined and twisted into great lengths by taking advantage of the tendency of materials to remember their natural condition."

He holds the twine so we can see it. "The lay of a rope is determined by examining the twist. See? . . ." He holds out a strand. "If you look down the length of a rope and the primary strands spiral in a clockwise direction, it is a right hand laid. Like this. See?" He bends down and holds it in front of each of us in turn.

"Now . . . if we do it by hand, we need to work together. First, of course, we need to get our material. We can either gather it

T

or buy a twisted fiber twine. What I have here is called jute, what burlap is made from."

He unrolls about ten feet of it. "We start by cutting three equal strands. Here . . . you," he points at Susie who happens to be sitting on the left in front of him. "Hold this end." She does. He stretches the fiber and cuts it with a jack-knife. Then he repeats this two more times, so he has three strands.

"Now, tie a small loop on one end of each strand large enough to slip a stick or finger through." He does this as he explains it, and directs Susie to hold all three strands.

"Now . . . you . . . and you . . . and you," he picks three others and hands each the other end of a strand, "you three pull your strands tight and twist them to tighten the natural twist of the twine." He stops Bobby. "Wait a minute. Here . . . you have to be careful not to let it kink." He adjusts the hands of each of those holding the twines until he is satisfied. "Now, bring all three strands together without losing the tension." He deftly controls the movements of his helpers. "Twist the three together in the opposite direction, while holding tension on the whole thing . . . see . . . okay . . . . The memory of the fibers will produce a simple three strand rope." He continues to pull each of the strands tight as the children try to follow his directions. Then he takes the newly stranded rope from them, ties off the end and swings the result through the air. "And," he says exuberantly, "just like that, we have rope!"

I wonder why rope has a grain. Same as our water hose. Always a pain to rewind that into a circle after using it. Same as electric cords . . . .

One afternoon we're told we're going on a hike to visit a nearby farm. "We have something special planned for you," Chuck says mysteriously.

T

A chorus of "What? Please, tell us, please! . . . please! . . . please!" is followed by a laughing "No! It's a surprise!"

What could it be? The counselors build it up. They say we're going to see an exotic creature. What does that mean? An exotic creature?

While we guess . . . a lion? . . . an elephant? . . . maybe a huge gorilla like King Kong? . . . they line us up, ask several times if anyone needs to go to the bathroom, and make sure each of us has a partner. Then, while we're still buzzing about the creature . . . Godzilla? . . . No, you dummy, that's just pretend! How do you know? . . . they lead us down the gravel entrance road onto Game Farm Road and turn us left.

Beneath a hot sun, we begin to make our way — first up a small hill, then down, then back up a larger hill, following the dirt road as it swings in a lazy curve to the right. Mike and Chuck and Susie have canteens filled with cherry Kool Aid they keep offering to whoever wants a drink.

The younger children continually fall behind, so we have to stop and wait for them to catch up. Birds announce us from the trees. Chipmunks, grey squirrels and occasional rabbits scurry in and out of the tall grass along the edges of the road. Grasshoppers, honey bees, dragonflies and various colored butterflies flit about. At one-point Chuck puts his hand on my shoulder. "Look." He points to a branch high in an ironwood tree. "It's a Red-tailed Hawk!"

So it goes. What I might have walked in thirty minutes by myself takes ninety, and the initial curiosity that energized the group begins to fade. The counselors don't seem to care. In fact, they often stop the group to show us some plant, animal, type of rock or insect we encounter. According to Mike, there is no rush, the journey is as important as the arrival.

T

But eventually we pass a thick patch of birch trees to our left, make one last sharp turn to our right and see the farm house through several large cottonwood trees on the right. This is all it takes to re-energize us. The monstrous creature awaits, somewhere in that farm, lurking . . . !

With the destination in sight, everyone is drawn toward it, even the younger dawdlers. It takes but a few minutes to reach the driveway.

There is nothing special about the place. As I wait for everyone to come together at the end of the driveway, I take it in, an old white farmhouse and some other building about the same size, both needing paint, straddle a fifty-foot dirt driveway that leads through them into a farmyard and through the farmyard to the open barn doors of an old red barn. Some large white geese and a mixture of white, light brown and orange brown chicken wander about the driveway and weedy lawn on either side of it.

Next to me at the end of the driveway, an oversized, dented, rusty mailbox sits atop a leaning, unpainted, wood post. I think to look for a name on it, but there is nothing, not even the usual address. About half way up the driveway, we walk into the shade of the two huge white oak trees that rise above the yard, one on each side of the driveway. Some kind of leafy bushes have been planted though not trimmed along the front of the house, which consists of a screened-in porch centered by a front door with a small front porch and two cement steps down to the beginning of a cement walkway, but this entrance does not appear to get much use.

While I've lived near farms all my life, I've not had much chance to be on a farm, just the one night I spent at the farm where Gordy grew up, which didn't amount to much more than

T

looking out on his farmyard from my upstairs window. I remember it satisfying my "Charlotte's Web" images. I still remember the teacher reading that book to the class a chapter a day. I don't know why but listening to her read that story will stick with me all my life, and whenever I remember it, I will feel happy.

Some of the children from Minneapolis are even less familiar with this world and are afraid to walk into the squawking geese.

"As long as you don't make any sudden or threatening moves, you don't need to worry," Susan says. "They're used to being around people, don't cha know." She crouches down, spreads her arms over as many of the smaller children as she can and walks them forward.

Once we get to the screen side-door of the house, Chuck separates and knocks. Immediately, a woman appears in the doorway and the two exchange greetings. As he turns back to join us, she smiles, waves and calls out a welcome before disappearing back into her house.

"Okay," Chuck says, his eyes sparkling. It's all set. Come on, now, everyone stay together."

Then it happens.

We reach the back edge of the two buildings and can see past them to the farmyard. I immediately register the larger equipment. To the right are two beat-up flatbed trucks, one with four-foot wooden stakes fitted on each side of its bed to keep a load of tree branches from falling off. To the left, an equally rusted, dark-green pick-up truck sits next to a large, rusty contraption that I assume has to do with planting or harvesting a crop.

T

A chestnut Irish setter barks and runs up to us, wagging its tail. Some of the children back away, but Mike steps immediately into its path, slaps his leg and calls out "Here boy, come on, over here." The dog eagerly pushes into his outstretched hands and he playfully backs it away from the group.

Though we can't see most of the animals, the sounds of a farm fill the air — horses snort and whinny, sheep and goats bleat, pigs squeal and snort, and cows moo. So do the smells, including a strong stench of manure.

Two men in overhauls look up from beneath the hood of a Ford station wagon, wave and head toward the barn. Most of the ground is dusty dirt, similar to the driveway, and the dust rises as they shuffle across it.

All in all, though few of us have spent much time on a farm, there is nothing overly exotic or unexpected. At the very least, we've all seen similar depictions on television.

"Look!" Chuck says and points to the large, green and yellow tractor sitting a bit back from the yard to the left.

We turn to him and then to where he's pointing. Two peacocks strut proudly out from behind it. Wow! We've never seen live peacocks! And these are huge!

No, they are not the monstrous creatures of our imaginations, not even the dangerous ones featured in those Saturday-morning-African-safaris-movies we've all seen. But because they are immediate, real, and seem so strangely out-of-place we are caught by surprise. Some of the children squeal.

Is it out of excitement?

Fear?

Both?

T

I'm not sure how to understand my own feelings. There is a sense I am living one of the curious episodes of The Twilight Zone. Indeed, it is as if two different worlds have inexplicably merged. No, not merged. The *real* world is still the world, but some entity from another world outside of the real world has found a passage into it. One of the seams of the fabric of the comfortable, known world of rural Minnesota has gotten pulled apart and two strange animals that shouldn't been in it have crossed over.

It's not the same as going to the zoo and seeing lions, leopards, elephants and all of those mostly African animals. They are caged. They are not part of my world. They remain a part of another world that does not belong in my world.

These peacocks are walking about my world as if they are a part of it.

The more I try to clarify it, the more I realize my explanations are getting in the way of what I experience. I sense it. Yes. I know I sense a strange, surreal feeling as these out-of-place birds strut casually about this farmyard.

On Wednesday morning the counselors take us into a barnlike building located at the top of the hill overlooking the natural amphitheater where we gathered on the first day. Inside, we find it's mostly one room with a high ceiling and a cement floor. There are some stacked chairs and long tables with their legs folded along one of the walls, and another wall has a counter fronting a large half wall that appears to have a kitchen behind it.

"Okay!" Chuck says enthusiastically, "Time for a Saturday night square dance!"

It's safe to say none of us shares his exuberance. I suspect he knows this and likely is not all that excited either.

T

Soon we are paired off and trying to follow a scratchy recording of some man talking fast . . . or . . . I guess . . . singing. Later, Chuck says it's referred to as 'patter,' which is a sort of talking and singing mixed together. At the moment, the counselors are busy moving among us, trying to keep us dosey-doeing and . . . whatever . . . to the music. If nothing else, it will give us a couple of catch phrases that bring a laugh for years to come. Here is the first of a string of verses:

It's not too good to be alone,
Iron sharpens iron, don't you know?
You lead, I'll follow - this could all change tomorrow,
Let me slip on through your fingers,
Take my hand, we're arm in arm and toe to toe,
We'll keep this all from being touch and go.

So swing your partner 'round and 'round,
Dosey the doe,
Put one foot in and one foot out,
Hokey the poke.

I never sort out why it is considered something we should experience at a day camp. In a way, it's a strange experience similar to that of the peacocks. I'm not sure what to make of it. Are the counselors really as excited about this as they seem? They put up a good front, but I can't buy it.

As with the unreality of the peacocks in my world, this square dance or barn dance or whatever it is also feels unreal. I know, again mainly from television, that once upon a time people in Minnesota and apparently all over the country or at least the frontier part of it gathered for these on Saturday

T

nights. The counselors say many of the smaller towns surrounding us still hold them and that my parents most certainly experienced them. Nevertheless, for me they are a part of the world of Davy Crockett, that distant past I've learned about by watching Disney.

I don't feel the strange juxtaposition in the same way I did for the peacocks, as this experience never breaks the barriers between the realities. These dances are more like the animals at the zoo, safely separated from my world, not really a part of it.

The main thing that we take from the experience are the lines "dosey the doe" and "hokey the poke," which we begin to say whenever we want to make an ironic statement or indicate we don't understand something. We find them so humorous that we start laughing before we even finish the phrase. The first word for either is enough. It's as if we've begun to develop our own private language. "Hokey the poke" and a shrugged shoulder has an insider's meaning we can't quite explain, but we all know there is something humorous about it.

As for the dancing, I will never experience a real square dance. I remember being taught the same dance or one very similar in kindergarten, and I performed *Skip to My Lou*, the best-known song associated with them, for my first piano concert.

I can't know it at the time, but I'm on the edge of a dramatically different world of music and dance, one that will become an obsessive drive to give life meaning.

In truth, I've already entered that world. Camp Christmas Tree is the world I've lost, a world that is real and yet not real – a world of childhood where square dancing, coonskin hats,

T

camp fires and Indians are real. It's the frontier, wild-west world I watch on television and act out in the woods of my neighborhood.

At the time, I have no idea Hollywood has created a pretend world of cowboys and Indians. It doesn't matter. In my childhood reality, I can still believe it. That's what I'm recapturing or desperately trying not to lose, and this day camp is surrounding me with it. Here, if I can just stop time, I can have my world back again.

In my real world, I've felt it disappear. I don't understand, but I know that there's an atmosphere here I no longer have when the bus drops me off at the end of the day.

My favorite group activity at the camp is capture-the-flag. I've been playing it in my neighborhood for years. It works much better at night, but since the camp has such deep foliage and trees, it works okay during the day. Besides, since I am the oldest, am already beginning my growth spurt noticeably younger than most, and have some natural abilities, I am easily the best at it. It's fun to be good at things, and as with music, I am not yet quite to the point where I see the complications beyond the simple beauty of a major chord.

It is one of those crystal-clear memories. Not only can I visualize it, I can feel the wet leaves and smell the wet bark from a brief cloud burst. The sun has returned and the sky is blue. I am directly above Chuck in a tree as he searches for me, so close I can reach down and remove his tan beach hat. I almost do it, because it's so funny, but don't. After all, technically, it means I'll be captured.

I don't know when I first realized it, but it was at a young age. Hiding up a tree works. People never look up. It will come in handy in more dangerous situations.

T

The second Monday, Chuck takes each group for a 90-minute demonstration of how to set up a campsite, mainly how to put up a tent, gather firewood and make a campfire. The site is about twenty yards down the path that goes by the swimming dock. There's not much to it, a small, rocky field with sparse patches of Chestnut, Limestone Meadow and Fringed Sledge trying to survive the trampling. A Yellow Birch spreads like a fat bush on the front left, and a patch of large, old Bur Oak dominates the woods to the right.

"All right, you," he says, pointing to three boys standing off from the rest of the group. "Over here. I want you to gather up the tent stakes and roll up the rope."

The way it works is that each group takes down the tent and puts out the fire before leaving the site, so the tent canvas, stakes and ropes are lying in a jumble, ready for the next group. The boys he directs are looking at something in their hands and whispering. Probably why he focuses on them.

One of them slides whatever he has been showing the others into his pocket.

"Alright," Chuck says, "so what's the prize? What's in your pocket?"

"Oh . . . nothing . . . nothing."

"Come on, you know everyone here saw you with something, saw you put something in your pocket."

"It's nothing . . . just a rock . . . nothing."

"Well," Chuck cuts him off. "It's a strange rock . . . yes sir . . . strange rock indeed."

The boy looks back as innocently as he can.

Chuck laughs. "Okay, you're making a fool of yourself."

The rest of us start to giggle.

T

"Ahhh . . . funny how you're the only one who doesn't seem to notice . . . but . . . your rock is an awfully lively one!"

Now the boy realizes there is no way out. He digs into his pocket and pulls out a frog.

"Let the poor frog go. How'd you like to be stuffed in a pocket, unable to move or even breathe."

The boy tosses the frog into the grass.

"Sure is a small frog," Jennifer says.

"It's a tree frog," Chuck says.

"What?"

"What?"

"What?"

Many of the children have never heard of a tree frog.

Chuck laughs. "Okay . . . time for a nature lesson. Tree frogs are much smaller than true frogs. They have pads on their feet so they can climb high into trees."

"What?" the chorus responds.

"Frogs in trees!"

"That's right," Chuck says. "During the breeding season, you can hear the males call from perches on vegetation in or near standing water. The females lay eggs singly or in small clusters, attaching them to aquatic vegetation."

"So . . ." a boy from behind me asks, "what happens to them in the winter? Do they just freeze?"

"Well," Chuck says, in most cases they find a cozy place to hibernate in a pile of leaves or under rocks or logs. Some can create their own antifreeze. Their liver converts glycogen into glucose and pumps it into their other organs to keep ice crystals from forming."

"Frogs give you warts," Billy says"

"No! That's toads!" Dave cuts in.

T

"Okay," Chuck says, "Time to get back to why we're here. Now, you three boys get at the tent." He continues through the rest us, giving directions to some for gathering dry grass, leaves, twigs and dead branches to start and burn a fire, and explaining to others how to clean and prepare the site for both the fire and the tent.

We never do get our tent set up correctly. Chuck has been through this many times, so instead of getting mad or frustrated, he laughs it off. "Enough. We can try it again another day. We're going to run out of time, so take down what you have and leave it ready for the next group."

The gathering of materials for the fire has been more successful. Chuck calls us around the fire pit, an uneven, five-foot, dirt circle surrounded by rocks. Most of the ashes from the previous group have been shoveled into two large, black plastic bags. Three larger, half-burned logs have been set just outside the rocks to be used again.

Explaining it to us as he works, Chuck begins building the fire with kindling – dead grass, weed stocks, leaves and twigs. Then he leans slightly larger branches in a tent-like structure over them.

"Now," he says. "This is the tricky part. If you practice it, you can start a fire by striking stones together. Flint works the best. It is even possible to start one by rubbing pieces of dry wood together, but you have to rub really fast. I don't recommend it. It takes a lot of practice, and if you try it will just frustrate you." As he talks, he takes two small pieces of flint from his pocket, kneels and begins striking them . . . click . . . click . . . click. I can see the sparks. But the dry stalks and bark they fall on aren't catching, click . . . click . . . click . . . Hearing our murmurs, he says without stopping, "You have to be

T

patient," click . . . click . . . click . . . The murmurs get louder. Someone giggles. "Patience!" Click . . . click . . . click . . . click . . . click . . . A small spark catches a leaf and holds. An edge of the thin bark above begins burning. He cups his hand around it . . . then blows gently on it to feed it oxygen and send it traveling along the edges of the bark.

No one is whispering or laughing now. We're all squeezed into a circle to see if it's going to work.

Then the red-and-yellow glow jumps onto another bit of bark hair and flames up. We respond with a group murmur of excitement. He carefully dangles dry stalks of grass over the flame. We hold our breath as he brings them as close as he can without touching the barely burning bark . . . .

The flames die down and failure is evident . . .

Then . . . Yes!

The flame catches!

He drops them quickly to avoid burning his hand. They immediately ignite more of the kindling.

We respond with a group cheer.

"Okay! Okay! See! Now calm down! We're still not done!" As the fire takes hold, he quickly adds more twigs, reaching right into the flames to place them where they'll catch. "Eddie, get me some of those branches over there." He motions with his shoulder to indicate a pile to his left.

I quickly comply. Each time he holds his hand back toward me, I supply it with more. The critical moment has passed.

"That's enough," he says to me as he stands. Then he places four of the larger, half-burned logs into flames, and familiar crackling and snapping sounds accompany a wave of heat.

He steps back and stands to admire it for a moment. The group is not as interested and begins to get rowdy.

T

"Come on! Settle down! We're out of time! . . . The next group's comin' in! So guess what! Now," he says and smiles, "we get to put it out!"

This is where we get the standard lecture about being sure not to ever leave a campfire burning, not even warm. "Smother it with dirt! Dig into the ashes with a shovel or a stick or whatever you have! Be sure there are no hot embers still ready to burst into flame. Throw water on it, even turn it into mud."

Smoky the Bear would have been proud of him.

One morning, Jeff takes our group on a nature walk.

"Come on," he motions us. "Over here . . . Come on . . . make sure everyone has a partner. Eddie, you walk at the back and make sure no one gets left behind."

We barely begin walking the path and he stops us. "Look, see," he waves his right arm across an area. "This patch . . . these tall weeds all along the left edge? This is Giant Ragweed."

"Huh . . ." I blurt out, "thought ragweed was just a general term for all kinds of weeds that cause people to get runny noses and headaches."

"Yes and no," he replies as he walks into the patch and breaks off a stem. "Ragweed is often used as a generic term," he stops to find another word, "a general term for all weeds that cause such problems, what is often referred to as hay-fever," another somewhat casual reference for allergies to pollen. Both ragweed and hay are actually just a couple of specific plants within many that produce such pollens. Plantain, nettle, mugwort, fat hen and sorrel are some of the others. Now, look .. . See how the leaves are opposite." He holds the stem up and shows us as he talks. "They grow up to a foot long and about

T

eight inches across. The larger leaves divide into three or five deep lobes. The edges are finely toothed . . . see?" He holds them out and walks through the group. "See how the surfaces have a kind of hair. And look, see . . . the stems are coarse, mostly smooth in the lower part with spreading hairs in the upper. The central stem branches from nodes along the entire length. The upper branches often reach heights equal to the main stem." He hands the stem to Billy and turns up the path. "Come on . . . we're just getting started."

And so the walk continues, Jeff stopping us every few yards to tell us about another wild plant. Though I've lived my life surrounded by these plants, I don't know most of their names and know almost nothing about their properties — which ones are edible, which poisonous, which cause rashes or in some cases help prevent them. I'm reminded of suffering from an afternoon of clearing away the undergrowth by the lake to create a great little fort, only to find out most of what I cleared was poison ivy.

My entire body was covered. It's impossible to relate how much I wanted to scratch, everywhere, arms, chest, face, legs, and impossible to reach back. Calamine lotion was the prescription — at best a lame solution.

Jeff stops us at a patch of wild blueberries, picks a handful and holds them out to us. "These are ready for picking in mid-summer and safe to eat. Minnesota also has a variety of briar berries — blackberries, thimbleberries and raspberries. All are safe, tasty snacks, but be careful about their thorny stems."

I've often stumbled on bushes of red and black berries and eaten them. This is an obvious one. But I've not thought much about eating the flowers, leaves, stalks and roots of other wild plants. I know wealthy people consider mushrooms a delicacy,

T

but I've been warned not to eat any wild mushrooms because some are poisonous.

Not much farther along, he points out a group of ostrich fiddlehead fern. "These sprout in early spring, and as soon as the stems reach eight inches, they are harvested and cooked, similar to asparagus. They're also used as ornamental plants in many offices and homes. . . .

As interesting as I find it at first, it starts becoming too much to take in, and his talk becomes the droning patter of a guided tour. My mind wanders.

The screen door bangs shut. JoAnn calls me, "Eddie! Eddie! . . . Eddie, I have something for you!"

I throw Dad's heavy pick aside and scramble across the clay to the wooden stairs.

"Eddie . . . . Eddie, you home?"

Up the stairs, left at the back-door entrance, up the final three steps to the main floor and a sharp right turn into the kitchen.

"There you are! What a grubby boy!" She sets her large wicker purse on the cupboard next to the sink and digs in it. "Here!" She pulls out a shiny, ceramic, white piggy bank that has decorations and Eddie on it. "I made you a piggy bank!"

My own piggy bank!

"And look," she turns it over, "on the bottom it has this plug you pull out if you want to get at your money!"

After dad's death, while digging through the junk in the small shed I find a dark brown, wooden box that's about six inches tall, six inches wide and eighteen inches long. The top half is connected to the bottom half with four small, rusted hinges. Inside, it's filled with odds-and-ends – screws, nuts,

T

bolts, washers, keys (some strung on circular holders, some random), and a number of Indian Head pennies. I separate these and put them in my piggy bank. As it turns out, they will come in handy to pay the two-cent cost of milk for my school lunches.

I almost didn't get to go on this nature walk, almost got a lifetime ban from Camp Christmas Tree. It happened the previous Thursday. I was walking up the back path to the hobby center and heard snuffling and crying from behind the fence blocking the view of the garbage bins. I walked around the fence and saw Paul sitting on an old bale of hay left next to the bins. His elbows were on his knees and his head was lowered into his hands, so he didn't see me.

"Paul," I said as I walked to him. "Paul . . . what's wrong?"

He immediately stopped his crying and wiped his face with his sleeve.

"Paul . . . what's goin' on?"

"Hey . . . come on . . . somethin's wrong."

"No, nothin' . . . everything's fine."

"Your cheek's all red. Did someone hit you?"

"No . . . no . . . I just . . . I just . . . I fell and hit my face . . . that's all . . ."

"Okay, who hit you?!"

He looked away.

"Come on!"

"It was Sammy. He said if I told he'd beat me up."

"Why?"

"I don't know. I was just walkin' up the path and he was comin' the other way. . . . and . . . and he shoved me down."

"Just pushed you down for no reason?"

T

"Yeah... I mean... I guess... told me I was blockin' his way... told me I better never block his way again or he'd beat me up."

"So... how did you get hit in the face?"

"I didn't... I... he... kicked me."

"Where is he?"

"I don't know.... he was goin' that way down the path..."

"Listen! Don't you worry about Sammy! You go into the bathroom in the craft building and wash your face and get yourself cleaned up! Got it!

He nodded. I was already turning.

I don't remember running around the fence and down the path, but I'm sure it was a quick trip. Sammy wasn't hard to find. He was standing beneath the large cottonwood tree to the left of the main administration building.

"Hey! Sammy!"

Sammy was a year younger than me, but he was the biggest boy at the camp, already weighing near 200 pounds. While he had a large frame and was clearly going to be a big man, he also already had a belly on him. It didn't matter, muscle or fat, his size was enough at that age to intimidate, and he knew it.

"What?" He must have known the answer before I even said it, but I wasn't paying attention to anything. I was focused.

"Come on, tough guy! You like pushing people down! Come on...! Try me!" I gave him an opening push, not meant to knock him, just to initiate the fight.

"What're you doing? You better watch out or..."

"Or what?" I cut him off. "Or you'll push me down! Come on, you chicken shit! Come on! Take your shot! It's the only one you're gonna get. Come on!"

T

"Look! . . . Here comes the counselors!"

I turned to see and he swung.

But even his trick wasn't enough. I was too fast for him, blocked his swing by sliding my left hand across his arm and hit him hard in the stomach with my right. He doubled over and I shoved him on his back. I immediately kneeled on his shoulders, ready to start pounding his face.

But then I was caught in a hammer-lock from behind and dragged off him.

It was Chuck.

He was not happy.

Paul saved me.

It took the rest of the afternoon to sort it all out, but in the end, Chuck got all three of us to agree not to say anything more about it. Fortunately, no one else had seen it. While such things often do get out, I wasn't too worried. Paul was embarrassed and since I had just become his idol, he wasn't going to say anything that might get me in trouble. And since Sammy's self-image was dependent on his tough guy stance, he wasn't about to admit what had happened. The only problem would be the possibility of Sammy making up a story to get me in trouble. Chuck was alert to that and emphasized to Sammy that he better not cause me any problems of any kind or he'd not only see to it Sammy got banned, but, even more effective, he'd see to it that everyone knew I had taken Sammy down, even Sammy's parents, which it was immediately clear was the ultimate threat to use on Sammy.

He immediately begged Chuck not to let his dad know he had lost the fight. It was strange. It confused me. I actually felt sorry for him. I wanted to comfort him!

T

Amazing! How can something so straight-forward end up being so complicated?

Since I'm lost in thought, I bump into the boy ahead me as Jeff brings us to another stop. We've been on the tour for about 45 minutes and arrived at a campsite. Some large sections of a tree trunk are arranged in three circles around a fire pit and Jeff indicates we should all sit. Once he has us in place, he sits on a stump that allows him to be higher up, so we can all see him, though it means some of us have straddle our trunk. "There are all kinds of interesting superstitions and stories attached to these plants. Perhaps you've heard some of them."

"Ladybugs bring good luck!" Sally says.

"Yes," Jeff says. "Ladybugs are named after Mary, Jesus' mother, who is referred to as Our Lady. She is often depicted wearing a red cloak in early paintings and the spots of the seven-spot ladybug, the most common type in Europe, are said to symbolize her seven joys and seven sorrows."

"What are the seven joys and sorrows?" I don't remember hearing about this in church or anywhere else. But something about things symbolizing other things interests me. I can't figure it out. Symbolic truths are true but they're true in a different way than literal truths. This connects to living after death. It makes no sense, nothing about religion makes sense. Yet . . . somehow . . . God is in control. He knows what I'm thinking . . . and he's judging me . . . but . . . if he knows my thoughts . . . then why do people pray out loud? And why do Catholics have to have a Priest talk to God for them? And . . . if he is all knowing and all powerful . . . why doesn't he control my thoughts? Every time, I try to think it through, I get confused. And I need to pay attention because Jeff is responding to my question.

T

"Let's see, the seven joys," Jeff says. "I'm not sure if I can remember them. There's the Annunciation . . ."

"What's that?"

"That's when the angel Gabriel told Mary she was going to give birth to Jesus."

"My parents don't believe in angels!" Billy says.

"Then they're going to Hell!" Gerald says.

I wonder . . .

Is Dad in Heaven? Can he see me? Is he watching me now? Is he proud of me?

Later that day, I see Jeff sitting on a bench, trying to fix a leather strap on his hat, and since it caught my attention, I ask him about fat hen weed.

"Oh, yeah, another catchy name," he says and laughs. "Fat hen has some medicinal properties and is a healthy addition to the diet, eaten much like spinach."

"Not my favorite," I interrupt.

"Yeah, a lot of people don't like it, but then there are many who do. And since Popeye gets his super strength from it, most everyone has at least heard about it. But since no superhero eats fat hen, only those really into nature and folk medicine or gourmet food have heard of it. The leaves are a mild laxative, and some find eating them or injecting the juice from the stems helps in the treatment of rheumatism. Also, some use the leaves as a wash or poultice for bug bites, sunstroke and swollen feet. Some believe the juice can reduce freckles . . . There!" He solves his problem with the leather strap and stands to leave.

"Do you believe in God?" I ask.

He stops and looks at me.

I look back.

T

"Of course! God's got everything under control. Even though we can't always figure him out, he's watchin' over us. Come on. The bus is waiting. You wouldn't want to get left behind."

Even the bus rides to and from the camp are fun because Bill rides with us and gets us involved in sing-alongs. It's where I first learn such songs as "On top of Spaghetti" and "?? Bottles of Beer on the Wall."

On top of spaghetti,
All covered with cheese,
I lost my poor meatball,
When somebody sneezed.

It rolled off the table,
And onto the floor,
And then my poor meatball,
Rolled out of the door.

It rolled in the garden,
And under a bush,
And then my poor meatball,
Was nothing but mush.

The mush was as tasty
As tasty could be,
And then the next summer,
It grew into a tree.

The tree was all covered,
All covered with moss,
And on it grew meatballs,
And tomato sauce.

So if you eat spaghetti,
All covered with cheese,
Hold on to your meatball,
Whenever you sneeze.

The final Friday afternoon the counselors gather everyone at the main stage for a formal goodbye.

They are in fine form, especially Chuck and Bill. And by now we've all been prepared for their bantering, so they have a group ready to laugh and clap and cheer. Spirits are high. Friendships have been formed. The upbeat atmosphere has been infectious and a group of children mostly prone to frowns has been transformed, at least for the moment.

Chuck begins a string of riddles, "Why did the farmer's wife tell the children not to play around the chickens?"

T

Bill is ready to play his straight man, at least initially. He makes a cartoonish, exaggerated motion with his arms to all of us to join him, "Don't know! Why?"

Chuck holds the moment as long as he thinks he can, then replies with a sly smile, "Because they use foul/fowl language!"

"Oooooooohhh!" The groan is a chorus of good natured jeers.

Chuck laughs. "Alright! Alright! You liked it! Don't pretend you didn't!"

Sharon interrupts. "What do you get from a pampered cow?" She waits for a response, but there is none. "Spoiled milk!"

We groan. The audience wants to join in. Jimmy yells from one of the top rows, "What do you call a cow with no legs?"

This one has already made the rounds and several of the children call out, "Ground beef!"

Sally, standing on her bench half way up, calls out, "what do you call a grumpy cow?"

Again, it's a joke that has made the rounds and several respond, "Mooooooooooody!"

Sharon has another, "What do you call a cow that has no milk?"

No one knows this one.

"An udder failure!"

No one gets it.

"Udder! You know . . . udder! . . . udder . . . an udder is the part of a cow where the milk comes from!"

"Ooooohhh . . . ." It's an underwhelming response. The children look at each other. Some are moving their shoulders to indicate they really don't get it.

Chuck jumps in. "What do you get when you cross an octopus and a cow?"

T

"I don't know," Bill says and motions for us to finish with him, "What do you get when you cross and octopus and a cow?"

"A cow that can milk itself!"

It gets a few laughs. "How about a chicken and cow?" he continues. No one knows. "Roost beef!" It doesn't go over well. "Come on . . . "Roost beef like in rooster!"

The jokes continue for a while, but it's clear we're getting restless, so Chuck slides the activities into a more formal goodbye. "All of us counselors have enjoyed getting to know you over these two weeks. We hope we've taught you some things about nature, and we hope you'll always remember your time here as a chance to have fun and make new friends. I can say personally that I feel lucky to have gotten to know you, and I'm going be sorry to see you go. But I will always remember you and those memories enrich my life."

Yes, it's true. I know I've been lucky because my church got together and raised enough money so that once-upon-a-time for two weeks I got to live in this happy world of once-upon-a-time.

I can see the orange buses lined up in the parking lot, ready to take us home one last time. Chuck continues to talk, but his words fade as I relive what is ending – the afternoon I sat in the crafts room and built an Alamo out of popsicle sticks, the cool morning I sat quietly in a canoe and watched a water snake sliding through a maze of underwater rocks, the day I won the horseshoe throwing contest and Chuck dumped a bucket of water over me as a joke congratulations for my victory, the day Bobby threw up from eating too many hot dogs, the day Sandy ripped her blouse and started crying, the day Jeff hit a softball into the woods past the field and Billy got burrs stuck all over his clothes fetching it, the day Jill wet her pants.

T

I'm startled out of my thoughts. It's Chuck's hand on my shoulder. He says in a soft voice, "Come on . . . time to go . . . ."

I've gotten so lost in my thoughts, I didn't even notice as the final ceremony came to an end and the children began being ushered to the buses.

Chuck gently rubs away the moisture beneath my eyes with his thumbs.

Crying?! I've been crying?!

"Remember that Red-tailed Hawk I showed you?"

I nod.

"Keep your eyes open. Next time you see one, you need to come and tell me about it. Okay?"

I nod.

"Promise?"

I nod.

But it's the last time I will see Chuck, the last time I will see anyone from those two weeks . . . from that world.

I no longer even remember their real names.

It's curious, though, I can still remember so much of it, those ten days. There a few experiences from that year of my life I remember as much as I remember that day camp.

As the bus wrenches itself down the exit road, I look out the window at the archery field, the stacked bales of hay . . . Funny, I thought when I was first told about the camp I would especially enjoy archery. After all I already had my own bow and I had practiced, so I would already know more than the rest. I imagined playing out my archery competitions, taking the roles of five competitors through a series of contests leading up to the world finale. But after the day it was demonstrated I never returned to the archery field.

T

The "real" equipment should have enticed me, made me feel I could at least pretend to live in a world where professional equipment is assumed.

For some reason I never took advantage of it . . .

There just wasn't enough time. There were so many things to do . . . the time . . . the days . . . the bus to take me home . . . before the morning had barely begun the afternoon kept coming to an end . . . my plans . . . my adventures . . . paths I wanted to explore . . . collages I wanted to make . . . the crafts . . . the endless crafts . . . carving designs in leather, burning them in wood, pressing them into tin . . . things to create each day . . . and . . . and . . . then . . . it was over.

Back in the real world I never thought to take out my bow and arrows. Like so many things that summer, archery disappeared from my life without there ever being a formal goodbye. It was just . . .
gone.

T

T

The Forbidden Pool

Kim bends down and whispers through the basement window, "Eddie."

I stop picking at the piano, walk over to the worn couch, step onto it to bring my face to the height of the window and pull back the short, flimsy, cotton curtain. The glass has long ago been broken and removed. "What's up?"

"Come on."

I pull myself up and through the window.

Kim stays in the shadows along the side of the house and then heads to the lake. I follow. We run slowly along the top of the bank above my dock and down the hill toward Lane Four.

Kim has it all thought through. There's an aluminum boat overturned on the bank. "Here," he says. "Help me."

Stealing!?
Borrowing . . . ?

Soon we have the light boat right side up and in the water. Two oars are stored on the floor, held in place by the seats. We use them like poles to quietly push ourselves away from the bank and out past the docks. "There's a swimming pool, across the lake, we can get into."

Trespassing . . .

"Where?"
"The Landing."

"The Landing?"

"Just past the creek on 110. Those five houses where 110 makes a sharp left into that S curve, on the lake side of the corner where 110 merges with West Branch Road."

"Oh, yeah, those rich houses in that wooded corner on the right."

"Haven't you ever seen the outdoor pool down the hill behind them, just off the creek, landscaped out of the swamp?"

"Never noticed."

"Well, it's left wide open all night long."

"Okay . . ."

"It's even lit! It's like a glowing pool of light all night long."

"They keep it lit all night?"

"To prevent anyone from sneaking into it."

"Makes sense."

"What's cool is that the pool itself is lit."

"The water?"

"Yeah. They have lights beneath the water so the pool glows."

The children clamor to hear the story. Mr. Orange looks down on them. So innocent. They won't understand.

"Please,"

"Please,"

"Please tell us,"

"Please," they urge him.

Children, he thinks. Always wanting stories.

He looks back at her. She has that sweet, ironic smile. He moves his head slightly and asks her with his eyes. Her eyes respond yes.

T

"Okay, okay." Let's see. Where to begin.

"Not his world," Mr. Orange's thoughts began coming out of his mouth. " A fantasy world. Only the wealthy had swimming pools. Those houses on the corner—only obtainable in that pretend world where dreams come true. . . .

Out on the dark lake I feel safe. No one can see us. Even if someone is standing in the shadows of the shore, just twenty-yards away, we're likely to pass unnoticed, or if noticed seem more a couple of ghostly spirits than two real boys in a boat.

Tom Sawyer and Huckleberry Finn poling our way through night.

Though it is a quiet night, a motor kicks in and we recognize the low rumble of the more expensive indoor motors coming from around the bend. It isn't going very fast, just trolling.

There is the chance its path might cross ours, and if it should gear and hit us directly, that likely means death, as we have no lights and will not be seen in time for it to swerve or slow. But the possibility is so slight it doesn't concern us. The only thing that might concern us is if it turns out to be water patrol, but that's also such a small possibility, we aren't worried.

We follow the shore until we reach the beach. The motor of the other boat stops. Either it is floating off shore, while its occupants enjoy the night sky and whatever else they have planned or it has docked. We fit the oars into their sockets and Kim begins rowing in a diagonal across the lake. I settle into the prow. Soon the night sounds of the shore fade and all we hear are the oars as they rhythmically groan and plunk into

T

the water with each new stroke—grroooan plunk . . . grroooan plunk . . . grroooan plunk . . .

Once we get far enough out we can see the dim lights of the speedboat. It is motionless, a dark shadow in the distance. As long as it remains where it is, we'll soon lose sight of it completely. We turn our gaze to the dark shore on the other side of the lake.

On the middle of the lake, the sounds from the edges are soft, a gentle background noise, but sound travels across open water, so we don't talk.

On occasion a fish breaches the surface. The oar holders groan and the oar blades rhythmically plunk in the water—grroooan plunk . . . grroooan plunk . . . grrooon plunk . . .

Though it isn't necessary, we take turns rowing—grroooan plunk . . . grroooan plunk . . . grroooan plunk . . .

As we approach the dark shadows of the opposite shore, we enter the range of the sound of the marsh crickets, and it quickly grows in volume, until it nearly blocks out the sound of the oars.

Small islands of marsh grass start to appear in the dark. We've reached the entrance into the lagoon that will lead us to the pool. Rowing doesn't work here. We stand and again use the oars like poles. We push through a large lily field, feeling with the oars to maneuver around shallow layers of rotting roots, sludge, large rocks and sunken tree trunks. It is a place that has not yet succumbed to the touch of human hands, as close as I will ever come to a prehistoric swamp. It won't take much to convince me that some of those creatures are still sliding through its muck and slime, especially on a dark night.

The swamp-grass gets tangled in the oars, and rather than making loud noises knocking it off, we bring the oars into the boat and pull off the wet weeds and clumps of gunk with our hands, hoping no blood-suckers, slugs, snails, salamanders, spiders, centipedes, or any of the endless other disgusting bugs get on us, not to mention beaver and water rats.

The water is generally still, but the shadows are alive with life, and as we quietly pole forward, we hear it from all sides. Bull frogs sitting on lily pads or half-submerged logs belch in low buuurrraps. A snowy owl hoots from the dark trees along the shore. A loon laughs eerily from the tall swamp grass to the right. Fish brake the surface, sending rippling splashes. Smaller swamp frogs splash into the water. We see the shadowy backs and heads of muskrats, the yellow-striped heads of turtles and the zigzag trails of snakes swimming on the surface.

The light of the moon always holds mysteries. So does the layered air of a swamp that flows through a summer night.

After half an hour, we begin pushing into where the swamp merges into the creek and surrounding land. We pass by small islands with basswood and hickory trees. I glimpse two mink slipping through a patch of sunflower stalks. The glowing eyes of a raccoon stare intently down at us from a tree branch, it's still form a silhouette in the moonlight. A cloud blocks out the moon. When its light returns, the silhouetted raccoon is gone. Then I see what looks like a common tomcat. Its eyes weave through the tall bulrushes, but it's too dark to be certain they belong to a cat.

Then we see the circle of light of the pool through the trees. It has an unreal quality, as if the result of enchantment rather than the work of human hands.

We climb out of the boat into the syrupy water, pull the prow of the boat into the bank and wrap the chain of the

T

anchor around the rough bark of a Red Oak. The ground is muddy, and I'm covered in the swampy slime nearly to my waist.

The five fingered, mitten like leaves of Sassafras rub against my face as I try to climb up the grassy bank, dousing me in its root beer scent.

The woman touches Mr. Orange. "Do you remember?"

He stops his story. "Remember?"

"The Sassafras, the days of the Sassafras."

"The early days," he says softly, "all those years ago."

"When God separated the double tree."

"Yes, in the beginning, yes, man and woman."

"Do you remember the transformation? The miracle?"

"The limbs morphing, becoming arms and hands and legs and feet."

"And the heads filled with knowledge."

"And souls . . . the unity of flesh and spirit."

"But the Sassafras didn't complete the metamorphosis."

"Perhaps they are the lucky ones."

"Without knowledge."

"Without souls."

"Without the awareness of self."

"Ignorant and innocent, without need of salvation."

"Come, come, let us not be sad."

"He is better for it."

The land is five feet above the water, and not much wider, a small peninsula with a string of trees jutting out into the swamp. On the other side of it is a wet field of wheat grass, twenty yards wide on a gradual incline to the backside of the

T

pool house, a small roofed building with three sides along one side of the pool. We can't see into it from where we are, but it doesn't matter. It's a safe place to hide from the view of the houses and roads.

We make our way through the thicker swamp grass, just outside of the light, to the back of the building.

We stop for a moment to gather our thoughts, make sure no one is about, and get up the courage to step into the light. I realize we're standing in poison ivy, but am too intent on the task at hand to worry about the likely results. I can see a patch of marsh marigolds with yellow, kidney-shaped leaves along the back edge of the cement platform base of the pool house. There's also a strip of poison ivy along the back of the building, through the grass and down into the bulrushes.

We lower our heads and shoulders and run to the back of the roofed structure. Our couching is pointless. Once we step into the circle of light we're visible, and the only reason no one sees us is because no one is looking. A swarm of gnats greets us, harmless but annoying. We make our way quickly to the corner of the building. Kim presses against the wall to furtively peek around it. I'm less careful and step out from behind him, exposing myself more in order to get a view. The lighted, mowed area of grass and weeds reveals no surprises. Not sure what we're anticipating.

We are trespassing.

We are on forbidden land.

Urged by the gnats, we step into full view and quickly pass the side of the building to the open cement surrounding the pool. Fortunately, the gnats don't follow us onto the cement.

Then . . .

There it is . . .

T

The forbidden pool . . .

It isn't a huge pool, twenty feet long and fifteen wide with slightly rounded corners. At the opposite end, the bottom slants up to a depth of two feet so one can walk into it. The pool sides are painted a creamy white, and there's an azure blue trim around the top. Nothing special, but the lights beneath the water make it glow—make it seem alive with energy. Though I know there has to be built-in lighting, I can't see it. Instead, the entire body of water holds a soft white light, as if the water and the light are one.

The pure voice of a Winter Wren sings a rapid sequence of notes, as if announcing our arrival.

It's a moment between moments, a timeless moment of balance. The adventure has reached its climax. I stand over the pool that holds the pure water of those who live on the rich lands on the other side of the lake. Is it really different than the unfiltered water I swim and fish and swallow? It looks different, looks softer and lighter—looks ethereal.

It's probably the light.

The light causes it to look different.

No sense in thinking it through.

I step into the pool and watch the ripples spread across its surface. Another step, another series of ripples.

I water feels softer, feels as if it's flowing into my legs . . . Caressing them . . . filling them with . . . with . . .

I'm three.

Mom sits above me, rocking Johnny to sleep.

She sings.

I hear her beautiful voice.

The voice everyone in church praises.

T

It is God's gift.
That's what they say.
God sings through her.
The baby Jesus.
I see him.
Outside the window.
Why?
What can it mean?

I walk into the pool . . . walk to the other end, where the water comes to my shoulders.
I stand in the light.
Now what?
What should I do now?

"Like swimming above the clouds," she says.
Mr. Orange remembers and smiles, but doesn't respond.

I sink into the water until I'm completely submerged.
I open my eyes as I often do in the lake. All I see is the light, as if the water and the light are one.
When I emerge, Kim has finished looking about the roofed structure and splashes into the pool.
I dive down and briefly raise my feet above the surface. When I resurface, Kim follows suit. We've entered the forbidden pool and completely immersed ourselves in it. We look at each other. What now?
Kim sends a splash of water at me and I return one.
Well . . . that doesn't work . . . seems awkward and forced . . . and pointless.

T

That's what we do at the beach or on the raft. It's out of place here.

Swimming doesn't really work either. We barely get started before we hit the other end of the pool. There is no diving board, so that's not an option.

"What do people do in swimming pools?" I ask.

"Drink," Kim responds.

"Huh?"

"There's a bar in the pool house filled with liquor."

The three walls with a roof built on the cement slab of the pool are mainly for the purpose of a bar.

"Well . . . let's check it out." I pull myself up and onto the cement platform.

Kim does the same.

The bar is attached to one of the walls and extends half way across the room. Against the other sidewall is a small wrought-iron table with a glass top that holds an RCA phonograph. A stack of albums, topped by one with a picture of Barbara Streisand, sits on the floor next to it.

The bar has a second level behind it for mixing drinks. Whoever last used it, left it in a mess—beer mugs, wine flutes, martini and rock glasses are interspersed with napkins, stir sticks, two ice buckets, wedges of lime, and a partially used container of olives.

"Look," I say, "Beefeater Gin!"

Kim is more interested in the beer, picks up a can of Hamm's and pops it open. He takes a drink, then picks up a second one and hands it to me. "From the land of sky blue waters," he says, mimicking the commercial as we click our cans together.

I take a drink and swallow the bitter-sweet, forbidden product of hops and barley. Kim takes a bigger swallow.

T

I take another, not really liking the taste, set my can on the bar and turn to the albums. "Wonder what kind of music they have?"

Kim slams the rest of his can, crushes it with one hand, and sets it on the bar. "Let's head out."

I pick up the Streisand album, revealing an album beneath it by Andy Williams of film theme songs, decide to take Kim's suggestion, and drop the Streisand album back on the pile. As I turn to follow him, I see the bottle of gin. "Wait."

Kim turns back. I take the nearly empty bottle, unscrew the top, and pour some into my can of beer.

Kim laughs. "You don't want to do that."

"Why?" I boldly take a full drink. It burns my throat and hits my stomach.

It doesn't stay there.

Not for a second.

My reaction is immediate.

I throw-up.

It's a good thing Kim has quick reflexes.

"Oooohhhhhhhhh . . . ," I moan, and follow it with a second heave.

"Come on," Kim says. "Let's go."

I wave at him with my left arm to signal I need a moment, kneel and roll onto my back. I'm about to pass out. I close my eyes. The sharp taste of pine needles isn't done with me yet. I roll on my stomach and have a series of dry heaves.

While I'm suffering my ill-gotten punishment, Kim sits on one of the bar stools to wait me out.

What have I done? I lie on my back and let the world disappear. If I remain motionless, it seems better.

T

I want to turn off my mind, but there is no off switch—the swamp, the weeds, the shadows, the snake . . . the snake, the snake, crawling through a tree . . . hissssssssssssing . . . saying something . . . something . . .

Then . . . it's gone.

I'm back, on the cement, in the light.

I roll over, testing my stomach. A bit queasy, but not bad. I push myself to a crawling position. No problem. Interesting. I rise to my feet. No problem.

Kim laughs. "Told you."

It takes two decades before I'm willing to drink gin again. In one of those quirks of life, a Beefeater gin martini, straight, up, with two olives becomes my favorite drink for a number of years, that sharp bite that once made me sick now an attraction.

T

The Dog Days of Summer

Summer drips into the hot, humid, days of August and the new school year approaches.

One hot afternoon, Mom says, "We're heading into the dog days."

"What are the dog days?"

She laughs. "They're the hot, humid days of August."

"But why are they called the dog days?"

"Hmm . . . don't know . . ."

I ask others. Carol says something about wolves howling at the moon in August. When Bob hears this, he says werewolves come out during a full August moon. I think they're both joking, but I'm not sure.

Keith says it has to do with dogs being "in heat." He's not sure how being in heat relates to it, but he believes it means dogs are mating, resulting in having puppies.

Possible, I think, but I'm not convinced.

When I ask Barney about dogs being in heat, he says "No, dogs go into heat in the spring, not the end of summer."

I later learn this isn't completely true. While it is common for dogs to go into heat in spring, most dogs go into heat twice a year, and it doesn't have to be in spring.

Vera gives Mom a Farmer's Almanac that has the following rhyme:

Dog days bright and clear
Indicate a good year;
But when accompanied by rain,
We hope for better times in vain

This doesn't help me any. I get it – if it rains in August that means it's going to be a bad year, but why.

"It's a prediction about growing crops," Mom says. "If it rains in August that means it will be bad for the crops, and the farmers will have a bad harvest."

"Why?"

"I'm not sure how it works, but it's late in the growing season, so it must be bad for plants if it rains when they're ready to be harvested."

"But what does it have to do with dogs?"

"Sorry, can't help you there."

It's one of those questions that adults might or might not try to explain but end-up telling me I'm too young to understand or there's no point in bothering with it.

While skimming a book on Greek mythology, I unexpectedly stumble on the answer, learning that dog days refer to Sirius, the dog star. One of the Greek constellations is named Canis Major, the Great Dog, thought to be Orion's dog, and the brightest star in the constellation, in the entire sky, is named Sirius, the dog star.

In late July and into August, Sirius appears to rise before the sun, and because of this, that time of year is when it is thought to have its greatest influence. Thus, this time of year gets designated the dog days in reference to Sirius.

The book also explains some of the negative meanings attached to it, possibly suggesting that Carol and Bob weren't completely making-up their responses.

In the Iliad, Achilles's approach to Troy references Sirius and gives it a negative quality:

T

Sirius rises late in the dark, liquid sky
On summer nights, star of stars,
Orion's Dog they call it, brightest
Of all, but an evil portent, bringing heat
And fevers to suffering humanity.

The Romans call these days dies caniculares, "days of the dog," and the star Sirius is called Canicula, "little dog." The excessive panting of dogs in hot weather is thought to place them at risk of desiccation and disease. In extreme cases, a foaming dog might have rabies, which can infect and kill humans they bite.

I see how all this has connections to werewolves. It is a bit of a stretch, and I'm inclined not to believe werewolves exist. However, I can't completely dismiss the possibilities, however tenuous. Besides it comes from a book, and the written word carries a lot of truth at the time.

Whether or not dogs are literally involved in any significant way with August, there can be no doubt but that it is a hot, humid month, a month that signals the end of summer and the beginning of fall.

Natalie Babbitt's Tuck Everlasting begins with a wonderful Prologue based on the hot, humid, still, silent days of August. She writes they are like a Ferris Wheel that has stopped at the top of the year, as if the yearly cycle of time itself has paused.

Yes, August does seem to be a pause in the incessant progression of time. Especially this August.

T

The Singularity

"Eddie! Eddie!"

"Huh?"

"Eddie! Wake up!"

"What . . . oh . . ."

Mom bends over my bed and gently shakes my shoulder. "Eddie . . . you awake?"

"Huh . . . oh . . . yeah."

"You were having a nightmare. You were saying something about getting out."

"Oh . . . I was reading . . . Must have fallen asleep."

"You were asking why you couldn't get out and you started screaming 'Come back!'"

"Hmm."

"It was as if someone left you or was leaving you. Do you remember anything?"

"No . . . I think there was some kind of music, like merry-go-round music."

"Strange. Anything else?"

"No."

"You okay now?"

"Guess so . . ."

"The singularity . . . that's what they call it." Jesus walks to a wooden bench beneath a blossoming olive tree and sits.

Mr. Orange walks over to the branch of another, cups a twig of blossoms and smells it. "When God breathed on the water . . .?"

"Genesis . . . the beginning."

"When natural and supernatural merged?"

"Some say space and time didn't exist before it."

Mr. Orange looks up . . . the Mount of Olives . . . "Are you a singularity?"

Jesus stands. "We used to meet here, eat, drink, laugh and sing."

"Gethsemane . . . the Garden . . . ." Mr. Orange feels something whenever he's with Jesus.

What is it?

Charisma? Some people have charisma.

Why? . . . They just have it?

Jesus is a man, perhaps better looking than most, but with no noticeable physical abilities. Certainly not athletic looking.

But there's something.

No . . . there is no halo . . .

That's an attribute employed by artists long after he died . . .

or . . .

didn't . . .

or did and was reborn.

No . . . he doesn't glow . . .

and yet he does?

T

There is no aura . . .

and yet . . .

A hand on the shoulder interrupts his thoughts.

"Come," Jesus says. "There's a raft on the shore of Galilee. Let us share some wine and bread, perhaps a story or two."

T

The Mirror Shatters

Mr. Balloon Man

The Fight

The Pit

The Mad Hatter's
Masquerade

Mister
Balloon
Man

Dad?

Mom?

Don't panic.

Think.

Push your thoughts backwards.

Come on.
Break through that wall.
It will all make sense.
You just need to wake up.

Yes, that's it.
You must be sleeping.
Having a dream.

Force your way out of it.
Keep calm.
Use logic.
Assess the situation, analyze it.

It's noisy . . . very noisy.
Noisy people all around me.
Hundreds of people.

T

Yet I'm alone.
I'm alone in the middle of a crowd.

A nightmare!
 That's it!
I'm having a nightmare!
That must be it!

Now just wake up!
Snap out of it!

Okay.
Keep calm.
Assess the situation . . .
The music . . . the loud music blaring from all around me . . .

Work backwards . . . work backwards . . .

Slow down.

Think!

It will come . . . it will come . . .

Did I fall?
Bump my head?
Am I waking from a concussion?
Where's Mom and Dad . . . anyone . . .
They must be near.

Think it through.

T

Think it through.

I must have just gotten turned around, separated . . .

Any moment one of them will appear, worried and relieved to find me.

But the crowd . . . such a confusing crowd.

Dark Shadow smiles. His white teeth sparkle in the darkness. He watches for a while, then speaks, "Dank corners, midnight crawl spaces beneath tattered, canvas skirts and the alluring entrances to exotic tents line the edges of the hard, bright lights of the Midway, a surrealistic circus dance of smiling middle-class families and mysterious, gypsy carnies — all merging on a late summer night in the innocent Midwest, both a gaudy playground and a macabre nightmare filled with a catholic array of people, a stage where the grinding sounds of the heavy machinery of the Farris Wheel and the Roller Coaster and the Death Drop mix with the high pitched squeals of those who pay to be frightened, where grotesque animals — sheep with two heads, a goat with an extra set of legs, a cow with no eyes, not even the sockets for them, sniff the discarded popcorn boxes and lick the remains off cotton-candy holders or kneel on the rough gravel next to a freak show tent that advertises a chance to see bizarre humans — flipper man, who has hands that look like fins attached directly to his shoulders, alligator woman, whose skin is scaly and green, four breasted man, who sits shirtless and bored, while sweat drips slowly down his neck and over his pale, unnatural breasts,

T

conjoined man, who is actually two men born connected at the waist."

He pauses and smiles.

The Mad Hatter laughs.

Other laughs come from the darkness:

"Hee hee hee,"

"Hee hee hee"

"Hee hee hee"

"Hee hee hee."

The Opium Queen's eyes sparkle.

Dark Shadow continues, "The lights are so bright they create an oasis in the middle of the darkness, an unreal world where thousands of humans pay money to throw balls at stacked bowling pins, and aim darts at dozens of red, blue, yellow and green balloons tacked to a damaged, white wall, and shoot streams of water out of plastic guns at tin targets to make tin horses run across a slotted, mock race track, and lean over the barrier of a tent-covered booth to try to get coins to land on slippery plates, and, if they are lucky, win cheap, stuffed animals of all kinds and sizes. Shouts, laughter and groans from young and old mix with early rock-and-roll songs that blast from tinny speakers."

"Hee hee hee"

"Hee hee hee"

"Hee hee hee"

"Hee hee hee."

T

"And there's Eddie. If you look closely, you can see him. There, just to the left of the ticket booth . . . see . . . by the Carousel."

Should I stay where I am?
Wait for them to find me?
If I stay where I am, they're more likely to find me."

But something isn't right.
I know my logic isn't right.
Don't know why, but . . .

Dad . . . Mom . . . they're not going to find me.
They're not here.

No one I know is here.
I didn't come to the Midway with anyone else.
I'm here by myself.
Alone.

Why?

Think!

Find a center, something. . . anything to make sense . . .

The people, all these people . . .

Someone . . . someone . . .

"Help! Help!"

T

No one notices.
It's too noisy, too random . . .

A space!
An opening in the crowd.

A large man in a larger-than-life clown costume steps into it.
"Balloons," he sings out in a deep, operatic bass, "fifty cents."

He frightens me.
He's too . . . too . . . too . . .
Like an evil cartoon character come to life.

My first impulse is to hide, merge into the crowd.
But I hesitate.
Why?

Perhaps . . .
I have to take a chance!

He's looking for children to buy his balloons so he's likely to notice me if I approach him, and he works here, so he might know.
Makes sense.
Still . . .

Oh . . . what's going on?

T

No time to waste.
He's turning away.

I rush to him. "Mister! Hey, Mister Balloon Man, please,
Mister Balloon Man!"

He doesn't hear!
And he's disappearing into the crowd!
Gone!

"Balloons," I hear his voice through the noise.
"Balloons for sale!"

"Mister!
Please!
Mister Balloon Man!"

I push into the crowd.

"Balloons the gift of color bring!" his deep voice booms out.
"Buy some color for your life!"

I shove into the people, squeeze between the bony hips of a
man and large purse of a women, dodge around a woman
pushing a baby carriage and rush through a small opening
beside a fat girl eating cotton candy.

The crowd keeps closing me off!

Then . . .
Suddenly . . .

T

There he is!
Directly in front of me!

I reach out and tug the back of his baggy pants.

He stops and looks back over his shoulder.
Yes! He felt me! He's looking for me!

Then he swoops ominously down at me, his nightmarish clown face nearly touching my own.
Startled, I jerk away. He quickly pulls back as well.

His eyes sparkle and he smiles, perhaps amused at the fright he gave me. I don't know.
It's unsettling.
I shouldn't have chased him!
Should have run!

His face and neck are painted white. His black eyes are surrounded with a blood red paint to match the red circles on his cheeks, fake red nose and exaggerated lips. His large, uneven teeth are a dull white, his orange eyebrows arch in clownish exaggeration, and his wildly curly orange hair grows out in all directions from a dirty red bandana.

Just a large man wearing a lot of clown make-up.
Or . . .

He chuckles, yet even his soft laugh has a full sound as if coming from a great cavern. There's something about it . . .
What is it?

T

Think!

He raises his large right forefinger and motions me to him. "Come, my child, there's no reason to cower, nothing to fear." His words are similar to his laugh, rich and musical with rhythmic spaces and practiced emphasis, a way of speaking that suggests duplicity.

I don't trust him. I know I should run. But something . . . something draws me to him.

"Please," I say. "Please, Mister Balloon Man, please, I'm lost. Please help me."

He laughs, such an ominous laugh, straightens up and knowingly detaches a balloon from the bunch he holds in his left hand. "Here's a bright blue one. See how big? With this balloon float you can, right up into the stars."

"Please," I say, "I'm lost! Can you help me find my family? Tell me where I am?"

"Only fifty cents," he continues, seeming not to hear my question, or, if he does, not to have any interest. A large, yellow handkerchief appears to grow out of a pocket in his old wool coat, and his brown-and-yellow patched pants billow out as he holds the blue balloon toward me.

I reach for it, but he pulls it back.

"Fifty cents!"

What is this game? "Please," I say, "Help me."

He smiles, his mouth resembling that of Alice's Cheshire cat. I know the only way I'm going to get an answer is to buy a balloon.

Fifty cents! Where will I get fifty cents? Ever since Dad got cancer and died there was little money. Putting aside sentimentality Mom even raided Dad's collection of

T

Indianhead pennies to have the two cents needed each day for my school milk money. Fifty cents might as well be a billion dollars.

"I have no money."

He looks away, no, he's not looking away, he's not looking anywhere. His eyes have a glazed blank look. He whispers something unintelligible, chuckles softly, hums, mutters disconnected phrases and sings bits of a song. Then from the disjointed monologue comes a clear sentence, "There's more about you than you realize."

"Hee hee hee"
"Hee hee hee"

Okay, now I know. This has to be a dream!
I'm going to wake up soon and that will be that!
This is all nonsense!
This clown is crazy!

He raises and lowers his clownish eyebrows, seems to be enthralled with them, as if he has just discovered he can do this.

I step back and look at the people wandering aimlessly about the Midway – women pushing strollers, young couples holding hands, children dodging through the adults, most smiling and laughing. Squeals come in waves as the Roller Coaster plunges down steep tracks, the Tilt-a-whirl swirls wildly, the Space Tower rotates 300 feet in the air and the Ejection Seat catapults thrill seekers into the night. Lights of all colors flash and the music of Elvis, Little Richard, Bill Haley and the Comets fights with the game barkers for

T

attention. I'm lost in a carnival world! I'm in the middle of an hallucination!

The dull clank of a bell joins the general noise. Someone has just brought a sledgehammer down powerfully enough to ring the bell.

I look at the balloon man. He's puckering his large lips, seems to be experimenting with different ways to push them forward in an exaggerated kiss.

My eyes grow wet and then my body begins to shake.

I can't understand.

What am I to do?

If it's all a dream, it won't let go of me.

If it's real, then why can't I remember?

Why is there no past, nothing leading to it?

I start to cry.

The balloon man leans so close I can smell alcohol and tobacco and grease paint.

"Child, child, child," he whispers. "So sure of your poverty are you."

My breathing stutters to an end of my crying, leaving the tears to trickle down my cheeks and drip off my chin.

He steps back and looks sternly down. "Stop it! Stop it! Stop it! Look at yourself! Embarrassing!"

I don't know whether to hit him or yell or run or what, so I do nothing.

He studies me. "The child the clothes do make!"

I look down at my clothes.

I don't recognize them!

What's this!

"Look at your clothes closely! Explore them!"

T

I'm not sure what he means. I look down, but don't see anything. What am I supposed to see? I began patting my shirt.

"Come on! Explore them! See what they give you!"

I stick my hand in my right pants' pocket.

"Ahhh, okay. Now you're turning."

I feel the cool semi-smooth texture of coins! My pants' pocket is full of quarters! I take out two and hand them to him.

He smiles, "So, not so poor as you think!" He carefully places the coins in his small red change purse, unties a balloon and hands it to me with a great flourishing gesture.

"Please, 'now' will you tell me where I am?"

"Why, don't you know?" He laughs and swings his arm towards the Midway scene. "You're in the Funhouse!"

"The Funhouse!? What's the Funhouse!?"

"Ahhhhhhhhhhhhh." He draws out the sound in his rich bass voice, and his eyes gleam. "The Funhouse is where you can buy balloons. Here, here's a bright yellow balloon, only fifty cents." He plucks the string of a yellow balloon from his left hand and holds it toward me.

Oh no! No! No! No!

What can I do?

I know I'll have to buy a balloon if I'm going to get any more information, so I take another two quarters out of my pocket and place them in his large palm.

He lets them rest there, studies them, drawing me into his intense scrutiny, and like a skilled magician, while his eyes focus my attention on the display, he slides his other hand into his baggy pants' pocket and again produces his plastic, red change purse, seemingly out of nowhere. In an exaggerated pantomime, he continues this strange performance, snapping

T

open the gold latch of the purse and carefully placing the coins inside. Then, in a movement so quick I do not follow it, he replaces the purse from wherever he has procured it, and apparently having completed this routine to his satisfaction, he detaches the string of a yellow balloon, hands it to me, and turns to go.

"Wait! Wait a minute! I bought your balloon! See! See! Here it is! I bought your balloon! Tell me what is the Funhouse!?"

He stops and turns back. "The Funhouse? Oh, yes," he says and laughs, as before, his rich voice evident even in the soft chuckle. "Why, don't you know, the Funhouse is where people go to get out of the rain."

"What?!" I exclaim, raising my arms and letting go of my balloons.

"Now see what you've done. Now you'll need to replace the balloons you so carelessly lost."

"Wait a minute!" I say. "I don't want any more balloons! I want to know how to get out of here!"

The balloon man smiles his Cheshire cat smile and turns to go.

"Wait! Wait a minute!" I pull four quarters out of my pocket. "Here! Here's a dollar. Stop your nonsense and tell me what's going on!"

"No dollars, just quarters," he says.

"A dollar 'is' four quarters!"

"Make up your mind," he calls back as he continues to walk away.

"Wait! Here, here's four quarters!"

He pauses, as if debating my anguished cry.

"Four quarters!"

T

He turns to face me.

I hold out my hand to show him the quarters.

He knows the moment is his, and he knows how to hold such a moment. As he studies me, it's as if the entire Midway has stopped. Everything is motionless and waiting expectantly for his decision. Indeed, it is as if the entire universe is holding its breath.

"Four quarters!"

With the slow, steady poise of a trained thespian, he swings his arms across his chest and up above his shoulders, as if telling an orchestra to be ready to perform. It is the moment, that moment when both the musicians and the audience are at his command.

"Please!"

He smiles, his eyes crinkling at the corners, his mouth wide, as if he indeed is the Cheshire cat and has just eaten a mouse.

"Well, bring them here and make it quick!"

I hesitate. The drama, the balloon man, the funhouse . . .

"Quick best you be! Dearly hesitation will cost you!"

I rush to him. "Here!" I push the four quarters toward his large palm.

He carefully takes them, one by one, examines each as if looking for flaws in a diamond, and slowly goes through his previous elaborate routine placing them in his coin purse. Then he takes the strings of two green balloons and hands them to me, not letting go of them until he is sure I have a firm hold. Then he steps back, looks me over and . . . and his eyes go blank and he starts the same disjointed comments and singing as he did earlier.

"Hee hee hee"

T

"Hee hee hee."

What! What! What! And he just threatened me about 'my' hesitation! I want to scream, want to snap him out of this latest meditation!

But I know it's 'his' world.

A verbal outburst will not work!

Logic will not work!

That's not the way to deal with him.

So I wait . . . try to be patient . . .

And I wait. The calliope of sounds annoys me . . . the flashing lights urge me to explode . . . scream out . . . to start swinging and swinging and swinging . . .

But I force myself to wait . . . and wait . . . force myself to be calm . . . to be patient . . . I began to withdraw from the noise . . . the busy lights . . . the . . . world of the midway . . .

I'm fading . . . fading . . . the sounds grow softer and softer . . . fade . . . until I enter silence . . . silence . . . a comforting silence . . .

The lights, the colors, the people, everything fades . . . soft . . . soft . . . soft . . .

And then it's gone . . . it's all gone . . . invisible and silent . . .

But in the silence, in the empty silence, I hear something . . . something . . . soft . . . soft . . . soft . . . somewhere in the silence . . . beyond hearing . . . I hear . . .

A melody . . . a lyric . . .

I hear it . . . something . . .

"Once . . . . Funhouse . . . . never . . . ."

"Once you . . . . the Funhouse, you . . . . never go . . . . ."

T

"Once you have been inside the Funhouse, you can never go back."

"What!? Never get out!? What, what, why, what is all this? What, what a sham! Here, here, take back your balloons! I don't want your damn balloons!" I push the strings into his hand.

He folds his fingers over them. "No refunds," he says and smiles.

"I don't care about refunds! I want some answers! What do you mean I can never get out!?"

He lets go of the strings of the two balloons. "It's too bad you don't want the balloons. Balloons to the stars can float you." He pauses, as if to let his words sink in or perhaps to consider his next action. Then he abruptly turns to go as if he has had enough of me.

I grab at him, and catch a handful of his shirt, but my hand goes right through it, as if it's not solid – an illusion, a filament of my imagination, a dream image.

"Hee hee hee"
"Hee hee hee."

This might be the end of it. In less than a second, he'll be engulfed by the crowd and lost to me.

It's a dangerous moment.

"Wait! Wait!" I yell into the noise of the midway. "Wait! Tell me why I can't get out!"

He turns abruptly! His face has a fierce, frightening scowl and his eyes glare! "That did I not say! More discerning you must learn to listen! Said I, can you never go back! A difference is there!"

T

The force of his anger hits me like an invisible wave of energy and I stumble backwards.

He vanishes.
Not into the crowd.
Into nothing.
I am alone –
Swallowed by the Midway's calliope
of swirling machines, flashing lights,
waves of laughter and squeals of fear
and delight.

T

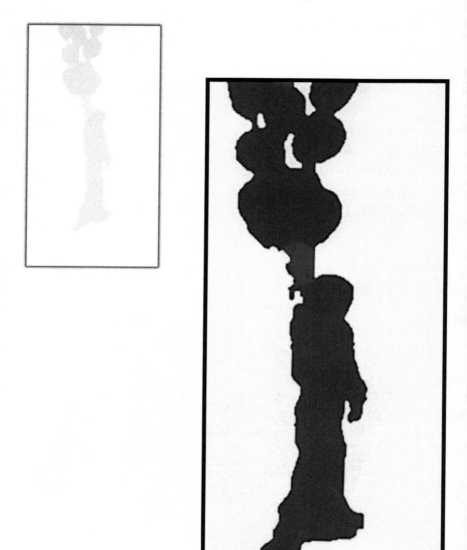

The Fight

Tom Porter's dad is one of those people who make me question Jesus' insistence on loving thy neighbor. I have no memory of him other than hearing his high pitched bitching at or about someone or something, and there's a general agreement in the neighborhood that it's best to avoid him. So it's no surprise that he's the instigator of my fight with Keith.

But though his actions are the spark that ignites the final fight, it is inevitable that this will be the final summer of my friendship with Keith. The reason we're friends is our mothers' friendship. While there's nothing wrong with our own friendship, our interests, abilities and personalities don't match. All along I've been seeing a more distant horizon than the one he sees, and this summer, without knowing it, I've already started walking towards that larger world.

As I've mentioned, Keith has the large build of his dad, Lenny, and like Lenny does not have a quick intelligence. I remember trying to get him interested in a baseball game I create.

It's a board game involving spinning a pointer over a circle of possibilities. To make the spinning board, I dig through some old wood piled in the basement, find a workable one-by-six and cut off six inches so I have a six inch square. I sand the edges smooth with a half-used piece of sandpaper.

For the spinning pointer, I cut four-inches off a piece of $\frac{1}{2}$ inch trim and attach it to the center of the board with a small nail. Great, I have my version of the spinning wheels common to board games. In some ways, it's even better, because those in the store games are made of cardboard, and mine is made of wood.

My plan is to make it even better by painting it, even painting some baseball images on it, but I never get around to doing this.

Now, I need a my exchangeable baseball players that I can slip onto the spinning board. I create a template with the appearance of a 45 record, and cut fifty pieces of construction paper into circles with circular holes, like large, flat donuts. I look up the batting statistics of baseball players, past and present, and draw divisions on my paper donuts that roughly match their percentages, varying the sections according to the number of singles, doubles, triples, home runs and walks each player is likely to get.

The game is ready. The two players chose the paper cutouts of the players until each has a team, one player for each position and a few reserves that can be used as pinch-hitters. The game is played similar to a real baseball game, spinning through nine three-out innings.

I'm excited about it.

Keith, however, is not interested in playing board games.

I play it by myself for a time, but find, as is often the case, I enjoy creating it more than playing it.

Another time, one of the rare times I'm in their house, we're in the windowed porch that faces the lake, and there is a cheap chess set sitting on a couch that has a brightly colored covering patterned much like Scottish sweaters. I try to get Keith to play because I've recently learned how, and he's been taught by Bruce. He gives it a try, but doesn't focus and make

T

numerous mistakes. It doesn't seem to matter to him. He's just bored.

I'm not sure our fight is inevitable. In fact, it's a more dramatic ending to our time together than seems likely.

Conversely, that it happens the summer after Dad's death matches my mental state. I am too lost in my darkness and too young to grasp the dramatic changes in me, but Peter Pan's Neverland has splintered into a frightening kaleidoscope, and I'm starting to strike out at the wildly changing chaos.

This summer, Keith, Tom and I play together more than usual. For a time, Tom's yard becomes a place for the neighborhood group to gather at night for such games as Hide-and-Go-Seek and Starlight/Moonlight. On one occasion Tom entices us to stand in his mother's tomato garden and throw tomatoes at passing cars.

I always remember times I've done something I know is wrong because I've let someone else entice me to do it. I would never do this on my own initiative. I am ashamed that I did it. I know many will think it a minor thing, one of those standard stupid things children do. Yes, it's wrong, but no harm done. Move on. However, for whatever reason, I have such a strong need to follow what I believe is ethically right, even at this young of an age, I cannot forgive myself. And it always involves the same weakness. I do not stand up against the instigator.

Tom teaches us how to decide who is "it" by employing a hand counting game: We all stand in a circle and hold out our fists. He taps each in turn as he counts out "One-potato-two-potato-three-potato-four; five potato, six potato, seven potato more." Whatever hand gets tapped on "more" is removed from

T

the circle and a new round begins. Finally, only one hand remains, and that's the first person to be "it." Variations are possible and often used to try and get around the obvious, that anyone who knows how to count can determine the loser before the counting even begins. I realize quickly this is exactly what Tom is doing and do stand up to him, resulting in a quick end to that night's activities.

We seldom go inside Tom's house. But one night when his parents are out, Tom takes Keith and me to his room. He wants to show us his collection of Mad magazines. Apparently, at least in his view, they are what those in the know read, and since he's two years older than me, he emphasizes he is letting me in on what young adults his age read. He also makes it clear that it's an in-thing to use the word "Fink," a word associated with the magazine. Apparently, my world never does become a part of the "in" group, as, though I hear it occasionally, it never gains much traction. In truth, by the time I'm Tom's age, profanity gets used a good deal more than such words as fink.

This is the summer Keith, Tom and I build our fort in the woods. It's something of a ritual for boys in our neighborhood. The woods is a natural playground for us. Three small caves, more just the beginnings of cave entrances, have been dug half way up the steep bank above the water. A "sort of" path runs halfway up the bank connecting them. There's another, more solid path along the top of the bank, and there's a small field in the middle of the woods with an oak tree that has been used by each generation in turn as the sturdy corner for a fort.

Now it's our turn. We take some of the wood and nails from my torn down garage, haul it up to the woods and hammer together an impressive fort for the circumstances. I would

T

venture to say it is the best ever built there. We even dig out a three foot deep basement. It is eight feet by six feet, tall enough to stand in, has a roof and walls to keep the rain out. We even take my dad's old fire burning stove and rig it so it's useable.

Then, I am out of town for a weekend.

When I return, I head to the woods to see how the fort is doing and . . . am devastated.

The fort is completely gone!

I run home and tell Mom. She says that Keith's parents decided they don't want us playing there, that they're afraid we'll start a fire.

"What!"

I head straight for Keith's house.

He's standing in his driveway.

"What happened to the fort!"

"Tom's dad told us we had to take it down."

"Why didn't someone talk to me?!"

"You weren't around."

"What do you mean?! I live right there! I'm always around!"

"Well, Tom didn't think we should tell you."

"What!"

"His dad doesn't think we should play with you anymore."

"What?!"

"The woods isn't our land. We were trespassing."

"The woods isn't anyone's land. Everyone plays there!"

"You'll have to talk to Tom."

"What about the money we had in the can?"

"Tom took that."

"What?!"

"Well . . . I have to go now."

T

"Hey, I want my share of the money!"

"You just go and leave me alone."

"What did you do with all of my wood!? . . . and my stove!?"

"Tom's dad hauled it to the dump."

"What!?"

"You'll have to talk to Tom."

"I'm talking to you!" I push his shoulder.

He makes an awkward attempt to push me back. But he's slow, and I deflect it. I charge into him, hitting his shoulder with mine and knocking him on his back in the ditch. He lies there, not sure what to do.

"Come on, gutless!"

He hesitantly crabs a few feet back.

"What's wrong?! Afraid to face me! Have to steal my money and my stove and my boards behind my back!"

It's obvious he doesn't want any of this to continue, but I'm not letting him off. So he rolls onto his knees and rises.

"You are a real loser!" I emphasize each word.

He steps toward me and takes a swing, but it's easy for me to dodge it. I hit him square in the stomach, and he bends over. Then I push him to the ground and he curls into a ball. I think about kicking him, but even in the rush of anger, I can't break whatever that code is inside me. So I turn and walk away.

It's the end of our friendship, one of the many endings that take place that summer. Life as I knew it no longer exists.

Many years later Mom will tell me that both she and Vera watched the fight from their respective houses. Vera thought Keith would easily beat me up. He was not only a year older, but he was noticeably larger and had his father's powerful chest and shoulders. Though Mom is against violence, she is

T

unashamed to say she was pleased I had proven her best friend wrong.

What neither they nor I can know at the time is that I've fallen into another world, and I would have fought to the death without fear or hesitation. But it has to be honest—everything done without succumbing to weak excuses or any form of cheating. It has to be fair and real. No pretense. No lies. All an excuse means is that I've done something wrong—failed.

T

The Pit

The stars shimmer in a black sky.

I tuck my light-blue, work shirt into my faded blue-jeans, buckle my heavy leather belt, lace up my old but still stout, black boots from a Salvation Army store and head to the Pit, a deserted gravel site west of town.

Large cottonwood trees surround the Pit, and even at night their shadows extend into it. Rocks, clumps of mud, and tall, thin shoots of prairie grass accent the rough road that runs along its top and circles down into it.

An owl hoots from the trees. It's a lonely sound, as if a sentinel is keeping watch over a clandestine meeting in the woods,

Except for the droning background of crickets, everything is silent.

I reach the gravel floor, walk onto it, and lie down on my back. The ground is cold, damp, and cracked like slabs of brown ice. I look into the heavens. The stars glitter and tremble, as if they're the tiniest of bubbles sparkling in the spilt nectar of the ancient gods, the gods before God. Yes, it is as I expect. How can it not be?

Time passes.

One must not rush God.

Then, it begins:

I stand on the shore of Jenning's Bay, next to the wooden dock I once swam off, caught crappies from, and sat on to dangle my feet over the water and watch the cumulus clouds drift above the point. I can't see the point now. A rare mist has settled on the lake. But I can hear the seagulls that live out their lives circling up from its rocks, and I visualize their lazy circles interrupted by rapid plunges into the lake to catch fish.

A boy of five swims in the lake.

Yes! Oh yes! I'm happy! The sight fills me with joy!

The boy turns to face me, but cannot see me. He has short, blonde hair, a white-blonde, and beautiful blue eyes, sparkling, happy eyes, eyes that match the blue sky. He smiles and his whole face lights up. It's a face meant to smile.

For no real reason, he laughs.

I laugh with him.

Does my laugh reach the night sky above me? The world of God?

Does that world know I'm happy? Does it care?

I call to him, "Hi. Can you hear me? Do you know I'm here? How can I tell you? How can I reach you and comfort you and protect you? You don't need to be alone and anxious. I can help you. I can tell you."

T

He doesn't hear me.

He turns away and dives into deeper water. I wait for him to reappear farther out in the lake.

Time passes.

He doesn't surface.

I am alarmed and step into the water to save him.

The water, my water, flows over my feet and legs. I feel it. My water.

How can one know the difference? Water is water . . . but no. Water is not water. This is the water I know. This is the water of my lake. It comforts me.

Something hits the back of my head. I turn. A beak stabs at my left eye and just misses it, cutting me below the eyebrow. I hold up my arms and stumble backward from a swirling mass of feathers with claws and beaks that rip at my face. I swing out with both arms. The air is thick – claws, beaks, wings and blank eyes. I cover my face. The whir of the wings! My arms . . . neck . . . chest . . . groin! I curl into a ball and lose consciousness.

When I wake, the white-gray light that hints at a pale blue sky and the summer dew of early morning gives the Pit a feeling of anticipation, the birth of the new day.

My left eye stings and my lip is bloodied. My cotton shirt is torn and stained with blood. My blue jeans are ripped down the left leg. My ankle hurts.

I stand. It's time for the long walk back.

A garter snake slides through the shadows and scattered fuchsia along a small pile of gravel.

I hear blue jays and titmice and other small birds as I circle to the top. A woodchuck studies me and then decides I've gotten close enough to pose a danger and slips into the prairie grass. I

T

hear a woodpecker from a thicket of cottonwood trees as I
followed the pit entrance through it and reach Game Farm
road.

It's about a mile walk to the main road. As I make my way,
I find the early morning has drawn numerous animals out of
the surrounding weeds. I see two skunks winding in-and-out of
a white patch of Juneberry. A perfectly still raccoon watches
me from the trunk of a fallen basswood. Chipmunk race across
the road into a patch of pussytoes and a gray squirrel lopes
along the top of an old fence that winds through the field
grasses and a scattered patch of sunflowers.

A male and a female pheasant peck at the gravel, but
immediately disappear into the wheat stalks as I pass. A red-
tailed hawk circles high above.

My walk seems to be helping rather than hurting my sore
ankle. I sit on the road and pull up the leg of my pants so I can
see if it's swollen. Perhaps, a little. Not as much as I thought
at first.

I know the next curve in the road will take me passed the
farm with the peacocks. When I get far enough through the
slow curve, the oak trees end, and the cleared land reveals the
old barn and farmhouse. I can't see the peacocks, and if the
owners are doing their morning chores, they are not visible from
the road. The only apparent life is a flock of white chickens
pecking about the driveway next to the side-door into the
house.

I wonder about the peacocks as I pass. They seem so out-of-
place in this world.

Even the small farm seems an encroachment on the
surrounding woods and meadows. While it has the quality of
an American version of a folktale cottage, it is, nevertheless,

T

an attempt to civilize, to tame the wilderness. Even the animals are not the same as the wild animals. The chickens I see are not the same as the wild pheasants.

It is a brief interruption, one I soon pass.

I see a gray wolf standing still and intent on a patch of open ground. I know it can be dangerous but is not likely to bother with me. Wolves steer clear of humans. Nevertheless, I keep my eyes on him as I pass until the road bends and he's out of sight.

Camp Christmas Tree, my brief haven. All I can see from the road is its sign above the dirt road leading into it.

I remember, and have walked well passed it before a small fox startles me back to the present. It runs through a patch of violets before disappearing into a thicket of birch trees.

I realized I've nearly reached the end of Game Farm Road.

Our Lady of the Lake Catholic Church has its graveyard, centered by a statue of Mary, on the corner of Game Farm Road and County Road 110. The sunlight is just rising above the horizon behind her as I turn right onto the asphalt highway and head toward town. When I reach the cemetery entrance, I debate walking up to her. I'm not sure why after all these years this is the moment I'm drawn in, but I enter.

It's eerie walking up the asphalt drive to her and I have to keep telling myself not to get caught in imaginings. This is nothing more than a cleared field. She is nothing more than a statue.

The next thing I remember is being back on the road walking toward town. Did something happen? Why do I not remember?

An occasional car passes, but I'm lost in my thoughts and not really wanting a ride. It's a slow walk, and my ankle hurts with each step, but I don't mind. I assume it's not a

T

broken bone or even a serious bruise. My life is filled with such bruises. There is no reason to think this one any different.

By the time I reach Mound, it is late Sunday morning. People are getting out of Bethel Methodist church, the church where I was baptized, the only church I've been in more than once or twice my entire life.

I recognize many of them, but they don't know me. Classmates who were confirmed with me at this very church – Jeannie Huff, Bill Ulrich, Rick Koehn, Wendy Hadden, Maka Gustafson, Linda Cox, Mildred Braun, Mike Curtis, Bob Fox. The Carlson family that took me in the night Dad died.

The men are dressed in suit-coats. They wear neckties. Their hair is neatly cut and combed. Their shoes are polished. The women wear dresses. Many of them wear high-heeled shoes. They wear pantyhose. Their hair is coiffed in chignon, bouffant, flips, and French curls. Most of them wear eye shadow, lip-stick and rouge. The children's hair is carefully combed and held in place; in some cases, it almost looks as if glue has been applied.

I limp slowly up the sidewalk, failing to avoid the spray from a lawn sprinkler that sends circular spirals of water across the neatly mowed church lawn and out onto the sidewalk.

Why is it on now?

One of the families passes me. The man, dressed in a light blue suit with a matching blue tie held to his light blue shirt with a golden tie clasp, walks between me and his wife and two daughters, pushing the daughters forward and away from me. The daughters are both wearing bright yellow dresses with big bows at the waist. Their light brown hair falls in streams of curls over their shoulders. The woman wears a blue dress and

T

light blue, high-heeled shoes. Two gold earrings in the abstract shape of a rose dangle from her ears. There is a hint of pink lip-stick on her lips and a touch of dark blue mascara above her eyes. Her eyebrows have been plucked, leaving two thin lines of black. Her cheeks have a slight red blush. I hear her mutter "so sad" as she passes me. I recognize them, but I'm not sure...

Something is different...

Then Mr. Carlson and his oldest boy, yes, that's who... approach, hesitate, but pass by. Others mill about, seem familiar...but...

I limp up the sidewalk to the front steps of the church. Bill's dad, yes, I know him, yes, Mr. Ulrich, in a light brown suit and yellow shirt, talks with the new minister, the one who replaced Reverend Voll. I forget his name. Mr. Ulrich is wearing a dark brown bow tie with thin yellow stripes running horizontally across it. His reddish hair is cut above the ears, and a razor-sharp part runs down the left side of his hair from above the left eyebrow to the back of his head. Mrs. Ulrich, wearing an orange dress that came to just below her knees, a white belt, white, high-heeled shoes, and a small, white hat, stands behind him. Her hands are covered by two lacy, white gloves, and she holds a white purse. She sees me and jabs at her husband in the back with her purse. He turns. She points her white purse at me. He thrusts his arm out to the side and rolls his eyes. The Reverend reaches out and grabs Mr. Ulrich's arm. A frown crosses the minister's face. For a moment, I think he's going to say something to me, but then he turns Mr. Ulrich towards the church and away from me. I hear him say, "We must pray for all of the Lord's children." I limp passed the

T

church to the corner of the sidewalk and sit down on the curb. The cement is hot.

Something has changed.

The two older ladies dressed in full-length dresses in bright flower prints walk passed me. I hear them talking about a church picnic. One of them is going to bring something called a split pea salad. I recognize them . . . have seen them in church . . . somewhere in my past . . . somewhere . . .

I hang my head between my knees and suck the blood that has started to dry on my lip.

T

The Mad Hatter's Masquerade

Mr. Bones Holds out his elbow. Mrs. Blood slides her arm through it, and they walk across the entrance into the ballroom, where they are immediately caught up in a waltz. It must be admitted they make an elegant couple swirling over the white marble.

When the music resolves into its coda through a series of sweeping, violin arpeggios, Mr. Bones holds Mrs. Blood's hand above her head, guiding her in a perfectly timed swirl to a final pose, much as if they were the delicate figurines, carefully carved from white marble and dancing on the top of a music box.

For an almost imaginary instant, time stops. Everything is still and silent, except the last lingering memory of the music and dance resonating through the ballroom.

Then the noise and movement returns. People clap. The conductor bows.

"So much fun!" Mrs. Blood says, still catching her breath.

"The dance floor truly is the great stage of life!" Mr. Bones adds.

"Have you seen Eddie?"

"In every sparkling reflection off every glass of champagne!"

They laugh. How can they not?

"Remember when we first met him?" Mrs. Blood asks and smiles.

"On the Midway."

"Yes, yes, yes. Such a broken, lost child!"

"It's been the journey of a lifetime."

"And we've been part of it."

"These memoirs – how many times did he begin?"

"And give up in frustration!"

"And begin again!"

"If he hadn't, we wouldn't be here tonight, laughing and dancing at the Masquerade of the Mad Hatter."

"Did you read them?"

"Read? I lived them!"

"Do you think anyone else will read them?

"If they want to join us."

T

CPSIA information can be obtained
at www.ICGtesting.com
Printed in the USA
LVHW09s1822040918
589117LV00001B/243/P